The Good Woodcutter's Guide

BAILEY'S IS A MAIL-ORDER WOODSMAN'S SUPPLIES COMPANY found-
ed by Bill and Judith Bailey in 1975. Bill was working as a timber faller
(feller), but was struggling with back problems due to a woods accident,
and Judith was working in a local sawmill. Through the years they had
identified a need for a company that would stock standard as well as specialty products for the woodsman, and sell them at discounted prices. They
borrowed $5,000 on their already mortgaged home in Laytonville,
California, and ran their new business out of their house and garage. The
first Bailey's "catalog" consisted of a single piece of paper typed at their
kitchen table, handed out to friends and relatives, and mailed to a few people in other states. Today Bailey's prints four editions (about half a million
catalogs annually) that range from 76 to 100 pages. Instead of a 400-
square-foot garage, they have a 16,000-square-foot warehouse in
California, and since 1984 they have also had a southeastern division in
Jackson, Tennessee. For a free catalog, call (800) 322–4539.

Now known as "The World's Largest Mail-Order Woodsman's Supplies
Company," Bailey's sells products for woodcutting, tree harvesting, woodlot management, log home building, and first aid, in addition to portable
saw mills, outdoor wear, and more. Many years ago, Bill and Judith also
made a commitment to sell reforestation products, including the world-
renowned TreePee II seedling protector. They always figured that if they're
going to help folks harvest trees, they better help replant them, too.

To further this mission, Bailey's has teamed up with Chelsea Green
Publishing Company to publish books about responsible, safe, enjoyable,
and productive forestry. These books are intended to be inspirational as
well as useful and enlarge our view of the complex relationships between
communities of people and healthy woodlands. Our goal is to ensure the
future of the forests, one of our most valuable renewable resources.

Stephen Morris   William G. "Bill" Bailey
President, Chelsea Green   *President, Bailey's*

The Good Woodcutter's Guide

Chain Saws,
Woodlots, and
Portable Sawmills

Dave Johnson

CHELSEA GREEN PUBLISHING COMPANY
WHITE RIVER JUNCTION, VERMONT

To Marcia, my partner in logging and in life.

Designed by Suzanne Church, Blue Door Communications

Printed in the United States of America
First printing, October 1998
01 00 99 98 1 2 3 4 5

LIBRARY OF CONGRESS CATALOGING-IN-PUBLICATION DATA

Johnson, Dave, 1932–
    The good woodcutter's guide : chain saws, woodlots, and portable sawmills / Dave Johnson.
        p.   cm.
    Includes index.
    ISBN 1–890132–15–2 (alk. paper)
    1. Chain saws. 2. Sawmills. 3. Fuelwood cutting. I. Title.
TS851.J64   1998
634.9'8—dc21   98–34466

Chelsea Green Publishing Company
Post Office Box 428
White River Junction, VT 05001
(800) 639-4099
www.chelseagreen.com

Contents

Acknowledgments vi
Introduction vii

1. Safety 1
2. Body of Work 13
3. Chain Saws 20
4. Saws and Accessories 35
5. Safety Equipment and Clothing. 45
6. Tools. 57
7. Starting Your Saw 69
8. Routine Maintenance. 75
9. Søren Eriksson and the Game of Logging 85
10. Felling. 89
11. Special Cases 106
12. Benching 119
13. Limbing. 124
14. Bucking and Bunching 130
15. Economics. 136
16. Selling Your Wood 141
17. Managing for Firewood 149
18. Wood Burning 165
19. Wood Stoves 172
20. Vehicles. 179
21. Should You Buy a Sawmill? 199

Afterword 210
Index. 211

Acknowledgments

I am indebted to the following people for their help and support:

Eric Johnson, who edited the manuscript and helped turn it into a book.
Ed and Helen Moberg, for reading and commenting on the contents.
And especially to my servicing chain-saw dealer and friend Clyde Samsel,
for his valuable comments and corrections.

Some of this material was published previously in different form in
Blair & Ketchum's Country Journal and in *Woodland Management,*
the magazine of the Wisconsin Woodland Owners Association.

Introduction

THE WOODLAND OWNER WHO DOES at least part of his own work with a chain saw is the person for whom this book will probably have the greatest appeal. This is more or less inevitable, because that is who I am. Still, there is much here for the professional cutter and novice alike. *Note:* I will be using masculine pronouns almost exclusively though I know that many of my readers will be women.

I live on my land and do all my own woods work. Like almost everyone who lives in a rural area and tries to make a living, I've had to "do what comes my way." This has included sawmilling, kiln-drying, logging, pulpwood cutting, tree planting, and firewood production.

For the professional or experienced woods worker, there is a good chance that some of the information contained in this book will be new to you and will lead you to a reevaluation of some work techniques. This can be important since, in repetitive work such as logging, a single small improvement can pay off handsomely over time.

For the novice cutter, the book can act as a guide as you gain expertise. Even after years of woods work, I find that whenever I read back over my source material I discover things I either previously overlooked, forgot, or was unable to fully grasp the first time I read them.

Finally, even though parts of the book may not seem relevant to you, I urge you to read it all the way through. Then, concentrate on those parts that apply directly to your work. The philosophy of work remains the same throughout the book, and perhaps seeing something written in a different way will bring home a particular concept to you and make it relevant to your own situation or circumstances.

I

● Safety ◖⌣

TO ME, SAFETY IS EITHER an integral part of the total work process or it is nothing. Therefore, I don't like to consider it separately.

If you want the final word on safety, the best place to go is to the owner's manuals supplied with quality chain saws. There is no group more obsessed with safety than the saw manufacturers. They know that they are selling a potentially lethal product, and they know that government agencies will continue to impose safety standards. They strive to anticipate these changes so their chain saws will be as safe as possible, yet will remain utilitarian and affordable.

Aside from chain brakes, and new, safer lower-kickback chains, which some manufacturers shortsightedly opposed in the past, I share the industry's viewpoint and concerns. I don't want my saw encumbered with guards and devices that make it less efficient. If you read anything here that seems to contradict anything your manual says, however, go with the manual. The manual writers have the benefit of worldwide experience with saws and logging, so they are the experts and will remain so, regardless of my personal opinions and observations.

In the United States, there are an increasing number of demonstrations and training sessions available for all levels of saw users. These are valuable sources of training and information. Many of the organizations that conduct these sessions also produce and sell videos illustrating their techniques. Some of these are pretty good as well.

Of course, you can always fall back on the old "learn from experience" method. Unfortunately, the trouble with learning from experience is that sometimes the "final exam" occurs on the first day.

About the worst source of safety information, in my opinion, is the kind of articles found in magazines that serve "country living" lifestyle readers. There are several of these magazines on the newsstand, and, even though they have printed articles by me, I wouldn't recommend most of them as reliable sources for logging and/or chain-saw-use information. To them, logging and wood cutting are more folksy weekend occupations, akin to gardening and composting.

Given the choice, most of these magazines will substitute folklore for fact. The authors seem to be either ignorant about modern techniques and tools or they purposely ignore them to preserve the idea of wood cutting as a colorful pastime for amateur, "back-to-the-land" types with their beat-up pickups, clunky chain saws, and blue jeans. That would be fine if it weren't so deadly.

Chain saws are inherently dangerous tools. There is only one chain saw joke I ever heard, and I think I'll tell it now and get it out of the way.

A chain-saw salesman was walking in the woods when he came upon a man cutting firewood with a bow saw.

"How much wood can you cut in a day with that saw?" the salesman asked.

"About a cord," the woodsman replied.

"How would you like to be able to cut five cords?" the salesman asked.

The woodsman was impressed, and the salesman sold him a chain saw.

Several weeks later the woodsman brought the chain saw back to the dealer.

"I not only can't cut five cords with it," he complained, "I have trouble doing even the one cord I did with my bow saw."

Puzzled, the salesman took the chain saw and started it up.

The woodsman jumped back, startled. "What's that noise?" he shouted.

Common Errors

I've observed and tried to train several people to operate chain saws. Each "student" has been different, but there are a few things they all seemed to have in common.

People starting out will invariably hold the saw as far away from their bodies as they can, and they will cut as far out on the bar as they can. This is understandable and indicates a healthy urge to get as far away as possible from what is obviously a dangerous tool. Unfortunately, it is exactly the wrong approach.

Real safety lies in keeping the saw close to your body and cutting as far back from the tip as you can. The tip area is the kickback zone, so the less cutting done out there the better. Especially when limbing, it pays to push the saw right up to where the limb is against the saw body when cutting. It pays to hold the saw up close to your body because you have much more control that way.

Inexperienced cutters tend to ignore the coast-down time of the saw. They act as if the chain stops when you take your finger off the trigger. Not so! Even a properly adjusted saw will stay at or close to cutting speed for a moment after you let go of the trigger. I think this accounts for many injuries to the left leg.

I have an acquaintance who sliced a big slab of muscle off his left calf muscle by letting go of the rear handle and allowing the coasting saw to swing around behind his leg. Safety devices won't save you from this sort of thing. Saws can't distinguish between wood and meat. I've never cut myself that way, but on several occasions I have felt a slight pull on my left pants leg and noticed a few small tears in the fabric there. These are not-so-subtle reminders to be more careful.

Sometimes, new cutters will simply press down on the trigger and hold it down while they swing the saw around, cutting off limbs. That is usually a foolish and dangerous thing to do. No matter how many limbs I'm faced with, I trigger the saw for each and every one. I never move from one branch to the next with the trigger held down.

Another bad tendency is to try and move to the next branch before the branch you are working on is completely cut off. This can pull the chain right off the bar, causing it to flip back at you.

New cutters are often reluctant to cut with the top of the bar. They feel that the proper way is to push the saw down, with the bottom of the bar doing the cutting. I did it that way at first, too. It seemed logical, looking at

Cutting with the top of the bar.

the saw and considering how other tools are supposed to be operated.

A chain saw is unique, however, and now I cut more than half the time with the top of the bar. This is actually safer than cutting with the bottom and often easier. If you are cutting with the top of the bar, the saw pulls into the wood, and any kickback will actually be a kick up or forward, into the cut, not back at you. (See the discussion of "kickback" on page 108.)

Finally, new cutters and people who are used to operating unreliable saws will gun the saw before starting a cut when they are just standing or walking about—like a hot rod driver waiting for the light to change. This is obviously dangerous and completely unnecessary with a good, properly adjusted saw. My saw is never revved up when it is not cutting except when my dealer checks it for proper rpm, and even then I wince when I hear it.

Many people say it's best to fell trees alone, but for us this is a two-person operation that includes felling . . .

Several Clarifications

Before we go any further, I should really explain a bit about my work. Several times I have referred to "my wife." I'm not going to do that any more. Her name is Marcia.

Our main source of income is from logs and pulpwood harvested from our own land. We do this year-round and we do it as a team. We do all the cutting together, then I do the "forwarding." She used to do that, too, but our work rhythm has evolved to where it works better if I do it.

Almost all our work now is second and third thinnings in red pine plantations. The process of bringing a stand of planted red pine to maturity involves regularly removing trees in the stand. Unlike some logging operations, we don't mark trees for removal ahead of time. Marcia makes those decisions as we cut. She selects the tree to be cut and indicates to me the direction in which she feels it should fall. I fell the tree while she inserts the felling lever in the kerf

. . . pushing (if the tree is very small) . . .

behind the saw in bigger trees, or pushes smaller trees over. She makes her selections by considering spacing, the form and health of the tree, and trouble-free felling. We always try to leave the biggest, best trees standing.

When the tree is down, if it is pulpwood, I begin to cut the limbs off as she measures 100-inch pulpsticks using a "stick" made out of ¾-inch plastic pipe. (This job is known locally as "running the stick.") As I move up the stem, Marcia shows me where the pulpsticks should be cut, and I mark those spots on the trunk with the saw. When we reach the spot where the last stick is about four inches in diameter on the small end, I make my last mark, and she moves off to the next tree, taking our equipment with her. I move back down the trunk, bucking the sticks as I go. Then I pile the sticks by hand and join her at the next tree she has chosen.

If the tree is large enough, we cut logs. Here I use a logging tape, which runs out behind me as I move up the trunk—again, limbing as I go. Marcia walks ahead of me with a "go/no-go" gauge. This is a U-shaped gauge that I made out of ½-inch plastic pipe. When she reaches a point where the gauge slips over the trunk, she slips it over and leaves it there for me to see. I look back at my tape and mark at the nearest point where I can get a full log without falling below the diameter limit. She also watches for "quality breaks." These are defects in the trunk, which will also affect our bucking decisions.

. . . *and bucking pulpsticks and logs.*

We are thus a woodcutting team, and have been for many years. Many people will tell you that it is best to work alone while felling trees. I'll have more to say about this later, although, in my case, it's irrelevant. There is no way Marcia is going to let me fell our trees without her being a part of it.

I'm sure there are some married people reading this who will wonder, not should we work as a team, but how we could work that closely for all those years. First and foremost, we have a common goal, which we both clearly understand and agree on: good, sustainable forestry with an eye to constantly improving the forest, so as to leave it better than we found it. Secondly, we have evolved a work rhythm that suits both of us and from which we rarely deviate. Marcia does her part and I do mine; she doesn't "help me in the woods." This is essential, not only for avoiding arguments, but for safety as well.

Finally, if we do disagree about something, we discuss our different opinions and then, no matter how it turns out, we don't indulge in "See, I told you so" recriminations. This latter stipulation comes up mainly with hung-up trees. Often, the best strategy for felling without the tree hanging up in other trees is not obvious. Marcia normally makes these judgments, but sometimes I disagree. If we have to argue about it, chances are neither way is foolproof and the tree would probably hang whichever way we went. So, when they hang, we just go about getting them down.

I try to avoid using the words "never" and "always" in regard to woods work, but they sometimes creep in nonetheless. There is a famous exchange in the Gilbert and Sullivan operetta *H.M.S. Pinafore,* which goes as follows:

Captain:	I am never known to quail at the fury of a gale, and I'm never, never sick at sea!
Chorus:	What, Never?
Captain:	No, NEVER!
Chorus:	Never?
Captain:	Hardly ever!
Chorus:	He's hardly ever sick at sea! Then give three cheers, and one cheer more, for the hardy Captain of the *Pinafore!*

That's an illustration of how you should view these words here. Read "hardly ever" for "never," and "usually" for "always." Woods work is infinitely varied and—I confess—I have probably done all the things I say you should "never" do and will probably do most of them again. You have the same choice. I am doing my best to point out the dangers in various acts, but in the long run, what you do is up to you.

Bear in mind that, in almost all cases, the safest way is the most efficient in the long run. But there are times when safety comes at the price of efficiency. When that happens, I will give both sides of the issue so that you can make an informed choice. What is an acceptable risk for some is foolhardiness to others.

Chain Brakes

At one time, I was the safety director of the Wisconsin Woodland Owners Association (WWOA). While in that position, I attempted to persuade the Wisconsin legislature to pass a law mandating that any chain saw sold in the state of Wisconsin be equipped with an inertial chain brake. The WWOA board of directors supported me on this, but the effort failed when we received no support from any saw manufacturer and open opposition from several American manufacturers and their trade association.

This is a copy of the letter I sent to the directors asking for their support:

A PROPOSAL

I believe that, when it comes to accident prevention, the inertial chain brake on a chain saw is equivalent to blaze orange for hunters and hardhats for construction workers. By itself, it can virtually eliminate kickback accidents, the most common and grisliest chain saw disasters.

It is almost foolproof and requires essentially no maintenance aside from an occasional cleaning. It presents no inconvenience to the user and requires no changes in procedures or habits. Like air bags in cars, it just sits there quietly waiting for a chance to save a life.
It can and should be used as a "parking brake" to ensure safety when carrying a running saw, but even if a user makes no intentional use of it, it will save him in most cases.

With an inertial brake, there is no need for other kickback protection devices such as safety chains, tip guards, "banana-nose" bars, etc. Moreover, all these other devices have drawbacks. Safety chains cut slower than professional chains; banana-nose bars can't be reversed to equalize wear; and tip guards prevent bore cutting and restrict the utility of the saw to a point where most users remove them sooner or later.

The inertial brake acts to stop the chain from rotating if it senses the saw swinging dangerously fast. It is claimed that it will stop the chain within a single· revolution. This is vital, since a kicking-back saw will hit you before it is possible to react. I have read that in one second, each tooth will hit you ten times, so there's no way to save yourself by yourself. With a 16-inch bar, that's over 300 strikes in that one second.

The brake itself is the latest step in a process that
started with the simple handguard. This protects your hand
from sliding down onto the chain. Not much, but better
than nothing. From here, the handguard evolved into the
standard chain brake. This brake will stop the chain if it
is activated by pressure on the back of the hand guard.
This was a big step forward in kickback protection. If the
saw were to rear up suddenly, the cutter's wrist would hit
the guard and activate the brake.

One of the shortcomings of this chain brake system was
that it didn't engage until it was struck--thus, it was
somewhat slow. An even greater problem was that if the
cutter was in a position where the saw could kick back
without his wrist contacting the guard, the brake wouldn't
engage at all. This meant that anytime the cutter was
holding the saw sideways, the brake offered no protection.
This was a serious flaw, because felling cuts are made
with the bar parallel to the ground and the cutter holding
the handle from the side. In this position, a kickback is
free to swing the saw back into the cutter's leg, unhin-
dered by the brake.

All this changed with the development of the inertial
brake. With this system, no matter what position the saw
is in, the brake will be actuated by the inertia of the
saw swinging around.

I have never cut myself with my saw, but I have experienced severe kickback. Several times, the force has been
so strong that it numbed my arm. I have used saws with
inertial brakes for several years now and have never had
any problems with them.

Since I started using inertial-brake saws, I've never
had an unstopped kickback. It is not uncommon to have
the brake engage while I'm working. It probably happens
several times a day. Often when it does, I can't see why
it did, but sometimes I will feel a kick and feel the saw
start to come back at me. It is then that I know that, had
it not been for the brake, I would have had a kickback to
deal with, with all the dangers that implies.

As far as I know, there are only three manufacturers that sell saws with inertial brakes on all their models in the United States: Stihl, Husqvarna, and Jonsered. The other manufacturers continue to sell saws that they know are not as safe as they could be and, I guess, accept the fact that a certain number of people will be killed and maimed by their products. Some manufacturers sell some of their saws with brakes--Sachs-Dolmar and Olympyk, to name two--but they continue to omit inertial brakes on some of their other models. Why, I don't know. I suppose there is some commercial advantage in this. Certainly, inertial brakes add something to the price of a saw, but there's no way to know how much. Inertial brakes are not optional; they are an integral part of the saw, so there's no way to tell.

My proposal then, is this: The state of Wisconsin should pass a law making it mandatory that all chain saws sold in the state after a certain date be equipped with inertial chain brakes.

I've been impressed lately by the way that states have taken it upon themselves to act in cases where they feel they should, without waiting for the federal government to lead the way. Wisconsin has been one of the states that has taken initiatives on its own, and I think this would be another opportunity for us to lead. I believe that federal law should insist on inertial brakes, but I'm not willing to tackle the issue on that level.

Government has acted many times on safety issues, most of them more controversial than this one. Seat belt and motorcycle helmet laws invariably raise issues of individual rights. However, there is no such problem here, since nobody is being asked to give up or adapt to anything. All the requirements are on the manufacturers. Unlike clean air legislation, no complicated scientific studies or technological breakthroughs are required. The technology is there, proven, and already in use. All that is needed is to force all manufacturers to do what some already do voluntarily. It doesn't seem right that manufacturers can sell saws here in the United States that would be illegal in the countries in which they are made. The trick, then, is to force them to sell the safer saws here.

If there are any valid arguments against inertial brakes, I've never heard them. It seems to me that the only reason to sell a saw without a brake is that you can either sell it cheaper or make more profit selling it at market price. To me these are not convincing arguments for compromising safety to this extent.

Chain-saw safety is probably not on any legislator's short list of things to do. Overall it doesn't affect large numbers of voters. Still, the ones it does affect, it possibly affects drastically.

As the writer of the Woodland Management safety column, it occurs to me that it doesn't make much sense to warn people about the dangers of kickback and explain ways to avoid it when a simple change in their saws will essentially eliminate the hazard. That is sort of like writing advice columns on how to brace yourself for a car accident instead of mandating seat belts in cars. The seat belts benefit everyone, while the advice protects only those who read and heed it, and then not as well as a belt.

Finally, I should close by saying that I have no interest in this other than safety. I don't sell or service chain saws and don't intend to start.

Thank you for your consideration.

Sincerely,

Dave Johnson

Since I sent this letter, OSHA has mandated that all saws under its jurisdiction be equipped with chain brakes. Not *inertial* brakes, unfortunately, but brakes nonetheless. This is a big step forward—a move that was actively opposed by some saw manufacturers, who succeeded in preventing the inertial brakes from being mandated but who weren't able to stop all progress.

The firmest opponent of chain brakes is Homelite. The company maintains that the "safety tip" that they include on their saws (Echo includes them also) is the only sure way to prevent rotational kickback. The brakes, it is pointed out, do not *prevent* kickback, they only protect the user from its consequences. Further, opponents say, the brakes are active devices which can—and no doubt do—fail. The tip guard is a passive device that requires no actions to engage it. It is always there and always in service.

These are valid arguments, which would be persuasive except that the guard so restricts the utility of the saw that, by Homelite's own admission, 85 percent of Homelite users remove the safety tip at some time. Of these 85 percent, only 65 percent bother to put it back on. These numbers far exceed any failure rate I ever heard of from chain brakes. Since an awful lot of the techniques discussed in this book cannot be used with the tip guard in place, I will say no more about it.

In response to a logger who couldn't believe that there were still manufacturers who were selling saws without even elemental safety features, I went to a local discount store and checked.

This store sold three brands of saws, all American made. None of the saws were equipped with inertial brakes. The three McCulloch models I saw all had the old-style brake. There were three Homelite models: of these three, one had an old-style brake. The other two had no brake at all. There were three Poulan models, and none of them had any brakes.

The Poulan models were out of their containers and were being sold with no manuals. There was a tag attached to each telling about fuel mixing and starting. The other saws were in boxes, and I couldn't tell whether they came with manuals or not.

These, of course, are saws marketed to the casual user, who, of all users, needs the safety features and instructions that are standard on the major European saws.

I know that neither McCulloch or Homelite put brakes on any of their saws until recently. They only did so then because OSHA regulations required brakes on all saws used on logging jobs. Even then, Homelite appears to have only put them on saws of a size that might be used by loggers.

To me, then, the first criterion for buying a saw is, "Does it have an inertial chain brake?" Personally, I would go further and ask, "Do *all* models of this saw have inertial brakes, and did they have them before the manufacturer was forced to install them?"

I don't understand how companies can install these safety devices on only some of their saws, but some do. How do they determine which saws need to be safe and others less so? Where do you rank in their thinking and why?

If you decide to go with a saw other than the three I favor, be sure that you get one with an inertial brake. This is not as easy as it sounds. Dealers who sell saws that don't have these brakes tend to twist and squirm when you ask about them. Some, I suppose, are genuinely ignorant about the difference between inertial brakes and regular brakes. Others know the difference but feign ignorance.

Luckily, there is a simple test you can perform to see if the brake is, in fact, inertial. With the saw shut off and the brake cocked, hold the saw above a stump or board, using only your right hand on the rear handle. Let the nose of the bar drop until it strikes the obstacle. When the nose hits, you should hear a "click" and the brake should engage. You may have to do this several times. You'll know you've got it right when you are able to recock the brake. Do this test yourself and be sure not to touch the handguard.

Stihl has introduced an additional feature to its braking system. The new system will actuate the brake in one of three ways: (1) in the way just described when the nose of the bar drops an obstacle; by hitting the guard with your hand; (2) inertially if the saw swings; and, now, (3) if your right hand leaves the rear handle. This last safety measure is accomplished by tying the brake into the throttle interlock on the rear handle.

Simply gripping the rear handle so as to reset the throttle interlock will reset the brake, no matter how it was tripped. Stihl offers this feature on two of its large, professional saws.

I've tried one, and it works fine. It's yet to be seen, though, how it will hold up in long service.

My only reservation would be that, if it caused any problems, some guys would tape the interlock device down, thus losing all the protection from the interlock and the brake system.

It does affect sharpening your chain, however. Since the brake engages when you are not holding the interlock down, you can't advance the chain while sharpening without depressing the interlock. This seems as if it would be really awkward. I think I would have to get a strap to hold the interlock down during sharpening.

My friend, who uses both hands on the file when he sharpens, says the locking of the brake might be a plus for him since he has a problem with the chain moving during his file strokes. Since I hold my file with one hand, using the other to hold and steady the tooth, this wouldn't help me.

2

● Body of Work ❨▲▲

IF YOU CUT WOOD, YOU USE YOUR BODY more than any tool you have, but I'll bet you know less about how it reacts to the strain you put on it than you do about your chain saw.

Even if you are curious about how your body works, you won't find anything of interest in logging books or magazines, at least not in American publications. Where you will find this information is in sports publications and in some forestry textbooks read only by students who will probably never actually do any of the things they read about. I guess it never occurs to anyone that an American in this day and age would subject his body to the stress that comes from hard work; for games yes, but for work no.

But those of us who cut wood for a living are out there, knocking down trees and bucking them up, and straining our bodies the same as any athlete.

In fact, woods work is as athletic as most sports, and what has been learned in sports medicine over the last few years applies directly to us. And a lot has been learned.

Stretching exercises are a good example. Some exercise manuals and tapes recommend doing these kinds of "warm-up" exercises before you start work. However, the current thinking is that you should definitely not stretch before you are warmed up. Cold muscles can tear when stretched, just as a rubber band taken out of the freezer will break rather than stretch. I have always felt that the work is the exercise and that there is no need to do anything prior to that. Now, the experts in sports medicine seem to agree: stretching before work is not only unnecessary—it's harmful.

If you work on the ground doing forestry work, your body can be compared to a bored-out "hot" chain saw. From the outside, you look a lot like the guy who works in an office, but inside, where it counts, your body is quite different. Your bones are stronger, thicker, and heavier. Your heart and lungs are up to twice as efficient as a nonexerciser. Your body contains several pints more blood and up to a mile of extra capillaries to get all that blood where it's needed and then bring it back.

As you get into shape, when you first start working in the woods or after a layoff, your bones begin to strengthen to take the extra strain you're putting on them. New bone is constantly being formed and old cells sloughed off. Normally, this process is in balance: what is being formed equals what is being sloughed off. When you start exercising, your bones build up and reach a new balance at a higher density.

This doesn't happen all at once, though. When you start working hard, cells are damaged and sloughed off faster than new ones can be formed, so that your bones actually become weaker on their way to becoming stronger. The bones are weakest after about three weeks. By the fourth week, the building process catches up, and the bones begin to move toward a new, stronger balance.

The Army used to lose about 5 percent of its recruits in the third week of basic training due to small bone fractures in their legs during marches. By easing off in the third week of training, they reduced this number to 1.3 percent in a trial conducted at Fort Bliss in Texas. After the third week, they gradually returned to full schedule. It might pay to keep this in mind if you have to lay off for a while. The final result of this process is that your bones break less easily than the average person's, and if they do break, they heal faster.

Bones don't do much for you, though, unless you can move them, and muscles do that.

When you start working, or "working out," the most obvious change in your body is an increase in your muscles. You notice this most in the "macho muscles" of the upper body: chest, shoulders, and biceps. These are not your most important muscles, only the most visible.

As you develop physically, fat tissue is converted into muscle tissue. Muscle tissue burns calories faster than fat tissue, so that if you eat the same diet as an average person, you will lose weight, or, looking at it another way, you can eat more without getting fat.

Swedish studies show that a manual forest worker burns between 5,000 and 6,000 calories per day as compared to an office worker who burns only 2,000 to 3,000 calories. Skidder and truck operators use up between 3,000 and 4,000 calories. Dieticians have added up the calories in old logging-camp menus and found that the lumberjacks of those days ate about 9,000 calories per day. Of course they worked 10- to 12-hour shifts, much of it with two-man saws.

I use my muscles every day, cutting and stacking wood, and yet I don't look like Mr. Universe. I make a muscle in front of the mirror and it doesn't look much bigger than it did before I started working in the woods, yet I exercise just about as hard as I can.

In actual fact, my muscles have changed. They haven't just become bigger, they've become more efficient. By doing the same work over and over, my stamina has increased. The blood supply to my muscles has increased so that oxygen can be supplied and wastes carried away at a faster rate, thereby increasing the amount of work I can do without tiring. The only way to increase muscle size is to lift heavier and heavier loads. This is how "bodybuilders" do it. Compared to woods workers, however, these musclebound weight lifters may have little stamina and might well be left gasping in the woods, trying to keep up.

The system that keeps all body functions going is lumped together under the name "circulorespiratory," and it consists of the lungs, heart, and blood circulation systems. The lungs add oxygen to the blood and remove waste gases from it. The heart supplies the pressure to move blood around the body, and the circulatory system—the arteries, veins, and capillaries—supply the channels through which the blood flows. All these components change drastically as you become more physically fit. They become stronger and more efficient, allowing you to do more work without tiring.

The ability of a muscle to do work depends on how efficiently it can burn sugar and eliminate the wastes formed by that burning. This in turn depends on how efficiently blood can be circulated through the muscle, and how quickly the blood can be cleaned and loaded up with oxygen for another trip. And that depends mainly on lung capacity.

If you are working efficiently, all these bodily systems are operating within their limits, and you feel fine. Your heart is probably beating about twice as fast as it is during a break, and your breathing is increased. Everything is in balance, though. Just where it balances is what fitness is all about. You can build these systems up through exercise to where you are just cruising along at work levels that would overload the average person.

Any time these systems balance, you are said to be exercising "aerobically." Push your body over the limit, however, and you are working "anaerobically." In an anaerobic condition, the blood cannot remove the waste (in this case, lactic acid) that is being formed by exercise in the muscles fast enough, and the muscles cease to function as they drown in their own waste.

Ever drag a log over soft ground and then collapse on top of it, panting when you finally drop it? That's anaerobic work. You can do it briefly, and we all do, but we pay for it by having to back off until our bodies can catch up.

People used to think that this was the way to build your body. The popular philosophy was, "No pain, no gain." No longer. The trick now is to operate just below this threshold, while in the process pushing the threshold higher. Go over the threshold, and you just poop out, and nothing is gained.

None of us is training to became an Olympic athlete. Our goal is just to comfortably do a day's work, make a buck, and have something left to enjoy the evening with. Nobody is going to spend money to wire loggers up to sophisticated computers so that they can figure out what their optimum work level is, but you can do pretty much the same thing on your own, simply by paying attention to your breathing. Since your body runs on oxygen, regulating the oxygen supply is the key to working efficiently.

Your body works like a stove. Even if you are full of fuel, you won't get combustion without enough air. Since you probably have plenty of fuel from eating regular meals, the rate of burning depends on your ability to supply air, and that depends on your lung capacity. Your best work level should keep you breathing heavily, but not panting. You should be able to carry on a conversation while you work and not run out of breath. The level at which you can do this is determined by how fit you are, and this is largely a function of lung capacity.

The amount of oxygen your body needs per minute tells you how hard the work is. For instance, cross-country skiing requires a maximum of about 6 liters of oxygen per minute. Forestry work requires about 3.5 liters per minute.

The Swedes have broken forest work down into separate tasks and rate some of them as follows, based on the amount of oxygen needed per minute for each activity.

- felling with a chain saw, 1.2 liters/minute
- delimbing with a chain saw, 1.2 liters/minute

- bunching (stacking) average-size logs over bare ground, 2.2 liters/minute
- manual debarking and/or felling with a buck saw, 2.5 liters/minute

These are average oxygen requirements measured over time. Maximums can be much higher for short periods.

To perform identical amounts of work requires identical amounts of energy, which must come from identical amounts of oxygen burned. The difference is in what portion of your lung capacity is required to obtain that amount of oxygen. It may take half the lung capacity of a young, fit worker, and all the capacity of an older, unfit worker.

Notice that age enters in here. Maximum oxygen intake capacity declines steadily as we age. An average 60-year-old's lungs have 30 percent less capacity than the average 25-year-old's lungs. This is an average, however, and there is wide individual variation.

Swedish tests on men of the same body size and varying ages show, for example, that "low" capacity for ages 20 to 29 is 2.79 liters per minute, while "high" capacity for ages 60 to 69 is also 2.79 liters per minute. Thus, it is possible to overcome at least part of the aging process by taking care of your body.

The following chapters of this book are all based on the premise that if you work smarter, you don't have to work as hard. Tests have shown it is not unusual for one cutter to take twice as many steps as another to produce an identical amount of wood. When you realize that these steps are made through slash and sometimes snow, and over logs, all the while carrying tools and sometimes pulpsticks, you know what a difference these extra steps can make.

Even if the same person does identical work, such as pedaling a stationary bicycle, the work rhythm he uses greatly affects the amount of work he can do without becoming exhausted. Consider the following experiment:

The subject first pedaled a bicycle for 5 minutes, took a 7.5-minute break and started again. He was exhausted after 10 minutes.

In the next test, he pedaled for 2 minutes with a 3-minute break. Working this way, he was able to continue for 24 minutes before becoming exhausted. He did two-and-one-half times better just by varying his pace, even though the ratio of work to rest was the same, at 2:3.

Finally, he tried pedaling for 1/2 minute and then rested for 3/4 of a minute. This way, he worked the entire 24 minutes with no sign of exhaustion.

When I analyze my normal woods-work routine, it turns out that, through good luck, I come pretty close to the ideal: I fell the tree, limb and buck it, stack the logs, fell the next tree, etc. This pattern also helps rest muscles, since different muscles are used in each of these activities.

Given a choice, the cutters I know would rather work very hard during a short workday instead of spreading that work out by taking it easier through a longer day. The researchers found, however, that it is best to spread the work out. Their ideal work cycle is: one hour of work, five minutes break, one hour of work, and then a long break. This would divide an eight-hour day into four two-hour segments, with long breaks between them.

You could do this by taking your breaks when you fuel your saw. If you considered the long breaks to be 20 minutes, you could take one every other time you gassed up. This would be three 20-minute breaks in an eight-hour day, which is equivalent to taking an hour for lunch, as many people do now.

With this scheme, you would take your lunch in three separate portions, eating a small amount each time. It's been said that "When the belly is full, the body must rest," and this is borne out by fact. When the body is at rest, about 60 percent of your blood goes to your brain, kidneys, and intestines and about 15 percent to the muscles. When you start working, about 85 percent goes to the muscles. The brain and kidneys get about 3 percent each, and if you are working hard, the intestines get just enough to stay alive; digestion simply stops and doesn't start again until you slow down. Based on this and on everyone's experience of after-lunch sluggishness, the Swedes may have a point.

As a topic of discussion, what you eat is obviously very important to your general health and way beyond the scope of this chapter. However, we should deal here with the working muscles, which get their energy by burning sugar. How you supply that sugar to them makes a lot of difference.

It used to be generally accepted that lots of protein was essential for hard work, and since steak and other red meat are good sources of protein, they were considered essential to a hard working person's diet.

We have since learned that the best source of energy to the muscles is not protein but carbohydrates. These are found, not in meat, but in cereals and pasta. The starch in these foods is converted to sugar slowly and feeds the muscles over a long period, thus enabling you to work a long time without running out of energy. This accounts for the ability of people from developing nations, whose diet includes almost no meat, to work long, hard hours without tiring. You need only to think of Vietnam and Korea to realize that this is true.

You can change your diet fairly easily to include more carbohydrates. Eat pizza instead of a burger and fries, spaghetti rather than steak, and pancakes instead of bacon and eggs.

Incidentally, what really counts is your diet over a long period, not just what you eat on a single day. Nutritionists no longer feel that athletes gain anything by eating special foods just before a big game or race. They have to keep at it to realize any real benefit.

Thirst is normally considered to be the body's way of telling you it is time to drink, but when you are sweating heavily, thirst is actually telling you that you should have had liquid earlier. Thirst indicates that your system is short of fluids, and, in order to stay at peak efficiency, you should "top up" regularly to avoid running short. Get in the habit of drinking water when you gas your saw. Think of it as regular maintenance for your body, like adding bar oil to your saw. You do that automatically every time you refuel; you don't wait for the bar and chain to tell you that you're running short.

Water is all you really need. Questions are now being raised as to whether the highly publicized "sports beverages" that athletes promote and drink while competing are actually any better for them than plain water.

You'll notice that I've said nothing about being obese and/or smoking. I assume that if you understand how your body works and all the benefits you can expect if you use it right, you won't need to be beaten over the head with horror stories about the effects of abusing it.

3

● Chain Saws ❤ ◆

FEW TOOLS HAVE HAD AS REVOLUTIONARY AN IMPACT on work as the chain saw. A modern chain saw in the hands of a skilled operator can do an incredible amount of work (or damage) with comparatively little effort.

Working with a chain saw is, at best, an athletic undertaking. Like athletics, skill and physical conditioning are important. Also like athletics, perfection is always beyond your grasp. You can improve with practice and training, but you never completely master the art.

Unlike most other power cutting tools, it is not possible to guard the most dangerous portions of a chain saw. Thus, physical danger is always present, not only from the saw, but from the trees.

A chain saw is more versatile than other power tools. It will cut equally well on the top and the bottom of the bar, right-side up, upside down, or any position in between. It is not restrained by cords, wires, or hoses and can be used as high or low as the operator wishes. In skilled hands it can be made to move and cut with almost complete flexibility. It can, in the blink of an eye, sever an artery and leave you to bleed to death in less than a minute.

Even though I have used chain saws for countless hours, I'm still sometimes awestruck by the work that a good saw will do. Maybe this is why people who use them a lot become sentimental about their saws. I'm as attached to my saw as I am to my old jeans and my Peace Corps backpack.

Don't ask me to loan you any of these. Such a tool demands respect and inspires real affection. It will receive both in this book.

Many features are found on all modern saws. Some are, alas, found only on foreign made saws—and not on all of them.

All saws manufactured these days have *anti-vibration mounts* to prevent the engine vibration from reaching the operator's fingers. These are rubber "cushions" that isolate the engine from the handles. (Some large saws now use coil springs rather than rubber for mounts). This not only lessens fatigue, it also prevents a condition known as "white finger disease." This condition was common among old-time loggers. Over time, the nerves in their fingers became damaged from the pounding they received. It was irreversible and resulted in the fingers turning white and feeling cold even in warm weather.

Saws made in the 1970s, when I started using them, allowed quite a bit of vibration to reach the operator. I don't think I suffered any permanent damage, but I was often bothered by tingling and numbness in my arms when I went to bed after working with my saw during the day. I have none of these problems today.

All saws have *mufflers*. These help, but are not sufficient protection for the operator. I never start my saw without first donning ear protection. By law, all chain saws used on federal lands have to have their mufflers fitted with screens to prevent sparks from flying out and causing fires. All professional saws now contain these screens. Most of them are easily removed, and people do remove them, thinking that they produce back pressure in the saw's engine cylinder.

I used to routinely remove the screens from my saws until I actually started a fire with exhaust sparks. After that incident, I replaced the screen and have left it in. I haven't noticed any difference in performance. I look at it occasionally to see if it is plugging up, but have never noticed any carbon buildup. (My dealer tells me that buildup will only occur if the saw idles for long periods of time. Mine doesn't do that). Some chain saw users are so obsessed with back pressure that they puncture their mufflers with screwdrivers. I don't have much to say to people who do that. Even if I did, they probably couldn't hear me!

Saws are all designed now so that the mufflers exhaust forward, away from the operator. That wasn't always the case. I hate to think of all the fumes I breathed over the years from saws with side exhausts and leaded gas.

All saws that I know of now have *handguards* either ahead of or attached to the front handle. On way too many saws, these are simply guards. They protect the operator's left hand from branches whipping back and stop his hand from contacting the chain in the event that it slips off the handle and is thrust forward. On the best saws, this handguard also functions as a chain brake.

The lower plate on the rear handle is not symmetrical. It extends out to the right side. This puts it in line with the chain. It is built this way to stop a broken chain from flying up and striking the operator's right hand. There are several other pegs and stops in the body of the saw that are also there to catch flying chains. You can see them when you remove the side plate.

There are, as far as I know, no left-handed chain saws. All of the saws we are concerned with look pretty much alike. We won't be discussing electric saws or "mini" saws.

Most modern, professional chain saws look about the same.

Like the guards just mentioned, chain saws are not symmetrical. The bar and chain always extend out from the right-hand side of the engine. Because the chain is driven by the crankshaft, this is probably the obvious way to configure a saw. This configuration also has advantages for the user. It allows the operator to turn the saw onto its right side when felling, making it easy to cut stumps close to the ground. A skilled operator takes advantage of the flat area in front of the engine to rest the saw on the trunk of the fallen tree while limbing. He slides the saw along, lopping off limbs as he goes, with the trunk supporting the weight of the saw.

Most saws have the oil and fuel filling holes on the left side of the engine, so that the saw is laid on its right side for refueling (refueling here includes both fuel and bar oil).

The *oil hole* is generally located toward the front of the saw, while the *fuel hole* is located toward the rear. In some models, both fuel and oil inlets are located side by side on the top of the engine. With this arrangement, it's easy to get mixed up and pour the liquids into the wrong holes. This is a minor problem if you pour gas into the oil tank, but a disaster if you fill the fuel tank with bar oil. Another advantage of side filling is that, if you slop the oil over, it doesn't run down onto the handle; instead, it runs down on the bar and actually aids a bit in lubrication.

Older saws vent the fuel tank through a hole in the filler cap. New saws vent separately. This is a nice improvement. With the old saws, fuel would run out of the cap when you tipped the saw on its side.

All saws now have automatic bar oiling. On older saws oiling was manual-activated through a push-button oil pump you worked with your thumb. Some saws still have a manual override in addition to the automatic feature. These are rare and we won't be discussing them. Some saws have adjustable oil flows; others are factory-set.

All saws now have *throttle interlocks,* which you must push down, normally with the palm of your right hand in order to accelerate the saw. This valuable safety feature causes no operating problems that I can think of, but, still, people disable them by taping them down. Why, I don't know.

All saws sold in North America start with a *pull cord* and *recoil mechanism,* which is bolted onto the left-hand side of the engine. I saw a picture in a magazine one time of Chinese loggers. Their saws didn't have the recoil mechanism attached. Each crew had one, which attached to the saws in some manner and then was removed after the saw started. It was passed around from man to man as needed. That's not a bad idea. I rarely stop my saw between refuelings, and it would subtract weight and allow for a streamlined design if the recoil mechanism weren't there. I could easily carry the mechanism in the purse I use for a tool kit.

All saws now have *"on-off"* switches. With some older saws, you had to choke the engine to stop it. All saws have *chokes* and *half-speed throttle locks* for starting. Some combine these features in a single starting lever. On others, they are separate.

All saws have *filters* on their oil and fuel pickup tubes. All saws have at least one air filter. Some have multiple filters.

Almost all saws now have *electronic ignition.* On top-quality saws, the ignition systems are warranted for the life of the saw.

All saws have *centrifugal clutches,* which permit the saw to idle without the chain turning and then to engage when the saw is revved. All saws drive their chains directly from the crankshaft.

All saw engines are single-cylinder, two-cycle engines and require a gas-oil fuel mixture. On top-quality saws, the mixture is 50 to 1, premium gas to two-cycle oil. Echo, at one time, made an opposed-piston, single-cylinder saw engine. Solo made a two-cylinder engine and Sachs-Dolmar used a Wankel rotary engine. I don't believe that any of these are still in production.

The two-cycle engine, with the gas-oil mixture and the all-position carburetor, makes the modern chain saw the versatile tool that it is. There is no crankcase oil to spill out when the saw is flipped over, and the carburetor delivers fuel evenly to the engine even with the saw upside down. Contrast this to the old saws you sometimes see displayed in dealers' shops. With these, you had to bolt the bar on one way when you were felling trees, then rotate it to buck fallen logs.

All saws drive the chain through a *sprocket*. In older saws, the sprocket and clutch drum were one piece. New saws use "rim" sprockets, which slide onto a splined shaft on the clutch drum. It is easy and cheap to change the sprocket now, which is a savings because sprockets need replacing more often than drums.

Bars are bolted to the engine housing using either one or two studs. Adjusting screws are provided to adjust chain tightness.

Chain

I'm looking at the box my latest chain came in. On the back it shows seven tooth profiles, all of which have names. These are broken down into more than fifty separate model numbers. The box lists four sizes of round files and one flat file. All these measurements are given in metric and English units. It shows four dimensions that are to be maintained on each tooth while filing. These are different for each of the styles. Some of these vary by as little as .005 inch, or five degrees.

We're going to be talking in detail about chain sharpening later, but the obvious first question is, how in the world can a person select the right kind of chain out of all these choices? You can, of course, simply trust your dealer to outfit you as he or she thinks best. You can also just accept the chain your new saw comes with. These are not bad options, but there are some choices you should make for yourself.

The chain profiles clearly show the buyer the compromises that have been made in each style. You might think that, if there is a superior chain, it should be the choice for everyone, but that is not the case, nor could it be.

Differences in chain styles trade off safety for "aggressiveness" and frequency of sharpening for cutting efficiency. There is also a special "skip link" chain for ripping. These are used mainly by operators of the so-called

Alaskan mills, which use chain saws for sawing boards out of logs. Standard chains plug up with the long chips produced by sawing with the grain, and thus these chains have every second tooth removed. (Note that I use the terms "tooth" and "cutter" interchangeably).

Carbide-tipped chain is available, but it is very expensive and can't be sharpened with a file. Its use is limited to special service, such as firefighting units. I can see where carbide *chain* is impractical, but why doesn't somebody make carbide-tipped *files?* I wear out more files than I do chain.

"Chipper" chain has round-nosed teeth. "Chisel" chain, by contrast, has teeth that end in a sharp point. This is an obvious tradeoff. Chisel chain cuts faster and easier; chipper chain doesn't have to be sharpened as often. There is a compromise chain as well, appropriately named "semi-chisel." Chisel chain—being more aggressive—is considered more dangerous to use. Possibly it is. The average user may not sharpen his chain either frequently or correctly, and thus chipper chain with its less aggressive profile and longer cutting capabilities is the proper choice for "consumers."

On the other hand, I feel that you *will* sharpen your chains frequently and correctly after reading this book, and that the methods described here will result in safe practices. For this reason, I will discuss only chisel chain.

All chain I use is sharpened with round files. However, there is a professional chain on the market that is sharpened with a flat file. It's called "square-ground chisel" or "chisel-bit" chain. It's supposed to cut 10 percent faster than round-ground chain and requires a special file and special techniques to keep it sharp. The files are expensive, and the techniques for sharpening are difficult to learn and time-consuming to perform. For these reasons, I have stuck with round-ground chain and that's what I will be talking about. (*Note:* You can convert round-ground chain to square-filed chain by filing the teeth down to a "flat" profile. I don't recommend you try that either.)

With all these tooth profiles, the basic cutter is the same. It consists of two main parts, the tooth itself and the "raker" or "depth gauge" portion (also called the "drag" in the South, apparently because it "drags" out the chips produced by the teeth), which is directly in front of the tooth. This often neglected portion of the cutter determines how deeply the tooth will cut into the wood. If you fail to file it as you sharpen the tooth, eventually the shortened tooth will not be able to contact the wood at all and the chain will cease to cut. If you file it down too much, the tooth will jam into the wood and either stall the saw or kick it back at you violently.

There is a new tool on the market which uses a flat and a round file

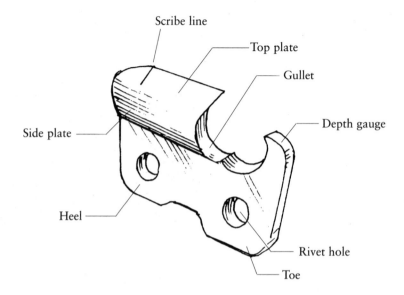

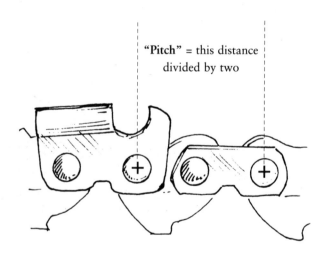

Chain profile.

together. It is said that, with this tool, you can file the teeth and rakers down in proper relationship in a single operation. If true, this is an interesting development.

On so-called safety chain there are additional "guide links" ahead of the teeth. These tend to ease the wood up onto the rakers for smoother cutting. Most chain now uses some form of guide link.

There is a definite difference in the performance of chipper and chisel chain and between safety chain and professional chain. The difference is so great that the American National Standards Institute (ANSI) requires that labels be attached to chain boxes to inform the buyer which type it contains. Thus, if your chain comes in a box, the box will have either a yellow or blue label. Blue labels signify safe chain, yellow, a more aggressive chain. (Stihl uses green and yellow labels.)

A well-maintained full chisel chain about halfway through its useful life.

You would think that the labels would be red and green, colors that we are used to in these situations. Not so. Apparently the industry was reluctant to admit that some chain could be dangerous with a red label. You might also conclude that, human nature being what it is, some people who shouldn't would opt for the red chain rather than choose the "sissy" green.

I really have no experience with safety chain so I don't know how it performs. All chain discussed here will be "yellow label" chain. Which type you actually use is up to you. Presumably you can do

Note the filed rakers.

everything with the one that you can with the other. It would make sense, however, to determine which type you actually have.

Because bars come in different gauges, chain does as well. The "drive links"—the links on the bottom of the chain, through which the sprocket drives the chain—have to be compatible with the groove in the bar.

In addition to gauge, chain is rated by "pitch." Pitch is defined as one-half the distance, in inches or millimeters, between any three rivets on the chain. Thus, the larger the pitch, the greater the distance between points, and the fewer—and bigger—the parts. Since the sprocket drives the chain through the drive links, different sprockets must be used for different pitches. The only two pitches we will be concerned with are ⅜ inch and .325 inch. Why one of these is in decimals and the other in fractions is beyond me, but that's the way it is.

In case your arithmetic skills are a bit rusty, ⅜ inch is larger than .325 inch. Usually smaller saws are sold with .325 chain and larger saws with ⅜. I use .325 chain but I have also used ⅜. I can't tell any difference in performance between the two.

One recent innovation in chain is a line scribed at an angle on the top surface of each tooth. I am told that this line is a limit line for use in Europe, where laws forbid sharpening chains beyond a certain point for safety reasons. That may well be, but for me it provides a reference line right on the tooth to use as a guide when sharpening. I'm not sure exactly what angle the line is (it's approximately 30 degrees), but if I adhere to it while sharpening, it results in a good tooth profile and eliminates the need for any sort of file guides.

There is one further sharpening aid I have seen. Some chain is assembled using a colored enamel link. This acts as a reference to enable you to easily tell when you have gone all the way around the chain while filing.

Dealers often have "two-for-one" sales on loops of chain. Watch for them. You should always keep a spare chain. You can also buy reels of chain, 25, 50, or 100 feet long, and make your own loops. This is a bit cheaper than buying preassembled loops, but not worth the hassle for most people, including me. You will also find good deals on an extensive selection of chains and tools in the Bailey's catalog.

Choosing a Saw

For me, deciding which chain saw to buy is an easy question, since the choice narrows down quickly to the big three European saws: Stihl, Husqvarna, and Jonsered. These three have always been the leaders in chain-saw innovations, especially in the area of safety.

Just below these, there is a large group of saws, all of them foreign-made as well. This group includes Pioneer, Sachs-Dolmar, Echo, Olympyk, and several others. There are some good saws in this group, and they are generally a bit cheaper than the Big Three.

Finally—and sadly—come the American-made saws. These manufacturers have spent all their creativity in recent years fighting improvements rather than seeking them out. Their saws are cut-rate products sold in discount stores and given away as premiums for, for example, opening savings accounts at banks. Normally, I am all for discount stores and cut-rate products, but these manufacturers have, the way I see it, resisted changes that add greatly to the safety of the user in order to keep their prices down. To me that is inexcusable, and after this chapter, I won't be referring to them again.

The main thing, in my mind, that puts the Big Three saws above all of the others is their development and use of the latest safety innovations. I don't believe these companies have done this because they are more conscientious than the American manufacturers. In fact I know that some continue to sell unsafe saws in Third World countries where there are no standards.

At least one of these manufacturers sold safer saws in Europe for years before introducing them in the U.S. I think the companies made these changes because laws in European countries have forced them to change, and it was cheaper to just market the safe saws here in the U.S. rather than produce separate models for each market.

In this country, the Occupational Safety and Health Administration (OSHA) has finally mandated several of these innovations—over the strenuous objections of American manufacturers. Still, even the OSHA regulations, brought into effect in 1995, fall short of technology that is now standard on the Big Three saws. Further, these regulations apply only to companies whose employees are covered by workers' compensation.

Saw manufacturers can, and do, continue to sell unsafe saws to the general public. The regulations thus have little impact because few, if any, professional cutters used the cheap saws that are now banned. It bears mentioning, however, that at least one American manufacturer has brought several of its models up to the minimum OSHA requirements and now boasts of this "important safety feature" in its advertising. This is the same feature the company resisted for years until it was mandated by law.

Although lack of safety features is my big concern with these saws, I have operated several of them and they are also slower and heavier than top-quality saws. In my experience at least, they require much more maintenance.

All three European manufacturers recommended at the beginning of this chapter have unique features on their saws. None provides a clear enough advantage, in my opinion, to sway the average user one way or the other. I'll discuss a few of them here, but don't let my ideas influence you too much. A quality saw is what you are after, and all three makes provide that more or less equally.

My main experience goes back quite a number of years and is almost exclusively with Stihl and Husqvarna. I ran Stihls for many years and then switched to Husqvarna for reasons I'll explain later. In my opinion, Stihl saws have several desirable features that "Huskies" lack. On the other hand, Husqvarna seems to be at the forefront of new technology. Many of these improvements are internal, however, and thus invisible from the outside.

One feature I came to like and depend on with my Huskies was a solid blue line painted on every saw. This was an aiming line which ran perpendicular to the bar, across the top of the engine. It proved to be a great aid in directional felling, and your eye was immediately drawn to it. Unfortunately, Husqvarna has now eliminated this line from its new models. I was told by a dealer that few people even knew what the line's purpose was, so the company eliminated it. He said that I could easily paint my own line on, but I don't think I should have to do that, considering what the saws cost.

Stihl saws feature one-piece mufflers. If the hold-down screws on the mufflers loosen, the muffler will shear off and you have to buy a complete new one. By contrast, Husky and Jonsered mufflers are built in two pieces, and it costs much less to replace the part that usually breaks.

Stihl uses a "through-the-side-plate" chain tightness adjusting system, accessible from the side of the saw. All other saws place their adjusting screws forward of the engine, alongside the bar. The Stihl method is much easier to use.

Stihl saw sprockets are mounted outboard of their clutch drums. Husqvarna and Jonsered sprockets are placed inboard of the drum. Husky engineers say they do this to put extra distance between the clutch and the bearings to keep heat generated by the clutch away from the bearings. Maybe so, but Stihl sprockets can be changed by the user. With the others, sprocket replacement is a shop job. In addition, it is hard to tell when the chain is in place. With a Stihl, it's easy. (Recently, several Husqvarna models have gone to the Stihl configuration).

Once in a great while, a tree will settle back on my bar so firmly that there is no way to extract the bar. When this happens, the only option is to unbolt the bar from the saw head and leave the bar and chain stuck in the tree. You can then mount another bar and chain, fell the tree, and reclaim your original bar and chain.

Even if you have a second saw with you, it makes sense to remove the saw head to avoid damaging it when the tree falls. With a Stihl saw, this is easy. With the others, you must work the chain up over the drum to get it and the bar off. This is not easy. Sometimes it causes you to spend more time at the base of a precariously balanced tree than is wise. This may sound farfetched (and, were I more skillful, not worth mentioning), but it does happen.

Husqvarna employs an air prefilter ahead of the main filter on some of its models. This is easily cleaned. The main filter is internal and requires you to remove the top cover of the saw to get at it. This is okay, but there's no easy way to see the main filter, so you never know when it is plugging up. Stihl uses only one filter, and access to it is easy.

All three saws use ports to pass warm air back to the engine intake during cold weather. With Stihl saws, this port is easily accessible, so you can regulate its opening during the day. With Huskies and Jonsereds, you need to remove the top cover. Since this takes time in the woods, the user is tempted to just leave it the way it was when he started. When I mentioned this difference to the Jonsered dealer, he shrugged it off. "Nobody bothers to open those ports anyway," he said. I do. (Some saws now attach their top covers with clips rather than bolts, making them easy to remove and replace.)

Husqvarna has recently introduced compression releases on its smaller saws, allowing the user to release the compression when pulling the starter cord. Large saws have had these devices for some time, but it was never felt that they were necessary on small saws. If they hold up and don't leak compression during operation, I guess compression releases on small saws would be a good feature. It's hard work pulling on a saw that won't start. My Huskies always do start, however, as did my Stihls.

Again, bear in mind that these are all external factors that really don't affect the overall quality of the saws, which is high in all three cases. I have little experience with Jonsered saws, but they have a good reputation. I see now that Jonsered (and Husqvarna) feature a "turbo" air-cleaning system. This arrangement supplies air to the filter and utilizes centrifugal force to throw off dirt and sawdust particles before they reach the filter. Stihl is introducing a similar system.

These systems do not actually "turbocharge" the engine—all they do is use centrifugal force to keep dirt off the air filters. I can't see where that would be necessary for most users. I clean my filters regularly and never have any problems.

All three of the manufacturers that I favor sell "professional" models and "consumer" models. Which you choose is up to you. I always buy professional saws. Sometimes there is quite a price difference between two models that seem to be almost equal. Over time, however, the extra money paid out for the professional model pays off for me. A day lost with saw problems will more than cover the difference in price. This is true even if you only use your saw occasionally. If you drive up to your land on Friday night planning to work on the weekend and your saw craps out with all the shops closed, there goes your weekend. How much is that worth to you?

To me, the two hardest jobs in the woods are pounding on a chunk of firewood that won't split and pulling on a saw that won't start. I'll have more to say about splitting chunks later, but spending a few extra dollars up front can almost eliminate saw starting problems.

Choosing a Dealer

The top three saws are enough alike, in my opinion, that the main decision comes down to choosing a dealer rather than choosing a brand of saw. Chances are you won't have much of a choice between dealers who sell the same brand. Manufacturers usually space out their dealerships so that they don't compete with each other. Some dealerships handle all three top saws, some two, but generally, the rule is, "Choose a dealer, choose a saw." This, incidentally, is why I went from Stihls to Huskies. I changed dealers.

I would never buy a saw from anyone other than a servicing dealer. If you do decide to buy a cheap saw from a discount house, bear in mind that all saws—even good ones—require maintenance from time to time. Discount houses don't do maintenance. It is the dream of all the servicing dealers I know to be able to simply tell people who bring these saws in for repairs to take them back where they bought them for service.

Most servicing dealers can't afford the luxury of turning down business, so they do the repairs. Often, however, they don't stock parts for cheap saws and have to order them. Since they aren't all that keen on repairing these saws in the first place, they are in no big hurry to complete the job. When they finally do they get around to it, they keep really good track of their time—charging the customer for all of it. Bring your cheap saw in on a busy Saturday morning and the best you can hope for is a repair tag with a low number.

By contrast, my dealer drops everything if I come in with my professional saw. He either repairs it on the spot or loans me a saw to use while he works on it. He does his best to get any charges under the warranty, and, on professional saws, that includes quite a bit. Husqvarna and Stihl warranty their ignition systems for the life of the saw, Jonsered for five years. These warranties include all parts and labor. Try getting that at K Mart!

So, how do you choose a dealer? First, of course, he should be a servicing dealer. If chain saws are not his only business, they should at least be a major part of it. I would avoid shops primarily in the lawn and garden business, which offer saws as a sideline. I prefer a dealer who actually uses a saw himself. In my area, several saw dealers also do some logging. These guys not only relate well to any problems I might encounter, but they are also a good source of tips and ideas to make the work easier and safer.

I would shy away from any dealer who, along with a major brand saw, sells dangerous, cheap saws. I would question his commitment to safety. I would look for a dealer who has professional cutters as his customers. I would look for a dealer who belongs to organizations that promote safe logging practices, and, ideally, a dealer who sponsors and/or participates in safety demonstrations and programs.

I would expect any dealer I chose to carry a full line of safety clothing. If the dealership was too small to support this, I would at least expect him to carry catalogs of safety equipment (the Bailey's catalog, for example, carries protective clothing at good prices). In either case, I would expect him to recommend safety equipment to new buyers and assist them in obtaining it if he didn't stock it.

I would expect my dealer to actively promote safe saw use by demonstrating safety equipment and safe saw operation. I would expect him to furnish safety manuals with any saw purchase and to promote their usage.

I am lucky that my dealer does all these things. That is why I switched saws and dealers. You may not be so lucky, but these are things to look for.

Safety awareness has increased dramatically in the last few years. A lot of this has come from increases in workers' compensation costs for businesses—primarily logging contractors—who employ chain-saw operators. In some cases, these rates run as high as 50 or 60 percent of an employee's wages.

Years ago, faced with these costs, employers banded together in groups and undertook safety programs to bring their rates down. These programs have been successful, and some groups have seen their accident and insurance rates drop significantly. OSHA has also tightened some rules, which has also helped.

Probably the one single factor responsible for helping saw operators increase their safety and efficiency has been the introduction of Swedish logging techniques to North America. Credit for this largely goes to one remarkable man, Søren Eriksson, about whom much more will be said shortly.

Along with better education for loggers and better safety equipment, there has been a change in attitude within the logging profession. The dealer I first dealt with carried no safety equipment, nor did he mention safety. "That just scares away customers, especially if their wives are with them," he used to say. Now he carries a full line.

Scars and bandages from saw cuts used to be macho symbols. I can remember a guy hollering across a crowded bar as he held up his bandaged arm, "My saw bit me." This was met by a lot of laughter from his fellow loggers and the other patrons. Another guy said he had spent his evening picking his blue jeans out of a cut on his leg.

You don't hear this kind of talk anymore. There is really very little excuse for these injuries. Everyone knows that now, and guys who do cut themselves tend to be sheepish rather than proud. The few times lately that I have met loggers who have been hurt, they have been willing to describe what happened to them, but always soberly, and with the aim of helping others avoid their injuries. That represents a huge change in attitude in just a few years time.

4

 Saws and Accessories

ASIDE FROM SAFETY, THE MAJOR CHANGES in saws over the last few years have been in weight-to-power ratios and increased rpm (revolutions per minute).

Speed is an important indicator of a good saw. Sometimes people who plan on buying cheap, slow saws will justify their decision by saying that speed is not that important to them since they are not really in any hurry. That doesn't wash. Speed is an indication of quality and power and has a big effect on overall performance. The chains on all modern saws turn between 13,000 and 15,000 rpm. That means the chain is traveling at 40 to 50 miles per hour. That's moving.

In my opinion, the best saw is the smallest saw you can get by with. For me that turns out to be a saw with about 2.7 to 3 cubic inch displacement. (Cubic inch displacement is the volume swept by the piston in a single full stroke. Basically, it is the diameter of the piston times the length of the stroke.) This is somewhat smaller than most dealers would recommend for the work I do—North American dealers, that is. In Sweden this size saw would be about right for the average logger.

Cubic inch displacement is about the most accurate way for the buyer to compare saws. It is true that engineering and quality control can increase usable power from a given displacement, but there isn't much else available to the buyer to better indicate what a saw can or cannot do. Engine displacement and no-load rpm together will tell you a lot. Note that this is "design rpm." All these saws will exceed this rpm by adjusting the saw to run beyond the design point. That's not a good idea, however.

Some people become obsessed with squeezing extra power out of a saw. One way to do this is to cut down on exhaust back pressure. There are places where you can send your saw to have it customized. Basically what they do is polish the exhaust ports to streamline the flow of exhaust gas out of the cylinder. I've never tried that, but I have changed carburetors and thus improved performance.

I have two supposedly identical saws (Husqvarna 242s) which have never really been identical. One saw always ran longer between fuelings and did substantially more work. This was important to me because I gauge my day's work by tanks of fuel consumed, usually running through two tanks in a morning. The dealer and I fooled with several things, such as changing mufflers. Nothing helped, though, until we replaced the carburetor in the less efficient saw. That made my two saws nearly equal.

Cheap saws are often advertised by bar length. This is meaningless. There's no relationship between the length of bar the seller chooses to bolt onto a saw and the power of the engine.

Effectively using Swedish methods of logging requires great flexibility and involves a lot of saw movement. For this, light weight is very important—more so than pure power. There are ways to glean more usable power out of a saw. Aside from proper engine adjustment, the simplest and easiest way is to concentrate on the parts of the saw involved in actual cutting. Bars and chains can make a big difference in performance—more so than fooling with engine ports.

The type of chain you use and the way you maintain it are critical to good performance. We'll devote some time to this subject later. Bars are also important, so let's talk about them now.

If you buy a new saw from a dealer, you don't have to just accept the bar and chain that normally comes with the saw. Most dealers will be glad to make up any combination you wish. My saws come with a 16-inch bar as standard equipment. I seldom use a 16-inch bar, however. I prefer a 13-inch bar. That's about the shortest bar of any quality you can buy. Sometimes even these have to be special-ordered, although they have become more readily available in recent years, perhaps as more people switch to short bars. Or maybe my dealer just stocks them for me. I don't really know if others are switching. I try not to hang around the saw shop. That can be an expensive pastime.

But if I did, I might see the ghost of Dr. Freud smirking as he saw men opting for long bars. I don't want to carry that thought much further, except to note that technique is often more important than length.

The main reason most guys give for wanting a longer bar is that they don't have to bend over as much or as far. This is certainly true if you bring the saw down to the fallen tree. It is a good deal less true if you bring the tree up to the saw. That's possible, and we'll get into it later in the book.

Assuming you can avoid bending, there are many reasons why short bars are better. For one thing, it takes noticeably less power to rotate the chain around a bar that is three inches shorter. That's a total of six inches less, when you consider both the top and the bottom of the bar. Because the chain is shorter and travels a shorter distance, it builds up less heat from friction. As a result, I never have to tighten my chain during a run and seldom at refueling. I never have to remove a link due to stretching, and I can't remember the last time a loose chain came off during cutting.

Short chains cost less than long chains, as do short bars. Theoretically, I suppose, you could argue that they also wear out faster so you come out even. This may be true, but there are so many things that cause chains and bars to die that it is hard to say that they "wore out" faster.

Aside from length, there are two basic styles of bars; "hard-nose" bars and "sprocket-nose" bars. Years ago, you could only buy hard-nose bars. These are just single pieces of steel, shaped, drilled, and machined to accept the chain. Modern hard-nose bars have Stellite-hardened surfaces at the nosetip. There are still people who swear by these bars and will use nothing else. Not me. I don't see why anyone would prefer a hard-nose over a sprocket-nose bar.

Sprocket-nose bars, as the name suggests, use bearing-mounted sprockets in their noses to lift the chain free of the bar as it passes around the nose. This greatly decreases friction. It also permits you to tighten the chain to "bowstring" tightness, basically eliminating chain sagging and the danger that it will flip off during use. The result is more power to the chain, less power lost to friction.

Someone, a few years back, invented a bar designed to automatically keep the chain tight. It used a sliding nosepiece backed up by a small leaf spring. Theoretically, when you first mounted your chain, you tightened it until the nose moved back as far as it would go. As the chain wore and stretched, the spring pushed the nose forward, maintaining a uniform tightness. Sounds like a really good idea. I don't know what happened to them. I didn't buy one because keeping proper chain tension wasn't a problem for me. Maybe that's what happened to them.

There are two types of construction on both styles of bar: solid and laminated. Solid bars are machined out of a single piece of steel. Laminated bars are made by spot-welding two steel pieces together to form a single piece with the groove around the outside. You can see the welds by holding the bar up and deflecting light off its surface. Solid bars cost more and are more durable.

There are also two types of sprocket-nose bars: those with replaceable noses and those that you throw away when they wear out. The most common problem with these bars is bearing failure. At one time there were bars that allowed the nose portion to be pried open and new bearings installed. This was a short-lived idea. Some bars now have replaceable noses that are riveted in place.

Which type of nose you use is simply a matter of economics. With normal care, you can probably replace three or four noses before you need to replace the entire bar. Replacement noses cost about 40 percent as much as a new 16-inch bar. It would seem to make sense, then, to go with the replaceable tips. Not necessarily, though. I can buy a new laminated, 13-inch bar for about 20 percent more than the price of a replacement nose. So why should I fool around with replacing noses?

Several manufacturers make a professional-quality, short-length, one-piece sprocket-nose bar. These bars are lighter and slimmer than the solid, replaceable-nose bars I was using. They cost about $20 each, so I can afford to carry a spare. This way I can change bars myself in the woods. To replace a nose is a shop job. That fact alone makes the one-piece bar a good choice for me.

As bar length increases, the cost goes up, whereas noses cost the same for all lengths. At some point, as you move to a longer bar, it makes sense to start replacing noses.

Another advantage to using "throwaway" bars is that you replace the whole bar each time. There are parts of the bar (such as the side rails) that wear in addition to the nose. I'm not bothered by these. I toss my bars before they start to cause problems.

Short bars weigh less than long bars. Shorter lengths are also easier to keep track of when you are limbing. Kickback forces are less because there is less length to provide leverage. Finally, with a 13-inch bar I can carry my saw holding only the rear handle, with my arm out straight, without the nose hitting the ground. That's handy sometimes.

Naturally, your choice of bar length will be influenced by the size of trees you will be cutting. It is possible to fell trees two-and-a-half times as thick as your bar is long. That's more than 32 inches with a 13-inch bar—almost three feet in diameter. While this is definitely possible (and I'll explain how later), it wouldn't pay to base your decision on doing a whole lot of it.

In general, your bar length should be sufficient to fell most of the trees you plan to cut without using special techniques. This would require a bar about two inches longer than the diameter of your average tree. Save the special techniques for special cases. Bear in mind, however, that you do a lot more limbing and bucking than you do felling (on average, 85 percent limbing and bucking and 15 percent felling), so sizing your saw for felling means you end up carrying around a lot more saw and bar than you use for most of your work.

At one time I considered buying a small saw for limbing and bucking and a large one for felling. I realized this was a kind of dumb idea and never did it. This idea not only represented a big expense, it also would have involved carrying two saws into the woods. Instead, I learned to use one saw for everything. I've come to believe that it is much safer to use only one bar length in all situations, mainly because I have a good feel for where my bar tip is when I'm cutting. If I were to switch off between different bar lengths, I would lose that instinctive feeling.

One way to add an extra inch or so to your bar is to remove the "timber spikes" (sometimes called "bumper spikes"). I suppose these spikes have a legitimate function in some large saws, but most people use them to buy leverage in order to force a dull saw to cut. If you use your saw right, they're just in the way. Take them off and throw them away. There is, of course, one final complication when it comes to buying bars. For no technical reason that I know of, bars come in three different "gauges" or groove widths. Location of the holes for bolting them to the saw also vary slightly. One gauge is as good as another, but you can't interchange these things. Bar, chain, and sprocket have to be compatible with each other and compatible with the saw. That is why you see all the complicated charts on the packages of discount store, "one-size-fits-all" chain and bars. One size doesn't fit all. It's good to keep the following maxim in mind:

> *If your saw is never too small,*
> *Then it is always too big.*

There is another type of bar that most readers of this book will probably never encounter—the "bow guide." These bars are used exclusively in the South instead of conventional bars. They are large, rounded tracks flattened somewhat at their front so that the cutter can fell a tree by simply pushing the guide forward into the trunk. Bow guides are a fast way to work if you know what you're doing, but they're also very dangerous and their use is limited to a few professional fellers. Don't try them.

But getting back to bar and chain gauges, I'm not going to try to sort all the variables out here. Take your saw to your dealer. He will know and stock what you need; there's no need for you to try and keep it all straight. As much as I use my saw, I've forgotten what gauge my bar is. My dealer hasn't, though, and that's all that matters.

I don't fool around with carrying cases. I don't know any professional cutter who does. If your dealer wants to include one with your saw, see if you can trade it off for something else, like an extra loop of chain. Some people use scabbards to cover the bar and chain for moving and storage, and these are probably a good idea. I always end up losing or forgetting them, however.

What I do is to cut a round cross-section, about six inches long, out of a six-inch diameter log. Set it upright and, with your saw, cut a groove about three inches deep in one end of it. This becomes the top, and you can then slip your bar into the groove when transporting it and it will stay put. I have two of these chain saw holders, one for each side of my pickup box, so I can set my saw down on whichever side I approach. Saves walking around.

Consumables

As stated earlier, chain-saw engines are designed to run on a fuel/oil mixture. They will run on plain gas, but only for part of one tank. Then they seize up. The two-cycle oil is a distinct color, so that you can easily see that it has been added. Your dealer can also see this if you take your saw back to him and swear that you did everything right and it still seized up.

With the saws we are talking about, you should use a 50-to-1 mix, and high-octane gas. This is what the manufacturers recommend. The saw might run just as well on regular gas, but using premium only adds about a quarter a day to my expenses.

A few years back, gas containing ethanol was ruining the diaphragms in saw carburetors. This was a real problem, since, if gas contained less than 10 percent ethanol, it didn't have to be labeled as such. Yet 10 percent was enough ethanol to do the damage, and I had lots of problems then. I don't anymore, though. The carburetor manufacturers have come up with some diaphragm material that resists ethanol damage. Be advised, though, that if you have an older saw, you may run into diaphragm problems as a result of ethanol in the fuel mix.

It is imperative that you store your fuel in a clean container that has not contained any other liquids. I made the mistake once of using a bar-oil jug for my fuel. I thought I had sloshed it out thoroughly enough with fuel mix, but some of the oil must have stuck to the sides, and I had all sorts of problems before I finally figured out what the trouble was. Actually, I never did figure it out. My dealer did.

Bar oil is usually sold in gallon jugs at saw shops and discount stores. Often it is reclaimed engine oil with an additive called Protexem. This additive causes the oil to become "snotty," so that it clings to the chain all the way around.

Bar oil is sold in different weights, just like engine oil, and the same logic applies: use heavy oil in summer, light in winter. The additive doesn't change the basic nature of the oil. I've known guys to add bar oil to their beat-up old truck engines and it worked just fine. Conversely, I've used plain engine drain oil in my saws and that works, too. Nobody recommends that practice, but you can do it. Engine oil doesn't lubricate as well as bar oil, though, and, if there is sludge in it, it could plug your oil filter and possibly damage your saw's oil pump. The repair cost if this should happen and the added wear from poor lubrication make it a rather silly option, but it's up to you.

Because it is so widely dispersed, it's easy to overlook the amount of bar oil that is actually sprayed about in a single day's cutting. I must easily release more than 50 gallons a year in my woods. I would like to avoid doing that if I could.

There has been quite a bit of publicity lately about using canola oil as a bar oil, and also as hydraulic oil in heavy equipment. The big appeal of canola oil is that it is biodegradable. Apparently a lot of it is recycled frying oil from fast-food restaurants. I've never used any, but a friend told me that he has and it works fine without additives in all weather. He said that he set his oil-flow regulating screw down 40 percent without encountering any problems.

I have also heard rumors that canola oil is going to be mandated in California. Stihl offers it in their new catalog, and it is available in Canada. At present, it is expensive, but hopefully this will change and we can all switch to it.

Problems are starting to arise with canola oil as its use increases, however. Since it is an edible oil, it attracts microorganisms, which feed on it. These microbes can plug filters in hydraulic systems, and potentially in saws. I understand that a "pesticide" of some sort is being developed to kill these organisms. If true, that would seem to offset the environmental benefits of using canola as a bar oil. Seems to me that the jury is still out.

One final consumable is grease for sprocket noses. The saw-using world breaks down into "greasers" and "nongreasers." I used to be a greaser, then I became a nongreaser. Now I am an "oiler." The books say to grease your nose at every refueling. I used to do that with the little plastic grease gun provided with my new saw. When winter came, I found that these plastic guns were splitting in the cold. So I bought a metal gun and envelopes of special grease. One week I ran out of grease but continued working without greasing. That eliminated a lot of hassle and seemed to cause no problems, so I just never went back to it. My bearings seem to last just as long without grease as they did with faithful greasing, and I don't have to monkey with special guns and grease.

I operated this way for years with no problems, but lately I've started to feel that it wouldn't hurt to lubricate those bearings once in a while, just to be on the safe side. Now I have an oil squirt can with a nozzle that pushes up tight to the grease hole in my bar, so when I maintain my saw in the shop, I give the bearings a squirt of whatever oil happens to be in the can. It can't do any harm and it's no trouble, so I do it.

Saw Tools

It used to be that you got quite a tool kit when you bought a new saw from a dealer. Not so any more. What you get now is a combination wrench and screwdriver and an Allen wrench. If you're lucky, you also get a file. That's about it.

My dealer longs for the good old days. "I really had some interesting repair jobs then," he says. He explains that people would tackle all sorts of repairs on their own. The result usually was a bunch of parts in a cardboard box that used to be a saw. Now, he says, people bring their saws in and he fixes them. It's not as much fun, nor is it as profitable.

With chain saws, like computers, "repair" usually means "replace." There's not much that can be repaired. Things either break or wear out and need replacing. Since you don't know which parts will fail—and when—it is not practical to try to stock spares, so most repair work is a shop job.

You do need the "scrench" (T-wrench) that's supplied with the saw, however. You need it to adjust chain tension and to remove the side cover for cleaning. You can change spark plugs with it. You need it to remove the fuel and oil caps for refueling. You can't get by without it.

You also need two types of files: a round file for sharpening the teeth and a flat file for filing the rakers. You need some sort of handle for the round file.

The correct file diameters for the two chain pitches are: 7/32 inch for 3/8 pitch chain and 5/32 inch for .325 pitch. Actually, all you need to know is the pitch of your chain. The dealer will give you the proper file.

The Swedes make double-ended files and the holders for them. This is what I use. You use one end until it is dull, then you turn it around and use the other end of the file. If you forget that you have used the other end, you can reverse them again later on, and, sure enough, the first side seems to be pretty sharp again.

You can also buy hand-held power grinders. One kind runs on regular house current. There is another kind that you can connect to your car battery and use in the field. I've tried both types and they will

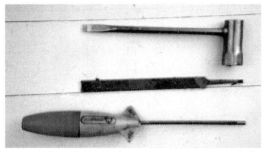

Essential tools for chain-saw maintenance include (from top) a T-wrench, flat raker file, and round file in a two-way holder.

do what the files do. That's all they will do, however. They won't improve poor sharpening techniques. If you fail with your file, you will fail with the grinder. Mine sits in my shop now, and occasionally I use it for other things, but I don't use it on my chain.

You can buy a hand tool designed to replace rivets on your chain while you are removing a link or making up a chain. I have one of these, too, but, as I said earlier, I now buy my chain in loops and never have to remove any links. My chain never breaks anymore. This tool sits alongside the grinder in my shop.

Spare Parts

I carry a spare spark plug in my purse. They cost a couple of dollars or less, come with the correct gap, and can be replaced using only the scrench.

When I used Stihl saws, I carried a spare sprocket and a snap-ring-removing tool. This only works with Stihls, because their sprockets are mounted outside the clutch drum. I think I used it in the field only once.

I carry a spare pull cord. I don't recall ever changing a cord in the woods.

I carry a spare chain.

If I am working far away from home, I will sometimes take a spare bar as well. Sometimes, rather than monkey with all this stuff, I'll simply take my spare saw.

You can buy a tool holder for your belt that has loops for files, a small screwdriver, and a scrench. I don't really see the point in hauling these things around. Since I can't carry my fuel and oil on my belt, I can't work far from these items anyway, so the few times I have problems while cutting, it's not a big deal to go back there when I need to make any adjustments.

I've had bad luck trying to do any repair work in the woods. Usually I lack a crucial tool or part, and I invariably drop small parts and lose them in the leaves or pine needles on the ground. Better to wait until you get home or, better yet, let your dealer do it. This will save you time and money in the long run.

5

● Safety Equipment and Clothing ◖◖

BEFORE WE TALK ABOUT STARTING AND OPERATING your saw, we have
to talk about safety equipment, because you shouldn't even start your saw
without—at the very least—ear protection.

A court in Michigan has ruled that logging is "an inherently dangerous
occupation." This statement has some sort of legal implications, which
don't concern us here, but the ruling bears out what everyone who has had
any exposure to logging already knows: cutting wood with a chain saw is
dangerous work, and it always will be.

Good safety equipment is expensive, but probably not more expensive
than the special clothing hunters routinely buy for deer and duck hunting.
If you hunt you probably have more invested for those few days a year than
you would spend to protect yourself working in the woods all year long.

Hardhats

Hardhats are probably the most obvious piece of safety equipment for
woods work. Their purpose and importance is self-evident, and everyone
nowadays seems to be wearing them.

It is possible to buy hardhats, safety glasses, and earplugs separately, but
few professional loggers do because they all come in a nice neat package in
a logger's helmet. These helmets all look pretty much the same though there
are differences.

At one time, all hardhats were suspended from harnesses using four
suspension points. Now, some manufacturers are promoting six-point

A professional logger's head protection system includes a hardhat, earmuffs, and a faceguard.

suspension. Is that better than four points? I honestly don't know. If six is better, why not eight or ten?

One innovation that I highly recommend is the ratcheting suspension, which is adjusted simply by turning a knob. Making size adjustments on the older hard hats was a major project. I once went over to a neighbor's place to fell some trees for him. I picked up Marcia's hat by mistake and, when I got there, had to fool around enlarging it to fit my head. The neighbor seemed really concerned. "Does that happen often?" he inquired. "What?" I asked. "Your head changing size like that," he said. I explained what had happened. He seemed relieved.

With the knob, it's easy to compensate for a bad hair day, a big night on the town, or a "Tree Farmer of the Year" award. You just click it open a few notches. Then, when things return to normal, you just click it back.

There are two types of face screens: nylon and metal. I much prefer the nylon. The metal screens are heavier and rust out in the winter when your breath condenses on the screen. You can rehabilitate a nylon screen if it is damaged by pulling the strands back in place with your fingernail.

One caution with nylon screens: Don't let the screen touch your saw's muffler when you take a break. The nylon will melt in an instant. (Incidentally, this is also a problem with extremely lightweight safety pants and chaps. They are also made of nylon and will melt if they come in contact with your muffler.)

Hardhats these days have an ultraviolet rating. Apparently, exposure to the sun over a long period of time weakens the plastic material enough to diminish the protection the hat offers. It's really unclear to me what this is all about. I just assume that, because most of my work is done in the shady woods, I don't have to worry too much about the UV rating and age of my helmet. I hope I'm right.

A sharp blow can also weaken a hat, so if your helmet is hit hard, either when you are wearing it or not, replace it. They are pretty cheap if you just replace the hat portion.

Try the hat on before you buy it. I once bought Marcia a new hat, and she couldn't use it because the screen didn't come down far enough and chips flew up under it, hitting her in the chin. This is a real concern with frozen chips. They really sting.

Finally, be sure the hat is comfortable. You will be spending a lot of time with it on your head. Get used to always leaving the screen down when you are in the woods, even when you are not working. The most serious eye damage I ever sustained in the woods happened when I was wearing my hardhat, but had the screen up. I was piling pulpwood and I dropped one of the logs on a pile. It hit a dry branch, breaking off a piece, which then flew up into my eye. The only time you should put your screen up is to spit. You won't make that mistake many times before you learn, especially in the winter.

Frost accumulation on the facemask screen is a nagging problem, and many times it causes me to leave my mask up when I'm not actually cutting because I can't see clearly with it down. It seems as if there should be some solution, but I've never run across one.

Some books I have read recommend wearing safety glasses as well as the face screen. My experience with safety glasses is that they quickly fog up when you start to sweat, so I don't do that.

As I mentioned earlier, you should never start your saw without ear protection. Hearing damage is cumulative over a lifetime. There is no such thing as getting by without damage. It just takes time before you notice it, and by then it's too late. Protect your ears when you drive equipment, as well; you need protection then, just as you do when the saw is running. Some people take the muff-style ear protectors off their hardhats in the summer and switch to earplugs, which they claim are cooler. I suspect they are right, but I don't do it. Some people recommend wearing both earplugs and earmuffs. I don't do that, either.

The soft muff liners lose their effectiveness after a while, as they become worn and the stuffing starts coming out. New liners don't cost much, so there's no excuse for sticking with torn ones.

Newer hats have earmuffs, which are individual rather than part of the faceguard harness. These will pop out of their holders if they are hit by falling objects. This is a safety feature; if a limb, for example, knocks off an earmuff, the hat remains on your head to protect you from any more limbs that may follow the first one.

There are several accessories you can buy for your hat. One is a sort of awning that covers the space between the top of the screen and the hat brim. This prevents dirt and twigs from falling down behind the screen.

Another item is a flap that extends down in the back of the hat to about shoulder height. This keeps rain and snow from sliding off your hat and down your neck.

These accessories are inexpensive and indispensable if you log in the winter. Without them, if there is snow in the tree branches and you fell the tree, a lot of the snow ends up down your neck. You can also buy cloth liners, which snap inside the hat and come down to cover your ears. The suspension system makes the hat sit up away from your head, which produces a windtunnel effect. This can make for a really cold head. I've never used these cloth liners. The ear protection seems to keep my ears warm, and I don't stay out that long on really cold, windy days.

Unlike a lot of safety equipment, protective chain-saw helmets grow on you. If you wear the ear protection for just a few hours, it's almost painful to run your saw without protection. The saw sounds like it's about to fly apart.

When you buy your hat, it's best to stick with well-known brands. Bilsom and Peltor are two popular ones. None of the component parts from one of these manufacturers will fit on the other maker's helmets, and nothing from lesser-known brands will fit on anything other than the hats they were designed for. I guess that's the free enterprise system at work, but this incompatibility can be really annoying when you need, for instance, earmuff liners and have to buy a whole new hat to get them.

Safety Clothing

You're not going to cut wood barefoot and naked. You're going to wear something, and it might as well be something that will protect you and conceivably even save your life. Safety clothing may do that, so you should buy the proper outfit and always wear it. I do this, and so does every serious cutter I know. For me there is a psychological side to it as well. Almost like an athlete suiting up before a game, putting on my safety clothing puts me in the mood for the task ahead. I don't wear this stuff any other time, so when I put it on, I ready myself mentally as well as physically.

The main purpose of most safety clothing is to protect you from your saw. There's nothing much available to protect you from the trees. The clothing won't protect you completely from the saw, either. At best, it limits the damage and allows you time to react should your saw come at you.

Modern safety clothing is almost as comfortable as regular clothing because it's made of specialized fabrics such as Kevlar and ballistic nylon. I've seen pictures of old-time safety chaps. They were made out of heavy leather and chicken wire. It's amazing that people could even walk around in them, yet the dangers of operating chain saws were recognized even then, and some people did make an effort to protect themselves.

Kevlar is the stuff that bulletproof vests are made of. It protects against saw cuts as well, but for a different reason. What it does is snag the chain and jam it up so completely with fibers that it stops. I checked this out once. I had an old pair of chaps I no longer wore. I nailed them to a log and drove my saw into them at full throttle. They whipped around violently, and the force of it tore the saw right out of my hands. The cut went clear through the chaps, but just barely. The fibers stopped the saw quickly enough so that it made a believer out of me. The chain was so jammed up I had to pry the side cover off, and it took about 15 minutes to pick all of the fibers out of the chain and sprocket.

This fabric is so efficient in jamming a saw because it is made of long fibers. Short fibers don't work as well. This is important to know: If you slice your pads, you should replace them. Fibers that have been cut will not function as well as before. In fact, they may not function at all; unfortunately, you won't know until it is too late. You should also keep your pads clean. Dirt and grit will wear through fibers, degrading their effectiveness.

The other fabric, ballistic nylon, is used where deflecting the saw is better than snagging it. This is mainly in gloves. Safety gloves have this nylon stitched across the backs of the gloves. If your hand slipped down onto the running chain, it would be better to have it bounce off than to snag the glove and pull it in.

The most important protection for most people is leg protection. Statistically, most saw cuts are on the legs, especially across the top of the right thigh. Thus, the padding is located here on safety pants and chaps, and down the front of the legs to the cuffs.

I prefer safety pants to chaps. You are not going to leave them in the truck, no matter how small the job is. You put them on when you leave the house and you leave them on, even if all you are doing is nipping off a small sapling in the roadway. With chaps, it's tempting to put them on at the job site and not bother with them in minor cutting situations like this. That, of course, illustrates the advantage of chaps. If you don't need them, you can take them off rather than haul around that extra weight when you are doing other work.

There are various styles of pants. The main difference between them is that some have removable pads, while others have permanent pads sewn into the pants. I use the removable pads. These slide down into pockets inside the pant legs and are held with snaps at the top. The advantage to these, of course, is that you can wear out the pants and, as long as they are not damaged, use the pads indefinitely. This not only saves you some money, it gives you some flexibility.

My pants come in summer-weight, double-knit polyester and water-repellent nylon for winter. I use the same set of pads for both. I use the winter pants without the pads for normal winter work. They are flannel-lined and eliminate the need for long underwear.

Sometimes when I'm splitting firewood on really hot days I will slide the pads out of my pants. This is much cooler, but it puts me in the same situation as with chaps. If I have to just nip off a limb, say, I don't put the pads back in.

There is one possibly serious flaw in the design of the slip-in pads, and that is that they aren't held firmly in place. A hit with a saw might very well simply push them to one side, allowing the chain to hit your leg. The pants are fairly loose and the pads have room to flop around a bit. In contrast, the permanent-pad pants I have seen fit rather tightly and wrap around the leg, as do the chaps.

I have never cut my pads, so I can't say whether the slip-in pads are really less safe. I talked to a guy once who said he knew someone who had cut himself wearing the pads, and that the pads did slip to one side. Such a third-hand account is not really definitive, but I think it could happen. Life, though, is full of tradeoffs and calculated risks. I've chosen to stick with the removable pads, but I don't really trust them. Maybe that's a good thing.

Even though some pants and chaps wrap around the legs somewhat, none of them wrap all the way around, so it's still possible to do yourself damage even with all of the safety clothing on. Also, as I said before, some of the super-lightweight summer pants are made of nylon and will simply melt if you let a hot saw muffler touch them.

Several companies now make shirts that contain Kevlar across the shoulders and around the neck area. I plan on buying such a top this summer. Still, I wonder if the thin layer of protection they provide would do much good. The pads on the pants are thick. With the shirts, it's hard to tell that there is any padding at all. Some protection is better than none, however, and the shirts are designed to be comfortable. That's probably an essential element in the wide acceptance of safety clothing: it is designed with the comfort of the user in mind, and it is attractive even without the safety features.

This winter was the first time that I bought and wore chain-saw safety boots. I've always worn safety-toe boots, winter and summer, even though the steel in the toes makes for cold toes in the winter. I've come to the point now where I *have* to wear hard-toe boots because I've developed the habit of using my feet as tools. If a log starts to roll where I don't want it to, for instance, my first instinct is to put my foot in front of it to stop it. When I'm bucking small logs, I will often put my toe under the log to take the weight and prevent the saw from binding as the two halves separate.

The cold toe problem and extra weight and size of these boots are just things I have become accustomed to. Again, it's a tradeoff. I've seen some boots recently that use fiberglass rather than steel for the toes. These are lighter and should be less heat-conductive than steel-toed boots. The ones I saw didn't have any ANSI rating on them, so I don't know how strong they are, but it doesn't really matter to me since I now wear chain-saw safety boots, and, as far as I know, all of these are steel-toed.

Regular hard-toe boots are a good deal safer than plain boots, but they really aren't sufficient for saw protection. There is plenty of room behind the hard toe for the saw to bite. There is also a pretty good chance that, even if you hit the hard part with the saw, the teeth will chatter back off the steel and end up in your upper arch.

If you take a look at the top part of your arch, you can readily see that there are few worse places to cut yourself. All the nerves, tendons, and blood vessels are right on the surface. So are the bones. No meat. A bad cut here could leave you limping through life with cold, numb toes. Not only is this a bad place for a cut, it is a likely place

This professional logger is wearing full personal-protective equipment, including chaps, head protection, and chain-saw resistant boots.

to receive one. When you are limbing a felled tree, you are constantly moving that saw around right over your feet.

The boots I wear now have several layers of Kevlar over the arch portion and in the tongue. In addition, the liners of my winter pac-boots have Kevlar in them. That is a good compromise for people who don't want to throw away a good pair of winter boots, yet need the Kevlar protection. Just swap your old liners for protective ones.

No matter what type liners you use, don't forget to take them out and dry them regularly. Damp liners quickly lose their insulating qualities.

Before I learned this, my liners got so wet from normal sweat that they froze to the boots. If the snow gets really deep, I wear gaiters over my boots. Usually if the snow is that deep, however, there isn't much work you can do anyway.

When the summer safety boots first came out, I resisted buying a pair. They were expensive—more than $200—and they came in styles I didn't like, with high heels and high-tops. These styles are popular with West Coast big timber loggers who walk on logs rather than around them. They all came with provisions for installing hobnails. I didn't like any of these features. The high-tops were too hot in summer, and the high heels constantly tripped me up on branches and litter on the ground. This was almost as great a hazard as the cuts they were designed to prevent. (In fact, when a survey was taken of which hazards loggers perceived as the worst, tripping came out number one, ahead of saw cuts and falling limbs.)

Now you can buy low-heel safety boots with eight-inch tops. The ones I bought cost about $150. They're very comfortable and seem like they will last a long time. (The brochure that came with them recommends treating them with Thompson's Water Seal preservative.) They have soles with deeply grooved treads, so you have to take them off outside the house, since the grooves pick up a load of sand and dirt every time you use them. I recently attended a logging conference where a new safety "boot" was being sold. This one buckled over the outside of a regular boot and looked like a big galosh. It looked awfully clumsy to me, but the salesman was showing a videotape where saws cut right through the conventional chain-saw safety boot!

The manufacturers of the traditional boot with the kelvar lining have taken this challenge seriously. They are issuing statements that say that they never said that their boots could withstand the full onslaught of a revved-up chain saw. They say that all their boots and other chain-saw safety equipment can do is to buy you time to react and thus minimize the injury.

So, safety equipment can protect you, but it can't protect you much. A good thing to be reminded of.

Chain-saw gloves have a layer of ballistic nylon across the back of the left glove. This is fine, but I work with my bare hands as much as I can. Søren Eriksson says that even in Sweden where, according to him, "everything is illegal" and you have to pass a course and get a license to operate a chain saw, it's okay to work without gloves if your saw is equipped with a chain brake. Mine is, so I do. Gloves are no good in winter, either. Mitts are what you need.

My saw has heated handles, and, if you plan to work in the winter, yours should too. I don't know why saw manufacturers don't push heated handles. You always have to wait for the dealer to special-order them, and then they seem to be only available in the winter. If you don't know about heated handles, nobody will tell you. In addition, not all saw brands have them, and those that do only have them on certain models. They add about 10 percent to the price of the saw, weigh about a quarter of a pound, and cause no problems.

Modern handle heaters are all electric. Originally they worked by passing exhaust gas through the handles. That caused problems and was abandoned. Both handles are heated. A switch is provided to manually turn the heat on and off.

These handles are not only a comfort item, they are important for safety and health as well. Warm hands grip better and warm fingers are less apt to suffer nerve damage from vibration. With heated handles, I can work comfortably with light deerskin mitts all winter. These mitts are only to keep snow and wind off my hands. I want the mitts to be thin because I don't want to insulate my hands from the handles. I buy mitts that are slightly oversized because there has to be room in them for my trigger finger to move freely. The triggers are not heated, so, if you use gloves, you end up with nine warm fingers and a freezing trigger finger. With the mitts, the trigger finger can snuggle with the others and stay warm.

The heaters only seem to work when the saw is revving up, not at idle. The only problem I have with cold hands when working in the winter is when the first tree hangs up and I have to pull on my felling lever to free it. Then I wish I had heavy mitts. The saw handles haven't had time to warm up, and my thin mitts provide little protection against the cold steel of the lever.

In the winter, I usually just leave the handle heat on all the time. In milder weather, I flip it on and off. Even in fairly mild weather, I will sometimes flip it on for a while to warm my hands early on. The handles are not hot enough to be uncomfortable with bare hands. Also, while we are sort of on the subject, I wear tennis wristbands in the summer to keep the sweat from making my hands slippery on the handles.

Marcia, of course, doesn't benefit from the handles. She used to take an extra pair of mittens out with her, which she kept in a six-pack cooler along with a canteen full of hot water. This gave her a nice warm change halfway through. She has switched to the "hand warmer" envelopes, which contain heat-producing ingredients. She says they work fine.

Dressing for the Woods

There is one other specialty item that I wear in the winter and that is a Helly-Hansen logging top. These large, roomy pullover tops are made of plastic fibers and, like wool, they retain heat even when wet. The outside (possibly inside) is pile and the inside (possibly outside) is smooth. I say this because I own two of them, which I bought several years apart. They seem to be identical except the older one is designed to be worn with the pile side out and the newer one with the pile side in. Actually, I wear both of them with the pile side out. The smooth side slides smoothly on my sweater and makes for easier movement than the pile side.

These tops have zippers at the neck and extra long tails so that you keep your kidneys warm even when you are bent over, which you often are. The main feature for me, however, is the sleeves. These are extra long; they extend down over your wrists and have holes for your thumbs to keep them there. The ends stuff into your mitt tops.

This is no coincidence. Your wrists are where the vessels carrying the blood to your fingers pass closest to the surface. If your wrists are bare, you lose a lot of heat from the blood on its way to your fingers.

We have an outdoor woodburning boiler for heating our house. Leaving my wrists bare is the equivalent of running the water pipes from the boiler above ground and without insulation.

The Helly-Hansen tops don't offer much protection against wind, so on windy days I wear a nylon shell windbreaker over them. I got mine from Goodwill. It says "Downtown Citgo" on the back and "Jim" over the pocket.

The tops are rugged; I've used mine for years with no problems except a torn seam under one arm. I repaired this easily using Super Glue.

These items—the logging top and the heated handles—all joined my collection gradually over time. Several years ago, when I first started work in the woods full-time, I realized that I was not equipped for winter work. Fortunately, about that time a number of catalogs arrived that offered just what I needed—or so I thought. I studied catalogs from REI, L.L. Bean, Norm Thompson, Damart, and others. Sure, it all seemed to cost a fortune, but after all, this was space-age technology, and we know that doesn't come cheap.

When I looked at the price our wood would bring on the stump compared to what it was worth stacked alongside the road, it seemed as if all this state-of-the-art clothing would pay for itself rather quickly. Surely, if mountaineering gear and special fabrics allowed smiling groups of people to sit around in snowbanks in their underwear, then I should do all right with it while working in the woods.

I read up on Thinsulate, GoreTex, polypropylene, and other insulating fabrics, finally deciding to order from Damart. I would have been better off at K Mart!

The stuff was overpriced and undersized. I had tops that rode up until they were nothing more than halters; bottoms that exposed my calves up to my knees when I pulled them up to the waist in a vain attempt to meet the tops; and mitts that quit long before the wrist.

Not only that, but polypropylene, which wicks away moisture as you sweat, stinks to high heaven after an hour or so of exertion. Why? I don't know, but it's a fact—albeit one seldom mentioned in polite society and never in the catalogs. I do note, however, that the new REI catalog offers a polypropylene deodorizer.

Bad enough that it shrinks, it also stinks! Now I knew why the smiling people in the ads were outside.

I tried outdoor clothing from other catalogs, too, but it was either too bulky for my purposes or simply couldn't stand up to the wear and tear that working in the woods produces. So I gave up on all of them, and now buy most of my working clothes from Goodwill. The only exceptions to this rule are chain-saw safety clothes and the winter tops.

Wool sweater vests at Goodwill cost $2.99 and provide as much warmth as down vests with half the bulk. Instead of polypropylene, I wear acrylic sweaters. There are always racks of these, and all of them, it seems, are made in Korea. I choose the finest weave available, and it feels really nice next to my skin. I always buy pullovers that button at the neck. My top also opens at the neck. This is a really efficient way to control body temperature, because regulating the opening at your neck can either release a lot of heat, or bottle it up to keep you warm. After a few minutes of work, I usually find myself opening the neck.

Acrylic smells as bad as polypropylene, but the used sweaters are so inexpensive that you can afford to buy a few and change them often. I don't know if acrylic shrinks. By the time I get hold of them, any shrinking has long since occurred.

For summer, I avoid cotton. Polyester is the way to go—textured polyester with an open weave, if you can get it. If I'm sitting or driving, for example, cotton is very comfortable, but if I am moving around and sweating, I want none of it. Cotton soaks up sweat and becomes clammy. With polyester, every little breeze gets right to your skin and cools it. Ideally, every item of work clothing I have on will be polyester. A drop of sweat from my forehead should end up in the toe of my boot. Sounds strange, but it's true.

Usually you can pick up polyester tee shirts with baseball team logos on them. Light colors are best—white if you can get it—but since you are working in the shade, it's not all that important. I like regular tee shirts with short sleeves. Sleeveless shirts don't provide enough protection against scratches. If the logos on the shirts are objectionable, you can wear them inside out.

Once, when I was a Peace Corps volunteer in South America, I taped a thermometer to my leg, covered it with a white tee shirt and stuck it out in the sun. After a while, the temperature leveled off at 100 degrees F. I tried the same thing with a black tee shirt. This time the mercury got up to 115 degrees F.

Shopping at Goodwill takes some getting used to. I started out at farm auctions, regressed to rummage and garage sales, and now have no problem fighting for items in the bargain barrel at Goodwill. As noted, the stuff is all preshrunk, and they have a great returns policy: just dump whatever you don't want in any convenient collection box. Still, if it bothers you at first, you could wear your hardhat with the screen down.

That's the big scoop on clothing. Do like I tell you and they may put on your tombstone what Marcia says she is going to put on mine: "Even on the coldest mornings, he started right up."

6

Tools

WE LIKE TO CONSIDER OURSELVES "live-off-the-land" loggers. We try not to take any more paraphernalia with us than we absolutely need. Yet even though I limit the number of tools I take into the woods, and paint them all blaze orange and electric blue, I still lose them. Better to leave most of them in the truck. I keep all the hand tools, such as files and the scrench, in a purse I bought at Goodwill. This is my second one. The first one was red patent leather. It wore out, and the one I have now is dove gray. It's harder to see than the red one, but it goes with all my outfits. It cost about a dollar.

About all I really need are the two files, the scrench, and a small screwdriver for adjusting the carburetor. The purse allows me to carry a few extra things, however. I carry a pull cord, bar nut, mirror (for possible things in the eye, not what you thought), glasses, Band-Aids, notebook and pen, and spare chain.

Simple manual tools are available that can make your work more efficient, while at the same time easing the strain on your back (and knees). There is a variety of these tools, since no single one works for all jobs, or all people.

Whenever I discover a new tool or technique, I tend to become enthusiastic about it and use it to the exclusion of my former tools and methods. This rarely works out. Most new things I have tried come with their own set of limitations. Usually, if I'm lucky, the new tool or technique will add to my arsenal, not replace parts of it. Even though I swear by the pulphooks described shortly, there are still times when the easiest way to move a log or pulpstick is to simply pick up one end and flop it over, leaving the hooks in their holsters.

For handling pulpwood, I use the Swedish pulphooks. They are the best small-log handling tool I have found, but require practice for you to become proficient. They also introduce their own hazard. Several times I have had a hook pull loose and sink itself into my wrist. This has always happened, though, when I was dragging a log, not picking one up.

If the hooks slip when you're lifting a pulpstick, it just drops. After being hurt pulling logs with the hooks, I started pulling with my arms straight out. That way, if a hook lets go, I just fall back. If you pull using your biceps and a hook lets go, your muscles will contract and pull the hook into your wrist before you can react.

The hooks are flat, with their points in line with their handles. They fit into holsters. This puts them where you can reach them easily when you need them, and keeps them safely out of the way when you don't.

They are also slim enough to fit into the saw kerf, and sometimes I will slip them in behind my saw if a tree I'm felling starts to lean back. This buys me some time to go and get the felling lever. I will also occasionally slide a hook in behind the saw when I am bucking a large log and the kerf starts to close.

Most professional felling levers have a fitting welded to them, which allows you to attach a pulphook and use the resulting tool as a cant hook for rolling hung-up trees. I use that a lot. Sometimes, however, I'll hang a tree that is too small to twist with a cant hook. When this happens, you can bore a vertical slot through the stem with your saw and stick a hook in each side, using this leverage to twist the tree down.

If I simply want to swing a log out of the way, I dig the point of one hook into the end of the log, pick it straight up and walk it around. You can move pretty big logs that way, especially if they are balanced on something like another log or a pulp pile.

The hooks are holstered with one tip pointing forward and one pointing backward. That's the position they should be in for lifting a log. Furthermore, the hooks are designed so that, if you dig the points in, the log can't twist either way because the shape of the hooks holds it. No matter which way the log tries to turn, it pushes against a hook and stabilizes. By using the hooks, my hands stay clean and dry, even when I'm working with pitchy trees like white pine.

It takes practice to become proficient with the hooks, but it's worth the effort. They are a truly versatile tool. Unfortunately, they are harder to use with really small-diameter logs, which is the kind you would normally start practicing with.

I have become so used to wearing these hooks that, when I cut firewood and don't wear them, I find myself "slapping leather" sometimes, like an old-time gunfighter who has checked his six guns at the saloon door.

Before discovering the Swedish hooks, I used a hay-bale hook to pull one end of the pulpstick up to where I could grab it and pick it up. This cut down on the bending, but there was no safe way to carry the tool. Because of its shape (the point is perpendicular to the handle), a bale hook is dangerous to carry on your belt, and, if it falls or you set it on the ground, it always seems to come to rest with its sharp point sticking up. This type of hook is sometimes advertised and sold as a pulphook. Don't buy one for this purpose.

For large logs, I used to use a set of ice tongs that I picked up at an auction. With them, I could move large logs by lifting one end at a time. This, along with rolling the logs with a cant hook, enabled me to maneuver them to where I could pick them up with a tractor. The tongs were big, so I didn't have to bend over very much. This worked pretty well, but the tongs and cant hook were heavy and awkward to carry around, and I spent a lot of valuable time looking for them when I needed them.

A well-designed, flat tong is manufactured in Sweden and is carried in the same kind of holster as the pulphooks. The tongs come in several sizes. I use mine for carrying firewood. They are also popular with some pulp cutters, who use them for dragging pulpsticks rather than lifting them. For firewood I use two tongs, carrying a chunk in each hand for good balance. My firewood chunks are almost three feet long and heavy, so this method works well for me.

It seems natural to grab the chunks on the end when they are lying on the ground, but I've found it is better to grab them in the middle. If you grab them on the end, the other end hangs down when you load them, and you have to raise your arms high to get them onto the truck. I don't bother with holsters for these tongs. I usually load my wood in one operation, so I don't put them down.

I also have a "pickaroon," which is essentially a light handle with a sharp steel point on the end, designed to drag pulpsticks and small logs. It's a useful tool, but has its own dangers. If it lets loose while you are dragging a log, chances are you will go right over backwards, probably landing on your back on a stump. Tools like this are always a tradeoff. They have to hold when you want them to, but they also have to let go when you need them to. Thus, they can't hold too tightly and, therefore, slip occasionally.

There is another kind of pickaroon that has a hook on the end rather than a point. These are used to roll logs, mainly in sawmills. I bought one of each, then cut them in half and welded the different halves together to make a tool with a hook on one end and a point on the other. This makes a heavy, unbalanced tool, and I wouldn't want to use it very much, but I carry it on my forwarder and use it occasionally for moving logs. It works okay for that.

Using a felling lever.

Aside from my saw and hooks, the one indispensable tool that I have is a felling lever. As I said, I use the type that employs a pulphook for a hook. I do a lot of thinning in pine plantations. The trees are close together, which is why I am thinning them. Often, especially in winter, when the branches are frozen, it's tough getting the trees down. There are various techniques for doing this, but the first attempts are always made with the lever, initially to try to force the tree down by prying in the backcut at the stump. If that fails, then I whip out a pulphook and use the cant-hook configuration to twist the trunk.

You can cut slots in the trunk and attempt to twist the tree down with pulphooks.

Illustrations in safety manuals show cutters prying on trees in the classic "save your back" stance, that is, both hands on the end of the lever, back straight, knees bent. It looks good in the pictures, but I can't seem to get it right in the woods. Instead, I put my left hand on the trunk and pry the lever with my right hand. I know that sounds like I would wrench my back, but it enables me to use my legs by sliding one of my thighs under the lever and prying with it. I can also use my leg to hold the angle if it becomes necessary to insert a wedge.

If you do pry or push trees over, stop when they start to fall. It doesn't pay to waste energy pushing or prying on a tree that is falling of its own accord. Better to use this time to move away from the stump.

The trees I'm cutting now are thick enough so that there is little danger of striking the lever with my saw when I insert it in the felling cut, so I rarely resort to a wedge. One less thing to carry. You have to be careful when cutting, though, since the lever is made of hard Swedish steel. All you have to do is to touch it with a running chain and it's good-bye chain.

I also use the felling lever to pry up the butt if the hung-up tree has slipped off the stump and dug itself into the ground. It's rather short for that use, however, and it's usually better to cut a stick or use a skinny pulp-stick if you have to pry the stem loose.

I also use the felling lever in a vertical slot, instead of the pulphooks, to try and twist down a tree that is too skinny to allow the hook to catch.

Books tell you that you should push "over the top" when twisting on a lodged trunk. That is good advice. If something should break or let go, or if the tree should let go suddenly, or if you should slip, you would be okay if you were pushing over the top. By pulling down on the lever, however, any one of these things could put you on your back under the falling tree.

The only problem with this advice is that you can't get much leverage pushing over the top. If you really want to put your back into it, you have to pull down on the lever. That's the way I usually do it. I'm aware of the added danger though, so I try and pull down and away on the lever, not down and under. I've had slips and breakages and will again. Usually when I fall, I fall straight down, not under the trunk, but I'm always aware of the danger as I fall and immediately try and scramble or roll out of the way. I know this sounds rather foolhardy, and I don't suggest you do it that way. But sometimes that's what I wind up doing.

In addition to my felling lever, I have an old cant hook that I bought at a farm auction. I used an oak sapling to put a six-foot handle on it. We call it "Ultimo" and keep it in the truck. Because of the curve in the hook, it will only work on big trees, but sometimes it saves the day. The hook is loose on the handle, and, if necessary, I can cut a longer sapling and really get some leverage. I cut the six-foot handle because that's about all the room I have between trees. It is also about the right length for a pry bar.

If the cant hook slips on the trunk, you can, as a last resort, bore a square hole straight through the trunk and stick a sapling in it to turn with. These are all tricks you can use with pine trees. They won't do you much good with hardwoods, mainly because they tend to have big, spread-out tops. You'll probably also want to avoid some of these techniques when cutting sawlogs. Pulpwood buyers don't care about holes and slots in pulpsticks, but there's not much market for logs with slots cut in them.

Swedish logging tools include a felling lever (top), dragging tongs (right), and a pair of pulphooks.

I have one final word of caution concerning the practice of twisting trunks to get them down. Once the trunk starts to fall, it is natural to try to slip the prying device off. That's okay, but don't carry it too far. If the tree hits the ground with the lever on it, it may twist and the lever handle will be flung violently around, possibly striking you or tearing the handle out of your hands. So, if retrieving your tool causes problems, just stand back and let it go. Chances are it won't be damaged.

People who thin branchy trees such as fir and spruce have worse problems felling trees than I do. A tool they use is called a "tree jack." The Swedish models cost almost as much as a chain saw and weigh around 35 pounds. They consist of a telescoping pole with a jacking device to extend the end. You place the tool on the ground with one end against the upper part of the hung tree, then you operate the jack to push on it. I've seen pictures of some homemade models as well. They all seem heavy and awkward to me.

There is another style of jack that is used in directionally felling big trees. This is a small jack used in lieu of a wedge when felling. After the felling cut is partway through the tree, you cut out a square at the rear of the cut and insert the jack. You continue the cut, jacking as you go until the tree falls. This type of jack is made in Oregon by the Silvey Company. Silvey jacks are available from Bailey's in a range of sizes from a single 28-ton jack to a 125-ton backpack unit.

There is also a tool called a "felling pillow." This is an air bag that can be slipped into the felling cut behind the saw. It inflates with a special attachment to the saw cylinder. Compressed gas from the cylinder enters the bag and inflates it as you saw, tipping the tree. A valve controls the flow of gas into the pillow, thus controlling the rate of tipping.

I mention these things only as points of curiosity. I've never seen any of them and can't see where I would ever use them. I doubt if most readers of this book would, either.

I do carry a small plastic wedge and use it sometimes, mainly to slip into a felling cut if the tree is too slender to safely use the lever. If you hit the wedge with your chain, it just chews up the wedge, leaving the chain undamaged.

I rarely drive a wedge to fell a tree in a direction that it is not inclined to fall. There is a whole science to wedging, and serious loggers who fell large trees carry several large wedges on their belts. In skillful hands, wedges can force a tree to go just about anywhere the logger wants. It's a tricky business, however, and beyond the scope of this book. As a matter of interest, a one-inch-thick wedge, when driven into a felling cut, will move the top of a 75-foot tree about six feet.

Using a felling lever/pulphook combination to twist a hung-up tree.

Staying now with pine trees, there are several other ways to drop hung-up trees. These all involve methods of sliding the butt out, causing the tree to break through the branches by its own weight.

On small trees, I pick the butt up with my hooks and carry it out. This can be really exhausting if you have to do it very often, or carry it very far. Often, the butt will dig into the ground when it comes off the stump, making lifting that much more difficult. In many cases, it just isn't possible. Some people put a smooth plank alongside the stump, and then push or pry the butt off the stump and onto the plank, using it as a track to slide the butt out. The Swedes have developed a fiberglass, double-ended toboggan. You pry the butt onto it, and it slides out, carrying the tree with it.

I use a scoop shovel in place of a toboggan, and it works just fine. It is one of the rare tools that works best when you need it most, in this case in the winter when the branches and the ground are both frozen. The first time I tried it, the tree hit the handle and broke it off. I put a rope on it instead and it works just as well.

The big problem with these tools is getting the butt onto the device. If the trees are small, you can lift the butt, but with bigger trees that's not possible. The easiest way is to put the shovel alongside the stump and then kick or pry the butt sideways onto it. The other method is to put the shovel behind the stump and slide or pry the butt back onto it. In our case, Marcia holds the shovel while I push. Even with the two of us, it isn't easy.

Sometimes I miss the shovel when I push, and sometimes she can't hold the shovel and the butt kicks off it.

When all goes right, however, this tool really works. Often just putting the butt on it causes the shovel to go racing off, taking the tree down with it. That, of course, can be dangerous. Once it starts sliding, you lose all control of it. All you can do is get out of the way. Sometimes the shovel moves in unpredictable ways. One of the first times we tried it, a trunk slid sideways and bent up the handle on my saw. Now, before we even start, I move my saw to safety behind a tree, and we both retreat smartly, just as we would from a falling tree.

Notice that I don't include an axe in my tool list. To me, the axe is a remnant of history and about as useful in modern times as a crosscut saw or a slide rule. I don't own one and haven't for some time. Almost anything you can do with an axe, you can do better and easier with a saw. And an axe is useless as a splitting tool since it always gets stuck. A splitting maul is much better. Loggers still lug around axes, however. They use them for driving wedges.

The first time I saw a demonstration by Søren Eriksson, he felled some big pines. Before he started, he "brushed out" an area full of sapling scrub oaks where he planned for the pines to fall. It didn't dawn on me until later that, as he was clearing these saplings, he cut some slender poles about six feet long. From some of the larger stems, he cut pieces about a foot long. Thus, before he even started his demonstration, he had a supply of pry poles and short thick clubs to use for driving wedges.

Even if he never needed these tools, it had cost him nothing to cut them, and, if he did need them, they were there. That's "logging off the land." Most people would think that they could wait and cut the poles and wedges if necessary. The problem with that logic is that, when you need them, it's because your saw is stuck, leaving you with no way to cut them. In woods work, there's no substitute for planning ahead.

I noticed another thing about Eriksson and the other trainers. When they were not using their saws, they didn't hold them up by their front handles or set them on the ground. They rested them on the ground on the points of the bars. Thus they didn't have to stand around bearing the weight of the saw when they weren't cutting, and they didn't have to bend over to pick them up when they wanted to resume working.

If you are cutting logs or pulpwood, you need a way to measure lengths. With logs, diameter is also important. There is a lower limit on pulpwood diameters as well, but it's pretty loose and easy to eyeball.

In Chapter 1, I explain a bit about measuring with a logger's tape and stick. There are other methods, though, which some people still use. For years, when all pulpwood in our area was cut by hand, pulp cutters worked in two-person teams. Usually a man would cut, and a younger brother or wife or girlfriend would run the stick. Sometimes the cutter would hire a stacker, who would run the stick and stack the logs as they went along. Sometimes cutters would work alone.

The big problem with solo cutting was measuring. It usually makes sense to measure as you limb up the trunk. If you do your limbing and then measure afterwards, you often either limb up too far, which wastes energy, or you stop too soon and have to go back up and finish it off. Either way is inefficient, so most people devise ways to measure as they go. Some cutters tuck a stick under their arm and drop it down when they think they have gone eight feet. Some throw the stick down ahead of them as they go. And some "saw measure."

With a 16-inch bar, three saw lengths comes out to about eight feet. Guys make marks on the side of the trunk with the tip of the saw as they go and then buck every third mark. Some people attach things to the handle end of the saw to make it four feet long, so they only have to mark once between bucking cuts. I've heard of using stiff pieces of leather and even car radio antennas, which can be telescoped in when they are not needed. None of these schemes, in my experience, works very well.

We always use our stick made out of PVC pipe. I cut it 99 inches long for 100-inch pulpwood. I put a coupling or cap on both ends and spray paint them blaze orange. This makes them easy to see and also alerts me if I cut an end off. This happens once in a while and can go unnoticed, which means you end up producing short wood. If your PVC pipe breaks, or if you accidentally cut it, you can always cut off a section of branch and slide the two ends together over it to hold it until you can get home and repair it.

Some cutters will use a small sapling cut at the job site as a measuring stick. If you do this, cut the top end at a point where there is a crotch of some sort. That way, if you accidentally cut the end off, you'll notice it. With a straight pole it is almost impossible to tell. Some people like to cut a fairly sturdy pole so they can use it for pushing trees over. With the extra height a pole gives you, you can get a lot more leverage.

The logs I'm selling now are 12 feet by 6 inches and 16 feet by 8 inches long. (The odd lengths are to allow for trim at the mill). To measure these, I use a logger's tape. These are called "Spencer tapes," since many are made by the Spencer Manufacturing Company. Other companies manufacture similar tapes. Tapes come in various lengths. Mine is 50 feet long. It attaches to my belt and I hook it onto the butt of the trunk. It then runs out alongside the trunk as I move up it, limbing as I go.

Because you can't tell until you get to the top just what combination of logs and pulpsticks a given trunk will yield, it's not feasible, in this instance, to mark as you go. You have to limb until you get to the endpoint and then

turn and see how best to buck the logs. The endpoint is usually determined by diameter, although, sometimes, a defect in the trunk will determine a switch to pulpwood.

I wrap colored electrical tape around my Spencer tape at the bucking points for the various combinations. By looking at the colors when I reach the limit, I know immediately what the possibilities are.

Next, I mark the endpoint with a saw cut and walk back down the trunk, pulling the tape down to the trunk and marking the points as I go. When I get to the final one, I flip the tape off the butt. Then I buck the trunk at the points I have marked.

Bucking a limbed stem. Note the measuring tape trailing behind.

The position of the trunk determines where I start bucking. If it's held up on an end by a log or pulp pile, I buck so as to leave the end resting on the pile, or log, until the final cut. The advantage is that the trunk is up, off the ground. If it is just the top holding the trunk off the ground, I will buck the top pulpstick last, even though that means walking all the way up to the top again. I will go to almost any means to keep the trunk up off the ground until the last minute. I don't like to bend over (actually, I don't mind bending over, it's the straightening up that gets me), and I don't like to worry about my saw hitting dirt. I'll do whatever is necessary to avoid these problems.

Working with a tape attached to your belt and reeling out behind you obviously restricts your movements somewhat. You almost have to stay on one side of the trunk as you limb. If you jump across, you will probably tangle your tape and, possibly, kink it. Sometimes it is tempting, with a long trunk and deep snow, to stack the top pulpstick when you cut it off, rather than walking back up and doing it after you have finished marking. That seldom works with the tape attached.

When you snap the tape off, you can't just let it reel back up on its own. If you do, it may kink as it whips around. You have to watch it as it comes back and guide it through your fingers. The tension in the recoil mechanism is easily adjusted by loosening and turning the cover plate. You should set it so that the tape comes back slowly and all the way.

If you kink or cut or break a tape, you can repair it if the problem is near the end. First, cut it at the break. Then cut the unattached piece off about four inches in from the hook. Tape the two pieces together with electrical tape. This makes a rather thick end, but it will still reel almost all the way in and you can still use it.

Obviously, a tape repaired in this fashion will no longer read right and you will have to move all your marking tapes to new locations. As long as you do that correctly, you're okay. You don't really have to know any points on the tape except the marked bucking points, so it's not really a big deal. It also shortens the overall tape, but usually problems occur near the end of the tape, so that probably doesn't matter. Even if your tape is not long enough to measure extra-long trunks, you can always snap it off and reattach it further up if you need to.

Of course, you can buy replacement tapes. They come with installation instructions. But, like all spring-loaded devices, it ain't as easy as they make it look. You can buy a tool to make it easier, but my dealer charges me a dollar extra for installing them. That's a dollar well spent.

There are various attachment hooks and "nails" sold for these tapes. Like most wood-handling tools, they have to hold when you want them to and release when that's what you want. The tapes don't come with hooks, so you're free to choose your own. I've fooled with the various pointed devices and found them wanting, especially when working with frozen wood. Usually it's difficult to push them into wood, so you push them in just inside the bark. The trouble is, if you push them in firmly enough so they don't pull out, it's hard to snap them out again when you need to. They are also hard to handle with mitts on, even the thin mitts that I wear.

The only choice, in my mind, is a spring-loaded, tong-like device. You push one of the tong points against, not into, the end of the log and pull the other end up and push it into the bark. This spreads the tongs apart and provides the holding power. The hooks snap right off when you flip the tape. They work just as well with frozen wood, and, for that matter, if there is the slightest roughness, they will even hold on rocks.

The logs we sell now can go down as small as a six-inch diameter, and I made my "go/no-go" gauge for six inches. I also made some for eight and ten inches since those are the limits for log-cabin logs. I made them up with tees in the center of the U's. If I am trying to decide whether it will be worth it to switch to the larger, higher-priced logs in a stand of trees, I insert a

long piece of pipe into the tee. This enables me to reach up into the standing trees and estimate whether there will be enough large diameters high up
in the trees to justify switching.

It's important to decide this kind of thing early on. Every log-sort you
make takes time and costs money. There is also a saying in the logging business that, "If you don't have a truckload, you don't have zip." A tractor-
trailer load is around 15 cords, so I don't want to start out sorting logs and
then discover I don't have a load. This is no problem for the big operators,
who can combine logs from several jobs, or for loggers who do their own
trucking, but it costs me the same to get a half load to the mill as it does a
full load, so I've got to watch it.

7

● Starting Your Saw ◗◆

THE CONVENTIONAL WISDOM THESE DAYS is that you shouldn't even start your saw without donning full safety clothing. I don't argue with that, and we've covered safety clothing already, in Chapter 5. Now, however, I want to talk about the saw itself, so aside from ear protection, I have no quarrel with simply starting the saw wearing what you have on. Dealers (who are not always the best role models when it comes to safety) do it that way all the time, many without even ear protection.

After filling both the fuel and oil tanks, put the choke-throttle lever on "start." This will close the choke and set the throttle to half speed. (If you have an older saw, you may have to do these things separately.) Put the "on-off" switch to "on." Using the back of your wrist, trip the chain brake. (There's no special sequence to this, just be sure it all gets done before you pull the cord.)

My owner's manual shows the classic, approved way to start the saw. Put the saw on flat ground. Put your right boot on the lower flange of the rear handle. Hold the front of the saw down with your left hand on the front handle and pull the cord with your right hand. However, I don't know anyone who starts a saw this way. For one thing, It's about as awkward a stance as it is possible to assume. Also, it's a real bummer trying to do this on snow.

There are several easier ways to start a chain saw. One common method is to stand up straight and tuck the rear handle in back of your left knee.

Hold the front handle with your left hand and pull the cord with your right hand. (You can also do this the other way around, tucking the saw behind your right knee.) This is much easier.

Starting a saw "by the book."

Another method involves tucking the handle behind your right knee.

A third method is the notorious "drop start": thrust the saw downward while holding it with your left hand on the front handle and pull the cord with your right hand. This is the method I use and it is the easiest method of all, since the weight of the saw is used to help pull the cord. The big objection to this method is that you really have no control of the saw. You are, in effect, flinging it around while holding it with one hand.

Neither of these two easier methods could be recommended if it weren't for the chain brake. If the brake works as it should (and mine always has), the chain will not turn and these starting techniques are safe. It's up to you, however. The risks and advantages of each method should be clear. If you feel that, because the brake is an active device and must be engaged to work, it is not safe to rely on it, then I must assume that you never drive your car into situations where you depend on the brakes to stop it. Same situation. Starting the saw against the brake also tests and exercises the brake, so there are other good reasons for doing it that way.

Whichever starting technique you are using, the first time the saw fires, open the choke by moving the lever. Continue pulling until the saw starts. When it does, gun the engine. This will kick off the starting speed control and allow the saw to idle. Then—and only then—reset the chain brake. Don't let the saw run long at a fast idle with the brake engaged. You'll burn up the clutch.

With a good saw, these starting procedures almost always do the trick. Sometimes, however, the saw doesn't start. Sometimes I miss the first firing and keep the choke closed while continuing to pull on the cord. This floods the engine and the saw won't start. When this happens, I can usually tell by the sound the engine makes as I pull the cord. It's a subtle difference, but it is a sound you can recognize even with earmuffs on.

The quickest and easiest way to clear a flooded car or truck engine is to turn it over with the accelerator to the floor. With a saw, this involves holding the trigger down with your right hand while pulling the cord with your left with the choke fully open. The saw will usually start after four or five pulls. Naturally, you leave the brake on during this operation. The saw will start slowly, even though the trigger is held down, and take a second or two to clear the carburetor before it comes up to speed, so the saw won't scream up to full speed immediately even if the brake should fail.

If the saw still doesn't start, there are a number of troubleshooting techniques you can try, but few of them will do you much good out in the woods. There isn't much point in diagnosing the problem if you can't fix it. Still, it's worth trying a few simple tests to avoid hauling the saw to your dealer to fix a simple problem you could have handled.

One thing you can and should do is to change the spark plug. Spark plugs don't cost much, and it doesn't hurt to change them occasionally anyway. If you don't have a spare plug, you can examine and clean the old one, making sure there isn't anything bridging the electrode gap. You can fool around to see if you get a spark by holding the plug against the cylinder—with insulated pliers—while pulling the

The notorious "drop start" method.

cord. If you don't see a spark, you can check all the wires you can see. You can spray all of the electrical system with WD-40 and after five minutes, try starting again.

You can also put a few drops of fuel directly into the cylinder through the plug hole and screw the plug in. Then check and be sure you filled the fuel tank. You can fish out your fuel pickup tube with a wire and see if it is cracked or if the fuel filter is plugged. These filters are white when they are clean, darkening as they plug. They can't be cleaned, just replaced. Indications of filter plugging are hard starting and the saw "leaning out" long before it runs out of fuel. ("Leaning out" refers to an air-fuel mixture that is "lean" on fuel.)

Finally, you can reset your carburetor adjusting screws to their original setting if you can remember what that was.

I've done all of these things at one time or another, with varying degrees of success. Usually, though, the time I spent doing these checks would have been better spent driving to the dealer's shop. Aside from flooding, which is my fault, my saws almost always start. If they don't, they need to go to the shop.

There are three adjusting screws on a saw. These are marked "H," "L," and "T" and stand for "high," "low," and "throttle." The "high" setting controls the fuel to the carburetor at cutting speeds; the "low" at idle speeds. The "throttle" setting adjusts the throttle stop, thereby setting the minimum speed at idle.

These are all set by the dealer on a new saw. The high and low settings are determined at the factory and are the same for all saws of that class. Usually they are one turn or a bit higher. Mine are each 1¼ turns. If you feel the need to adjust your saw in the field, the first thing you should do is reset these screws to their initial settings. The only way to be sure you are correct in the settings is to take it to your dealer and let him set it with his tachometer, but you can fool around with it in the field, if you want to.

After the initial settings, with the saw running, run the throttle screw in until the saw will idle. Next, screw the low screw in until the engine speed starts to fall off due to a lean air-fuel mix. Note how many turns—or partial turns—you made. Now open the low screw until the rpm starts to fall due to excess fuel to the carburetor. Note how many turns this took. Then, set the screw about halfway between the two endpoints.

Next, lower the throttle setting until the idle rpm is nice and smooth. You may have to fiddle with the low adjustment as you do this to get the best-running mix. The low and high limits on idle setting are (1) failure of the engine to idle and (2) the chain turning. Anything between these two is okay for now.

There are two reasons for setting the idle first. Number one is that the low screw is open all the time and thus affects the high speed. Number two is that you want to be able to idle the saw while you are adjusting the high speed.

The main problem with high speed adjustment in the field is the danger that you may "lean" the mixture out too much. In two-cycle engines, cylinder lubrication is accomplished by mixing oil with the gas. The more gas you supply to the engine, the more lubrication the cylinder receives. Lean this mixture out too much and the cylinder will receive inadequate lubrication. This can result in excess wear to the cylinder, or, in really extreme cases, it may cause the engine to seize up. The only way to be absolutely sure that this will not happen is to set the rpm to the factory setting with a tachometer.

If you adjust the high speed screw, be sure your air filter is clean before you start. If you adjust the screw with a dirty air filter, you won't have any problems until you clean the filter. Cleaning the filter will increase the air flow, thereby leaning out the mixture and causing the cylinder lubrication problems mentioned above.

Never rev your saw up without the bar and chain attached. Without the restraint of the chain, the engine can overspeed and cause the clutch drum to fly apart. If it does—and it well might—you will be standing right in the path of any flying shrapnel. (In this case, "never" really does mean never.)

I do fool with my settings in the field and have never had any problems. If you choose to do the same, here's what works for me. Holding the trigger down all the way, I run the high screw in until I get the maximum, no-load rpm the saw is capable of. Then, I back it off until it growls a bit. There is a point in between where it produces a nice, clear, smooth sound. That's a bit too lean. Open the screw just a little more and you will be okay. Your final adjustment should not be far from the initial setting.

When you are finished, the saw should run and idle in all positions. It should go from idle to top speed smoothly, without any hesitation. The final proof, however, is in the cutting. Cut for a while with your screwdriver handy and adjust as needed to get the best performance you can. My saw rarely needs any sort of adjustment at all. If it needs anything, it is usually just a tweaking of the throttle screw.

On really cold days, I bring my saw into the house at night. This makes for easy starting in the morning. I heard somewhere that this wasn't a good idea, since condensation was apt to form in the carburetor when the cold saw was brought inside. It's never been a problem for me though.

I should note here that if you are starting your saw for the first time, make sure that the pump is delivering oil to the bar. It's easy to check. With the saw running, simply point the bar tip down at a leaf or stump and gun the engine. You should see oil flicking off the tip onto the surface. You only have to do this at the initial startup or if you think you are having problems. Ordinarily, the fact that you have to fill the oil tank with each refueling tells you all you need to know.

(Incidentally, the above example illustrates why you should always wear all your safety clothing. I was just going to have you start your saw, and now I'm telling you to gun the engine with the tip pointed down at a stump. Get that tip too close to the stump and you have a classic kickback situation. This sort of thing constantly sneaks up on you in the woods. The only defense you have is constant vigilance. "Alert-Alive!")

You can probably turn your oil consumption down a bit from the factory setting. To find the optimum oil setting, logic would suggest closing down on the oil adjustment screw until the chain starts to seize on the bar and then open it up a bit. I've tried this with my saw, and the screw will only close so far, preventing me from starving the bar for oil. This feature would also prevent me from taking advantage of the 40 percent less oil consumption canola oil promises.

Bar oil consumption is greatest when the saw is operated in short bursts, such as when limbing. If you are cutting large trees where you are running the saw steadily, in wood, for long periods, you may wish to increase the oil flow. This is no problem as long as you don't open it up so far that the oil runs out before the fuel and seizes the chain when you go back to short bursts.

Everybody, at one time or another, has to take his saw to the shop. You can save yourself time and money if you do it right. Before you go, you should completely clean the saw, especially the air filters. If you don't do this, the dealer will have to do it for you, and this will cost you time and money. No matter what the problem is, take the saw assembled, complete with bar and chain. The dealer will not operate the saw without the bar and chain. If you don't bring yours, he will have to hunt around and fit a spare onto your bar. Again, time and money are at stake.

Try to troubleshoot the problem in a general sense before you take your saw to the dealer. Explain to the dealer what the problem is, what you have tried, and the results of your tests. That's it. Don't tell him what he should do to fix it. If you tell him, for instance, that the carburetor is the problem and ask him to replace it, he may do just that. Then, if it still gives problems, it's your fault, not his. He just did what you told him.

Finally, think ahead to things you may need and get them while you are at the dealership. This will save you a trip later on. I always need two-cycle oil, files, bar oil, or a chain.

It would be great if you could bring your saw in at times when the mechanic is not very busy—any time but Saturday morning, for example. I never succeed in doing that. That's one of the big problems with working on Sundays. If anything goes wrong or if you need anything, you are out of luck. You can't even drop the saw off to be worked on during the week.

8

● Routine Maintenance

OTHER THAN CLEANING, SAWS REQUIRE LITTLE routine attention. About all you really have to do on a regular basis is clean around the sprocket area and the air filters. How often you will need to attend to these areas depends on your work habits. I clean both at every other refueling. This cleaning routine is more frequent than is probably necessary, but it works out for me, because two tanks constitute a morning's or an afternoon's worth of work. I do the cleaning in my workshop, not out in the woods. I try to avoid taking anything apart in the woods.

I outfitted an old building on my farm as a workshop. I installed a wood burning stove with the idea that I would warm the place up for doing my saw maintenance. I never used the stove, however, and finally took it out. The reason is that it only takes about five minutes to perform all of the work I usually do on my saw, and it was taking at least that long to get the stove going—longer, really, because I then had to wait while it heated the shop.

Instead, I bought a heat lamp and set it on my work bench. It provides enough light to work by and warms my fingers as I work. It's a good solution. If I have extensive work to do, I will set the saw under the lamp for a while before beginning. I never go off and leave the light on. It's pretty hot and could start a fire, especially with all the gas around. Also, I'm very careful when I put my saw under the lamp, usually placing just the bar portion directly under the bulb.

There are basically two types of air filters. One is cloth and the other fine-mesh wire screen. I prefer the screen type. My saw came with a cloth filter, but I had the dealer change it. My manual says that the cloth filter is needed for very dusty conditions, which I don't have. My quarrel with cloth filters is that you can't tell by looking whether they are dirty or not, and you can't tell if they are clean after you have cleaned them. With the screen type, it's easy. All you have to do is hold it up to the light. It's easy to see whether or not it is in good condition. You can also fix any tears or punctures with glue.

Normally I just brush my screen off with a toothbrush. If it looks dirty, I take it apart and rinse it off with WD-40. I don't have an air compressor, so I can't blow it out. When I think of it, I put it in the washer with my work clothes. That really does the job.

I take the side plate off the saw and gouge out any sawdust that may have collected inside with a screwdriver. This is especially necessary with wet winter wood. Usually I don't remove the bar, but just clean out the plate side, especially around the brake area.

With a new saw especially, I go over it occasionally and check all screws and bolts for tightness. Any problems should be attended to immediately. There is nothing spare on a saw. To keep the weight down, the manufacturers have eliminated everything that is not essential for the saw to run. The only exceptions are safety items like the brake and throttle lock. The saw will run without these features, and so it is tempting to put off getting them fixed on the rare occasions when they give you trouble. For safety's sake, however, don't put it off.

I don't bother cleaning out the groove in my bar or the oil holes, ignoring them unless I am having problems there. It's a fact that you should rotate your bar regularly to equalize the wear on the grooves. However, I don't worry about that, either, believing instead that the law of averages will ensure that the bar gets rotated as I go about my regular maintenance routine.

When you take your bar off, be very careful when you reassemble the saw to ensure that the chain tension adjusting screw lines up with (and fits into) the hole in the bar. If you tighten the nut (or nuts) on the side plate without these two items lined up properly, you will bend the adjusting screw and have to replace it. Also, don't use the cover nuts to force the screw into its hole. Tighten the nut(s) "wrist tight." Don't put your whole weight behind the wrench or you might strip out the stud. If it strips out, you can have it fixed once by having the dealer drill out the original hole and put in a helicoil insert. After that, I don't know.

Tighten your chain "bowstring" tight. This means that when you pull it off the bar it should snap back and ride on the bottom rail. I have read all sorts of warnings about not tightening a hot chain and releasing the chain tension when you shut the saw down, so as to avoid stretching it. With a short bar and chain, this is not a concern. Before tightening the chain, lift the nose of the bar up and hold it up until you're done. This takes whatever play there may be out of the bar and ensures a good tight chain.

I check the pull cord occasionally for fraying. Cords usually fray where they leave the bottom of the pulling handle. If I notice any wear there, I just pull the cord a bit further through the handle and tie another knot in it higher up to put a new section in the wearing position. You've got a much longer pull cord than you actually need, so you won't miss that inch or so.

If I find it necessary to do much more than that with my pull cord, I either tie a temporary knot in it down low or grab it with a pair of vise grips to keep it from slipping out of my grasp and flapping around inside as the recoil spring unwinds. You don't need that on a freezing morning. It's not all that hard to replace a pull cord. The manuals all tell you how, so I won't bother here. Each saw is a bit different in this respect.

Every saw contains three running parts: the bar, the chain, and the sprocket. These wear on each other, and the wear on any one of them directly and immediately affects the other two. Users tend to either not understand this fact or to ignore it. A lot of chain-saw owners seem to feel that the chain is the only wearing part on the saw, and that, if they can squeeze maximum wear out of their chains, they are ahead of the game. It's not that simple, however.

There are all sorts of combinations people have come up with over the years in an attempt to equalize the wear on these three essential parts. Mainly they involve alternating chains to equalize wear. My book says to alternate two chains and then change the sprocket when both chains wear out. In other words, two chains per sprocket. There are other, more intricate schemes that include the bar in this schedule. I don't do any of them. I can never remember when I changed my bar and sprocket. I change my chains when I can't sharpen them anymore. I change my bar when it fails, usually when the roller-nose bearings seize up. I change my sprockets when I can see that their drive teeth are worn down to sharp points. They say you should never run a new chain on an old sprocket. I ignore that also. I have had sprockets break while cutting, but it's rare. Usually it's wear that does them in.

Aside from replacing worn chains, the best thing to do is always take your saw along when you visit your dealer for any reason. Ask him to inspect your bar and sprocket and do any necessary maintenance work.

With the sprocket, this will mean simply replacing it if it is worn. There are several things a dealer can do with a worn bar, however, which will bring it up to snuff. Aside from the bearings, bars give problems through wear in their grooves. If these grooves wear unevenly, the saw will cut off to one side. This is usually not noticeable in small timber, but if you are trying to fell a large tree, you may find that your felling cut either sweeps up or down and misses the notch elevation. Equalizing this wear is the reason for rotating your bar regularly. If the dealer sees this problem, he can grind the grooves down ("true it up") until their sides are equal. This is a simple job and well worth doing.

Another problem is simply the wearing and spreading of the groove itself. If the groove becomes oversized, the chain will wobble and make for erratic cutting. You can buy tools to squeeze or pound these two groove halves back together, restoring the proper clearances to provide support for the chain without causing undue friction.

These items are easily repaired, and should be. If you bend your bar or overheat part of it, thereby annealing the steel and making a soft spot, you are pretty much out of luck. You can bend your bar by prying with it, or if a tree falls on it. I've tried to straighten bent bars, but usually with little success. You may be luckier. There's no secret to it. It just doesn't work.

You can overheat a spot on your bar, usually on the tip, if a tree tips back such that its weight squeezes the groove together. This causes friction with the chain, overheating that spot. You can usually continue to work with a bar damaged in this fashion, but not for long. It will tend to continue to overheat in the same spot.

Since I have gone to throwaway bars, most of these concerns have disappeared. My bars simply don't last long enough to have a lot of these problems. Still, I do have my bar ground every time I take the saw into the shop. I notice an improvement in performance after grinding, but then, I think I notice an improvement whenever I change the oil in my car, too.

The main thing causing wear on the bar is a dull chain. If you have to bear down on the chain to get it to cut, it quickly wears itself out, taking the bar with it. The obvious solution, then, is a proper sharpening of the chain. Insufficient oil flow can also damage both chain and bar, but a dull chain is, far and away, the most common problem. By trying to get a little more out of a dull chain, people end up getting a lot less out of their bars, which generally cost several times more to replace than chains.

Chain Sharpening

Chain sharpening is the litmus test of true woodsmen. How it came to be that way, I don't know, but there it is. You can either sharpen a chain, or you can't. It's easy for me to say now that there isn't much to it, but, if I look back, I remember how long it has taken me to be able to do a workman-like sharpening job and how many gadgets and techniques I went through before I finally got as good as I am.

There are just a few general rules about sharpening, but dozens of notions about how to do it. In my book, Rule Number One is to sharpen at least every time you gas your saw. Rule Number Two is to never let anyone else sharpen your chain. This includes your dealer.

I almost never sharpen a dull chain. I almost always touch up a sharp chain. I'm like the butcher who whets his knife every few strokes, as opposed to the housewife who lets her knives get so dull they won't cut, and then puts them on a grinder. I have to admit that I do that with knives, too, but not with my chain.

If you follow this rule, it automatically rules out dealer sharpening since you are obviously not going to run down there after every tankful. It also explains one of the reasons I advise you to sharpen your chain yourself. You are the only one who will do it that frequently.

Okay, you say, but why not take your chain along once in a while and let the dealer give it a good sharpening job? Or, since you hopefully don't have to run to the dealer that often, why not just take it down to the hardware store? They've got the same machine the dealer does, and they charge a buck less, two bucks less if the chain is off the saw.

Well, if you take your chain to the hardware store and give it to the high school kid working there, he will put it on the machine, select the shortest tooth and grind them all to that length. That's what the book says to do. There's nothing really wrong with that rule, except that it's not necessary. If each raker is the proper height for its tooth, all the teeth will cut properly, and the chain will cut smoothly regardless of whether some teeth are longer than others.

It seems odd that the same dealers who grind all teeth down to the length of the shortest one will, without hesitation, completely remove a tooth to shorten a chain. If removing a tooth doesn't adversely affect the cutting of the chain—and I don't believe it does—why should running with a short tooth affect it? I don't believe it does either.

That brings us to the biggest problem with the hardware store. It's not that they grind too much off the teeth; it's that they don't take the rakers down. They just grind the teeth. This is true of some dealers as well, but, even if they do it right, I avoid them.

I bought a bench chain grinder once, but have since sold it. I quit using it once I learned how to file. It was just too much work to take the chain off the bar every time I wanted to sharpen it. This was not the only problem, however.

I thought I could use the file most of the time, and then go to the grinder occasionally if my filing got out of whack. Makes sense. I tried it, but ended up with the same problem I had when I was taking it to the dealer occasionally. When I would try to file the chain after grinding, the file would chatter along the tooth and I would see scratch marks on the file. At the time, I felt that this was somehow due to "impurities" in the metal of the tooth, but then I noticed that the only time I had the problem was after using the grinder. It gradually dawned on me that the problem was that small "stones" were coming off the grinding wheels and embedding themselves in the chain teeth. Then, when I went to file, these "stones" were scratching my files and preventing me from doing a proper job. That's when I sold the grinder.

Usually, any article about chain sharpening starts out by explaining what each part of the cutter does and the proper angles you must maintain while sharpening to allow each part to do its job. I'm not going to do that. This is mainly because I never got it all straight and don't want to take the time to look up and write down numbers that are meaningless to me just to confuse (albeit, possibly impress) you.

If you can hold a file straight while you run it across the tooth and keep it more or less parallel to the line on the tooth, you can do the job without knowing much of anything. Practice, above all else, is the key.

Success thus begins at the saw dealer's shop. Especially if you are new at it, demand that any chain you buy or get with your new saw have the angle guide line scribed across the top of every tooth. This basically eliminates the need for file guides or any other filing aids. Buy special chain saw files from your dealer. Don't try anything else. Get a good handle and put it on. For me that means the two-way Swedish files and handles. (I don't bother putting a handle on my raker file. I use it a lot less than my round files, and it works fine just as it comes out of the box.) Make sure you get the proper size files for your chain, or you won't have any luck at all.

"Real" loggers sharpen their new chains before they use them the first time, not trusting the factory to do a decent job. Amateurs wait until they absolutely have to before sharpening the first time, fearing (perhaps correctly) that they will never get it as sharp as when it was new and that each sharpening just makes it worse. I use my chains right out of the box, but I sharpen them after the first tankful, just as I would a used chain, even though they show no sign of dulling.

Aside from waiting too long between sharpenings, there are two basic problems people run into when it comes to keeping a chain sharp. Number One is that, through ignorance, they don't file the rakers. Number Two is that they have trouble maintaining the proper angles on the top plate. This is mainly because most people can't seem to file both sides of the chain the same, since most people are either right-handed or left-handed. It is very common to see chains sharpened to an extreme point on one side and almost straight across on the other.

If you don't file the rakers, they will gradually prevent the teeth from hitting the wood at all, and you will be correct in observing that, "The more I sharpen it, the duller it gets." Actually, the chain isn't getting "duller," but it might as well be. If, on the other hand, you file the rakers down too far, the chain will bite too deeply and either stall or kick back at you violently.

You don't have to file the rakers every time you sharpen the chain. You do, however, need to check them every four or five sharpenings. You do this with a little tool called a raker gauge. After sharpening, you simply place the raker gauge across each tooth and file off whatever part of the raker sticks up through the slot in the gauge.

Good raker gauges have two slots, one for winter and one for summer, because frozen wood is harder to cut than unfrozen wood. Ideally, if you are cutting frozen wood, the rakers should be a bit longer so that the tooth takes a smaller bite and doesn't chatter in the cut. Using the proper slot in your gauge assures that this is so. If your gauge only has one slot, don't worry about it. The difference in the two lengths is so slight that the average cutter won't notice any difference. The important thing is that you maintain the rakers, not the small difference between the two slots.

Because the raker eases the chain into the wood, it works best if the filed portion of the raker is rounded off to provide a smooth transition. As you continue to file the raker with your gauge, the top portion flattens out where it originally was rounded. This is easily corrected by rounding off the front part of the raker corners, with the gauge removed, every few filings. You do this freehand with the raker file. Just round it without filing any off the top. This too is not critical, but it's a good thing to do.

In tooth filing, the only angle you need to be concerned about is the top plate angle. Holding the file level as you sharpen will take care of the rest, within limits that are perfectly acceptable for the average user. The specs for various chain types will sometimes call for a 10-degree angle on the file and vary between 30 and 35 degrees on the top plate angle. Just ignore all of that. I doubt if you would ever notice the difference in performance between these specs even if you could adhere to them, which you can't. Just hold the file level and follow the scribed line. Do that and you will do a good job.

Obviously, you file only on the forward stroke. You do all of the teeth facing one way, then you turn the saw around and do the ones facing the other way. This is where it can become awkward, and where most of your problems will arise. If you are right-handed, you will file the teeth pointing to the left with a straight, forward, stroke. You will file the right-facing teeth backhanded. The average person finds it difficult to maintain the same angles using these two different techniques.

When I sharpen on the bench in my workshop, I put the saw straight across the bench in front of me with the nose of the bar facing to my left and sharpen the right-facing teeth with a backhand stroke. Then I rotate the saw 180 degrees, step slightly to the left, wrap my left arm around the saw

body and do all the left-facing teeth with a straight, forward stroke. You can do it this way in the woods as well, but not as easily.

A good way to sharpen chain in the woods is to sit down with the saw on your lap. Sharpen the right-facing teeth while bracing the saw on your left thigh. Now, flip the saw upside down and do the rest of the teeth. This works really well for me. It's worth

Filing on a bench or other stable surface.

practicing to get it right. You can do it sitting on a log, the tailgate of your truck, or right on the ground.

When you have finished, every point on every tooth should be sharply pointed, and all the top plate angles should closely match the scribed angles. The underside of each top plate cutting edge should be roughened from the file strokes, not smooth and shiny. The teeth should be almost all the same length. At the very least, they shouldn't be consistently longer on one side than the other. If this is happening, you have to even out your filing pressure. Maybe you have to take two strokes on one side while taking one on the other, for example, until you can eventually get them evened up.

For obvious reasons, the best time to do this, since you're putting the saw in your lap and turning it upside down, is after the saw has cooled and before adding fuel and oil.

If you use the correct size file, the top 20 percent or so of the file should stick up above the top plate as you sharpen. When you file, don't press down on the file. Press straight ahead with a slight upward bias, probably around 10 or 15 percent. This will ensure that the underside of the cutting edge is being filed (see the diagram on page 26).

Conventional wisdom says that you should always use gloves when filing. I never do that. I hate working with gloves. Dealers never wear gloves. I try not to pull the chain around the bar with my fingers, but, when I do, I always pull with my fingers on the back of the cutters. That way, if my fingers slip, it's unlikely that I will slice them.

How do you advance the chain without pulling it? As I sharpen each tooth, I move my file to the back of the cutter and push with the file to line up the next tooth. If I have to tighten my chain, I wait until I'm through filing before I do it. That way it's easy to advance it using just the file. I rarely cut myself.

I file with one hand and grip the tooth with the other. Some people file with both hands on the file, one on the handle, the other on the tip. That looks like a good method to me, but I am more comfortable using just one hand. If you do it this way, be sure the chain is fairly tight. If it is too loose, it will wobble in the groove and you won't get a good results.

You should figure out a way to know when you have sharpened all the teeth on one side. When you touch up a sharp chain, you can't really tell which cutters you've done by looking. I keep track by counting. With a 13-inch bar, there are 14 teeth per side (and 28 rakers, which are all filed from the same side). That's easy enough to keep track of. Some people mark

"Lap filing" is a good way to sharpen a chain in the woods.

the tooth they started on with a gob of grease or a crayon mark. Spray paint works too. Either way, don't worry too much if you lose track. It won't hurt to sharpen a tooth twice or miss one. It won't be the same one each time, so it will average out.

The proof of all this attention to detail is in the cutting. Chain saws are not cabinet-making tools. They should cut aggressively, produce big chips, not fine sawdust, and throw them a long way. One major chain manufacturer once supplied a sort of sieve device with its consumer-market chains. You were supposed to put your sawdust in this box and shake the box. If the sawdust was fine enough to get through the holes, it was supposedly time to sharpen your saw.

That wasn't a bad idea, except that the size of the chips is a function of how far the tooth bites into the wood, which in turn is a function of raker height, not sharpness. Since most hardware stores don't file the rakers, having the saw sharpened just made the situation worse.

Finally, chain is pretty cheap considering the work you get out of it. Don't be fanatical about getting the last mile out of every chain. Sometimes you can use a chain down to where the teeth break because they have been filed down to nothing. I don't usually get that far. I will generally damage the chain so severely at some point in its life by hitting a rock, a frozen chunk of dirt, or my felling lever that it isn't worth my time and effort to bring it back. This point, naturally, depends on how much chain I have left. I will work pretty hard to restore a new chain; considerably less to reclaim an old one for a few more tankfuls.

9

Søren Eriksson and the Game of Logging

AFTER YEARS OF LOOKING AT ADS for "Illustrated Swedish Manuals" in the back pages of magazines, I finally sent for one. It was about cutting pulpwood.

Shortly thereafter, I attended an exhibition of "Swedish techniques and practices." It was put on by a slightly built, middle-aged man with a bad back and an accent like your Uncle Ole. He wore baby blue pants and an orange jacket, and what he did was cut down trees. Boy, did he ever cut down trees! Like I'd never seen before. His name was Søren Eriksson.

Eriksson is the leading proponent of Swedish manual logging methods in the United States and Canada. He is also founder of the "Game of Logging." He has logged and trained logging crews all over the world in safe, efficient manual methods of timber harvesting. I've heard him described as the world's first millionaire pulp cutter.

Eriksson doesn't do tricks with his chain saw or perform feats of strength. What he does is apply "ergonomic" principles to woods work. He is obviously very skilled, but the main appeal for me is that he demonstrates and explains his every action so that you can understand what he is doing and actually apply it to your own woods work.

This is not a case of Eriksson possessing skills that the rest of us can marvel at, but cannot do ourselves. Remember those mail-order vegetable cutting gadgets on TV that the demonstrator uses to make roses out of potatoes and cut two-foot spirals out of a single carrot? You buy one and all you can cut is the end of your finger. Eriksson's demonstration does not leave the viewer with that kind of frustration. He teaches not just a set of techniques, but a philosophy.

Most woods work in North America has traditionally been just bull work: young, strong, guys muscle their way through the timber until they either are hurt or their backs give out, at which point someone else takes over. Nobody ever taught anyone else how to cut pulp and firewood because it was assumed that there is nothing to learn: just put your back into it and go. Well, it isn't so, and Eriksson's demonstrations over the years have shown that it isn't.

I guess the main thing I learned was that pulp cutting can be a profession and should be approached in a professional manner. I've applied this philosophy to all my woods work in the years since I saw my first demonstration, and I can truthfully say that my efficiency has improved at least 25 percent. Not only do I get more work done, but it is done more safely, and I enjoy it a lot more.

What impressed me the most from the first Eriksson demonstration I saw was the felling of a big, branchy, leaning red pine. About one hundred interested people, as well as several local television crews, were standing in a semicircle around the tree. Eriksson not only felled the tree safely with that crowd around, but at the point where his felling cut was almost completed, he stopped, shut off his saw, and explained what he had done up until then. I'm sure he used gestures in his explanation, but I doubt if anyone saw them, since I'm sure every eye was on the crown of that tree, expecting it to fall at any minute. It didn't. It fell when he wanted it to, where he wanted it to, against the lean into a clearing.

This was all several years ago. Now there are numerous logging trainers giving classes and demonstrations, some of them employed by Eriksson's Game of Logging. I don't know how many of Eriksson's techniques were actually developed by him, and it really doesn't matter. What he did was to introduce this philosophy to general audiences on this side of the Atlantic.

The Game of Logging has become the premier logger training operation here. It now includes training for "Urban Logging" and "Logging for Landowners." Its main focus, however, always has been—and continues to be—the individual, professional logger.

In fact, the Game of Logging has developed into a nationwide contest with state and regional winners competing for a $10,000 national championship prize in an annual competition. This is unique in the logging profession. The competition doesn't include hot dog stunts like "hot saw" competitions or wood chopping. The stress is on professional skills and, above all, safety. I can think of nothing that has done more to upgrade loggers' skills and professionalism than the Game of Logging and Søren Eriksson.

Having said that, I must tell you that I am glad that I attended the original demonstrations conducted by Eriksson, and by Dan Tilton of Tilton Equipment, a distributor of chain saws. There were probably other instructors around as well, but these are the two I know of.

Søren Eriksson explains filing technique to a group of Game of Logging students.

These days, the field has pretty much been taken over by certified Game of Logging instructors. The instruction usually is "hands-on," with the students practicing each technique as it is taught, leaving ample time between courses to allow the students to practice their skills in their work.

This method of teaching is, in most ways, surely superior to simple demonstrations with the attendees watching but not participating. One downside, though, perhaps inevitably, is that the courses have become more expensive and they concentrate—at least in my experience—solely on the items and techniques that appear in the Game of Logging competitions. This narrows the focus down to where the student succeeds by doing exactly as the instructor teaches. Any ideas the students may have are dealt with by the instructor explaining why they are not acceptable. No deviations from the Game of Logging doctrine are allowed.

This is fine as far as it goes. The techniques taught are, no doubt, the best and safest, and the training is effective. The problem I have with it is that no one technique is applicable in all the situations you run across in the woods. The best books I have seen on these subjects are the ones put out by the Swedish Forest Operations Institute. In these booklets, several solutions are presented for most problems, and they say "Don't marry any one technique." Eriksson's earlier programs usually demonstrated several techniques for most things. I have the impression that this approach has been lost now: the one right way for everything has been determined, and that may be all that is taught.

Still, the Game of Logging is, without a doubt, the best thing that has ever happened to logging safety in this country.

10

● Felling ◖▴▴

I MAKE MY LIVING WITH TREES. I plant them, cut them down, and cut them up. Of all the phases of this work, felling trees is the most difficult and dangerous. Yet every day, untrained people casually gas up their chain saws and set themselves up as loggers. It's ironic that, in a profession which has a higher accident rate than deep-tunnel mining, the most hazardous work is performed mainly by amateurs.

In the grim statistics of logging, chain saws account for most of the injuries, but trees are responsible for most of the deaths. Safety clothing and equipment can protect you somewhat from your saw, but nothing will save you from a falling tree if you're in its way.

Yet, if you are careful and realistic in your work, cutting wood can be a satisfying and rewarding task. Woods work should not be exciting. A good day in the woods is an uneventful day. A Chinese curse is said to be, "May you live in interesting times." A woodland curse could be, "May you have an interesting day." Your day should be productive and satisfying—possibly even fulfilling—but not, I hope, interesting.

Make it simple, make it routine, make sure everyone understands it, and don't change it without notice. These are literally words to live by.

Whenever possible, I do my saw work first, when I am fresh. I find that, when I become tired, safety is one of the first things to go. I stumble more and take risky shortcuts. I tend to reach with my saw rather than setting myself firmly and directly in front of the work. I am less alert to danger when I am tired, and my judgment isn't as good as when I am rested.

I try to keep in mind that what I am doing is dangerous. Often it doesn't seem that way. Things go smoothly day after day, and it begins to seem like any other job. My mind starts to wander, and I become careless.

I make sloppy notches, and the trees fall a bit to one side or the other. I just glance up at the tree rather than walking all around it to look for potential hazards. Rather than positioning my saw correctly to cut a limb, I'll poke at it with the tip of the bar, and so forth.

I have to force myself to concentrate and remind myself of the statistics and the people I know who have been hurt or killed doing exactly the same thing I am doing. If all else fails, I think of this book. I don't want it to start by announcing that the author was killed cutting wood, even though that might sell a few extra copies.

The work is easily broken down into separate operations, such as felling, limbing, and bucking. For firewood, it's felling, blocking, splitting, loading, and hauling. In a way that is unfortunate, because it suggests that these are independent tasks. In fact, each depends to a large degree on the others. You won't ever become very efficient unless you keep all the tasks in mind.

It may seem that felling a tree with a chain saw is a prime example of technology overpowering nature. Not so. You will find that nature is very much in control, and that there are definite limits to your influence over it. If you are clever you can use natural forces to assist you, but if you work against nature, you do so at your peril.

A good general rule in felling any tree is: Avoid "must" situations. Don't get yourself in a position where you *must* cut wood today even though it's windy, or where you *must* cut a tree even though it looks chancy, or where the tree *must* fall in this direction, even though it appears to lean in that direction. Felling trees is an art, not a science, and many things can go wrong with little warning. Before starting, always ask yourself, "What would happen if this tree fell the worst possible way?" Ideally, your answer should be, "Nothing very serious." Remember, standing trees are seen fore-shortened: they are always taller than they look.

I fell trees using the "open-face" method. I used to use the traditional method of cutting a thin wedge out of the trunk, but open-face cutting is much safer and easier to control. It is also easy to learn, and you can use it immediately upon learning it. Practice will perfect your technique, but even first-timers can use the open-face method to advantage.

With this felling technique, you modify the wedge cut. It is more a process of flattening the trunk on one side than one of removing a wedge.

A tree standing straight up on level ground will pass through 90 degrees as it falls to the ground. If you make a notch of 90 degrees, the notch will close at the point where the tree hits the ground. If you make your notch less than 90 degrees, the notch will close and break at some point during the tree's fall. From that point on, the tree will fall freely, out of control. If you make your notch greater than 90 degrees, the notch will not close and the trunk will remain attached to the stump after it has come to rest.

There are times when each of these conditions is desirable. It is important, however, for you to decide which situation you want and to be able to control events to produce the desired result. You can only do that by controlling the angle of the notch. And you can't do that with the traditional thin wedge.

A 90-degree notch.

To make a removable, conventional wedge that far into the tree, the notch width always ends up somewhat less than 45 degrees. As a result, trees notched in this fashion will free-fall after they have fallen about halfway down. This is not always a good idea.

The second problem with a deep notch is that it is hard to ensure that both notch cuts meet. It is always bad practice for one of the cuts to extend beyond the other. Open-face notches can eliminate both these problems.

Here's how the open-face method works:

Position yourself to the right and slightly behind what will become the open face on the trunk, facing the direction you want the tree to fall. This will usually put your left shoulder against the trunk. Sight along your saw, holding it with the bottom of the bar tipped slightly back toward the trunk. If your saw has a felling guide mark on it, sight along it. If you have no mark, try to find a line on your saw that is perpendicular to the bar—often the back edge of the top cover—and sight along it. If none of this works, you can make your own line out of tape. See that it is perpendicular to the edge of the bar at a spot on the saw that is convenient to sight along. Run it across the top of the saw and down the left side.

Bear in mind that your line of sight is not the trunk, but a line to the right of the trunk. This line may be a foot or more to the right of the center of the trunk. Thus, you must be aware that the actual falling path of the tree will be that much to the right of your sighting line. If you aim exactly where you want the tree to fall, you will be off to the left. This may not matter much with short trees and distances. As these dimensions increase, however, the inaccuracy becomes significant. If you are aiming between trees, aim between the trunks, not the tops. It's easier to aim straight ahead

The proper stance for aiming with the saw.

than it is to look up into the tops. If the tree leans heavily to one side or the other, you need to aim away to compensate for the lean.

Next, make the first cut almost straight down into the trunk, cutting into the tree at only a slight angle, maybe 15 degrees. Continue this cut until it reaches the height of the stump you wish to leave. Then make a horizontal cut at the bottom of the first cut to remove a tall, slim wedge that flattens the trunk about one-fifth of the way into the tree. The wedge will probably be about four to six inches tall and about two or three inches deep, depending on the size of the tree. The point of this notch is the front face of the hinge on which the tree will pivot as it falls (see the "key" on page 109).

The falling path will be perpendicular to the flat face of the open cut. It is important that the two cuts meet. If either cut extends into the trunk beyond the junction point, it could cause problems later, especially if the horizontal cut goes deeper than the intersection. You can guard against this by looking down into the first cut as you make the second one. You should be able to see the chain cutting into the kerf of the first cut and stop it at the point where they intersect.

At one time, people were taught to make the felling cut an inch or so higher than the bottom of the notch cut. The rationale was that this protrusion would act to stop the butt from sliding back on the stump as it fell. Some safety manuals still advocate this.

The argument on the other side is that, with the open notch, the hinge will hold almost all the way to the ground, making this protrusion unnecessary. This school of thought holds that it is more difficult to

The wrong way: aiming with your ass.

accurately gauge the thickness of the hinge if the cuts are not at the same elevation. This is not a trivial matter. The OSHA regulations were held up for several days while this point was debated. Eventually, OSHA settled on "at, or slightly above" the notch.

I come down on the same-elevation side. Actually, this is a goal, not a rule, for me and probably for you. I seldom take the time to ensure that my cuts will match exactly. The most important thing about the hinge is that it be the proper thickness, and the most important thing about the two cuts is that the horizontal cut does not extend beyond the notch cut.

When the open-face notch cut is complete, and you have removed the wedge, start the felling cut on the opposite side of the trunk at the same height as the bottom of the notch. The notch cuts are made from the right side of the tree using the bottom of the bar as the cutting edge. If there is a definite lie to the tree, make the felling cut from the side of the trunk away from the lie. That way, if the tree should fall sideways, it will fall away from you and your saw. ("Lie" is a logging term for the way a tree would fall naturally: it takes into account wind, branches, lean, snow loading, and other factors.)

The felling lever can save a great deal of valuable time and effort.

To determine the lie of a tree, it is best to walk all around it. Failing that, you must at least view it from two sides 90 degrees apart. You should not only look for the lie on your inspection. Look for dead limbs and possible dead trees being held up by the tree you are going to fell, or ones that are in the line of falling. Check for shelf fungus on the tree if it is a hardwood. These are called "conks" and indicate rot in the trunk. Felling a conked tree will often cause it to break at the level of the conk, with the broken-off top possibly swinging back toward the stump.

If the tree is straight and there are no other problems, make your felling cut from either side. As soon as there is room behind the bar, insert your wedge, or felling lever, into the cut. I just tap the wedge in with the heel of my hand, since its only purpose is to prevent the tree from tipping back and pinching the saw should wind or other factors force it back.

I make all my cuts while standing, and don't kneel by the tree. I make the felling cut from a crouch, with my elbows resting on my knees.

The felling cut should stop about 1 to 1½ inches from the notch. It is vital that you go no further. These 1 to 1½ inches provide the hinge that prevents the tree from falling sideways and guides it on its way to the ground. At this point, the tree should tip and fall. If it doesn't, push it or tap the wedge in a bit, or pry it over with the felling lever.

The proper thickness of the hinge is a function not only of the tree species, but of weather conditions. Frozen wood breaks more easily and cleanly than normal wood. Thus, in cold weather, your hinge needs to be thicker. Using the open-face method, I can usually fell a tree about 45 degrees on either side of its lie. I usually depend on the lie of the tree to tip it. I never depend on wind to help me. Wind is a fickle friend, often stopping or changing direction at critical times. When felling trees, the best wind is no wind at all.

I use wedges and a felling lever to prevent the tree from rocking back and pinching my saw, and to "help" the tree fall. I seldom intentionally try to force a tree to fall against gravity by driving wedges or prying with the felling lever. Sometimes, though, I read a tree wrong and it tips back onto the wedge. In these situations I drive the wedge and try to force the tree over. If this fails, I look for the best direction I can hope to put the tree. Then I move about four to six inches up the trunk and repeat my notching and felling cuts from there. That may work, but it often results in a hung tree.

In all cases I complete the felling cut before leaving the vicinity of the stump. It is imperative to remain at the stump until the tree is falling. Once you start your felling cut, you are committed. Don't start felling unless you are sure you have enough gas and oil in your saw to finish the job. It is extremely dangerous to have to leave a partially cut tree to get fuel, or a tool, or to move the truck if things have gone badly and it appears as if the tree may hit it.

It is not, however, dangerous to stop your cutting to reevaluate things. There is no hurry. You can stop to check the trueness of your cut, or to sense any changes in conditions, or just to get your breath. What you can't safely do is wander around away from the trunk.

As the saw proceeds into the wood, be alert to easier-than-expected sawing and changes in the color and texture of the sawdust. These hints can indicate rot or hollow spots, which could cause the tree to fall unexpectedly. Encountering any of these things is a good reason to stop and reevaluate the situation.

As your felling cut approaches the hinge, look on the other side of the tree to be sure that the tip of your bar is not leading the saw end. If it is, you may be cutting into hinge wood, and the tree may fall in an unexpected direction.

Adjust your cutting as necessary to leave a uniform hinge. You can use the aiming line as a guide. The felling cut should be in a direct line with the notch cut. If they are, the hinge will be uniform. Wiggle the wedge with your fingers. If it seems to be loosening, the tree is going in the right direction. If it has tightened, beware: the tree is tipping backward. Watch the handle of your felling lever if you are using one. If the cut is opening, the handle will start down toward the ground. If it is closing up, the handle will rise.

I always carry either a wedge or a felling bar. If you try to fell without a tipping aid of some sort, it is tempting to cut too much into the hinge to make the tree easier to push over. This is dangerous. Cut just a bit too much and the hinge wood may break, leaving you with a standing, severed tree, free to fall in any direction and completely out of your control.

As the tree starts to fall, I always withdraw my saw and retreat back at a predetermined 45-degree escape path away from the direction of fall. If trees shift as they fall, they will usually kick straight back or jump off to one side, so the most dangerous areas are directly in back of the trunk or alongside it. (I was watching a "National Geographic Special" once about a tribe of Stone Age natives in the Amazon rain forest. A man in a loincloth was chopping down a tree with a stone axe to clear land for planting. When the tree finally started to fall, he retreated at a 45-degree angle back away from the direction of fall.)

Note that I withdraw the saw and take it with me. (The native took his axe, too.) This goes against most recommendations in saw manuals. They say to leave the saw. My response is: Nobody would suggest that anyone risk his life to prevent damage to a saw. On the other hand, saws can cost more than an average weekly paycheck, so it is foolish to risk destroying one needlessly.

I think it is safe to assume that the people who will sell me a new saw if mine is destroyed, or will sell me parts to fix any damage, are at least a bit more willing to put that saw in harm's way than I may be. Leaving the saw at the stump may have been more reasonable when saws were big and heavy and when felling techniques were, possibly, riskier. I always try to withdraw my saw as the tree starts to fall, but if it binds in the cut, I leave it.

Several times, I have watched as a tree bounced off the stump and onto my saw, crunching up the handle, which is no small expense when you have heated handles. Each time I have thought that, maybe, if I had stayed just a moment longer, or pulled a bit harder, I could have taken the saw with me, but deep down I knew I did the right thing.

Some manuals say that if you retreat with your saw, you should shut it off. I don't do that. To me that is a distraction at a time when I don't need one. Newer manuals say that whenever you walk with your saw you should snap on the brake. That can be done with a flip of the wrist, and it is a good habit to get into.

I don't believe that it is necessary or even desirable to shut the saw off before putting it down or handing it to another person. Even with the brake on, some authors contend that this is dangerous. What, they ask, if the brake were "accidentally bumped" and reset as a result? Wouldn't that be hazardous?

In all the thousands of hours I have operated chain saws with chain brakes, I have many times had the brake actuate accidentally, but I have never had it accidentally reset itself. Try it with your saw. Can you see how it could accidentally reset?

If you can, you have a better imagination than I do, but let's say that such a thing could happen. Still, in order to hurt yourself, you would have to simultaneously depress the trigger lock and the trigger; then you would have to drive the saw into your body, while revving it. So, in order to hurt yourself, these things must happen in this order:

- The chain brake must reset itself;
- The trigger lock and trigger must be depressed simultaneously;
- You must, while depressing the trigger lock and trigger, drive the saw into your flesh.

Add to this the fact that, every time the saw is turned off, somebody must restart it if work is to continue. I would guess that the odds on hurting yourself while starting a saw are about the same as the odds on hurting yourself by allowing it to idle with the brake on.

Authors who maintain that you should shut the saw off when you are not actually cutting seem to think that a "running" saw is a real danger. They seem to equate "running" with full-speed operation when, in actual fact, "running" consists of idling if you are not cutting. If your saw is properly adjusted, it should just sit there putt-putting away until you trigger it. That doesn't seem very dangerous to me.

Over time, I have come to feel that the best way to retreat from a falling tree is to simply turn your back and walk briskly away. I don't run and I don't look back over my shoulder. I don't stop and I don't walk backwards to watch it fall. If I'm sure the tree was falling in the right direction when I left, distance is much more important than any sort of evasive action I might take.

The most important thing you can do, when leaving the scene of a falling tree, is to continue to walk without tripping or deviating. It's like a matador who turns his back on the bull. I know it's tempting to watch the tree go down, and some loggers I respect say that in advance of cutting, they select a "peeking" tree, which they step behind to watch the fall.

After the tree has hit the ground, pause for a moment and look up where the tree has fallen. Occasionally a limb will break off, either from the fallen tree or an adjoining tree, hang up, and then fall shortly after the fallen tree has passed through. These are the infamous widow-makers (in our case, widower-makers, as well) that killed so many loggers in the old days, before hardhats became a logging requirement.

There are also regional hazards associated with felling. In some areas, mainly in the South, trees may be festooned with vines. Sometimes these vines are strong enough to actually sweep the trunk up off the ground as it falls and leave it hanging and swinging around. Even if they don't do that, vines may well divert the tree as it falls, causing it to fall to one side, or to hang up partway down. They may also pull dead branches off surrounding trees, or pull dead trees down with them.

With the tree safely down, take a look at your stump. Did the tree fall where you aimed it? Was your hinge uniform and the proper thickness? Was your felling cut at the same height as the bottom of the notch? That's one of the nice things about these techniques; you can evaluate your performance each time and make corrections as you go. Tree farmers I know will often take me on a walk through their woods. They point out the trees to me, but, I have to admit, I find the stumps more interesting than the trees. By looking at the stumps, I can tell what technique the cutter used. Then, by standing directly behind the hinge portions, I can look up and see where the trees landed. It's not always directly ahead of the hinges.

It is easier to get the horizontal cut to meet—but not go beyond—the notch if the intersection is out where you can see it rather than somewhere about a third of the way into the trunk. It is also easier to aim. Old-timers sometimes cut their notches as they would have with a crosscut saw. They stand facing the tree and look over their shoulders to aim. That is called "aiming with your ass," and it will never get you any accuracy.

These old-fashioned cutters—and there are still plenty of them around today—usually make their horizontal cut first and then cut down to remove the notch as they did years ago with an axe. There is no way you can obtain a correct angle this way. (I continue to say "never" and "no way" and generally that is so, but of course there are always a few individuals who become so skilled at doing things the hard way that they make it appear easy. They are rare, however, and I doubt that you are one of them.)

Most logging nowadays calls for a higher degree of felling accuracy than it did years ago. Most of the work old-time lumberjacks did was clear-cutting. Here accuracy was not very important. As long as the trees went down it didn't matter a great deal just where they landed. This is still true on some jobs, mainly large clear-cuts in the West. Loggers are assigned a "strip," and they fell everything in it outward from the "face." Selective felling and thinning calls for much more accurate methods.

By placing the hinge well forward in the tree, you give your wedge and felling lever more leverage when forcing the tree over. This is an advantage. It can, however, become a disadvantage if the tree settles back on your saw. Now, the leverage is in the other direction, forcing all the weight of the tree back onto your bar. When that happens, you wish you had made your hinge where the weight would balance, that is, the center of the trunk. Maybe that's why the old-timers did it that way. That still doesn't make it right, though. Get the wedge in early, and you can use that leverage to your advantage.

The Swedes have used time-lapse photography to document what happens when a tree falls. They have shown that the direction the trunk will take is determined solely by the forward face of the hinge. The holding power of the hinge is a function of its thickness and length. Uniform thickness is almost always what you should strive for. The one exception is where a tree has a heavy lean to one side. In these rare cases, there may be a fear that the weight of the tree will tear the hinge and cause the tree to fall sideways. To prevent this, it might be prudent to leave a slightly thicker hinge on the side away from the lean to strengthen it. If the hinge holds, however, the tree will fall in the direction determined by the forward face, not by the thickness difference.

Another way to deal with this problem is to drive a wedge behind the hinge on the heavy side of the lean. This will take some of the weight of the lean and help to keep the hinge from breaking.

If you go too far with your horizontal notch cut and it cuts into the hinge, you will, in effect, have two hinge faces. The first is where the horizontal cut ends, somewhere further into the trunk than the face. Because this is simply a saw kerf width, it will close up very quickly as the tree starts to fall. This may very well break the hinge before the tree has fallen more than a few degrees, possibly in a different direction than the face of the notch. It may also close up before the tree has gone over far enough to break the hinge. In this case, the tree will stop falling at that point. If that happens, you will have to go back up to the stump and cut the hinge to allow the tree to continue falling. This is dangerous. It is therefore vital that the two notch cuts meet. A safety book I have says that overcutting the notch is the number-one safety problem in tree felling.

There is a variation of the notch that everyone who fells trees should know about. With small-diameter trees, it is possible to avoid removing the notch wedge. It will simply bend over as the tree falls, causing no interference. This saves making the horizontal notch cut. It also eliminates the problem of matching up the notch cuts.

I use this method exclusively in felling small pines in my plantations. I learned about it in a Swedish manual. They called the lip that sticks up a "sloven." I looked up "sloven" in my dictionary and it said it described a woman of loose character, as in "slovenly." Make of that what you will.

This technique has other benefits as well. If the tree hangs up, and you have

A "sloven" on a red pine stump.

to push, it prevents the butt from slipping forward off the stump. This is quite a plus. Often when you try to push a tree, the butt will slide off in the forward direction. This decreases the angle of the trunk. If the tree hangs early in its fall, as often happens when you are trying to fell a pine tree that is crowded between two others, the butt sliding forward can put the trunk right back up straight, or, in some cases, even result in a lean backwards. The sloven helps prevent that.

If you are trying to slide the butt sideways off the stump onto a shovel, the sloven acts to guide the butt. Sometimes, in fact, when the stump wood is frozen and slippery, the forward thrust of your chain (if you are cutting with the top of the bar leading) will slide the butt along your bar onto the shovel if you cut the hinge so that the butt rests on your bar.

If you plan to twist the tree to try and free it, you have to cut the sloven or it will prevent the butt from turning freely. If you plan on twisting the trunk, you must also cut into the hinge. Before you do this, decide which way you are going to twist, then cut the hinge from the opposite side, leaving a corner on the side you are going to twist toward. This corner will give you a pivot point to roll the trunk on and will prevent the butt from sliding off the stump and digging into the ground. It's a lot easier to roll a tree if the butt is not on the ground. In addition, the corner will keep the hinge from breaking and dropping the butt down onto your bar.

I realize that this paragraph, in some ways, contradicts what was said in the previous one. The difference involves the use of the shovel. What this really points out is the need to decide how you plan to proceed before you do any cutting. The main problem with using the shovel is getting the butt onto it. It's worth the effort, though. Even if the shovel doesn't slide, it keeps the butt from digging into the ground, and thus makes it much easier to twist the trunk.

If you hang around people in rural areas long enough, you will, sooner or later, hear about legendary woodsmen who can fell trees starting in one direction to clear an obstacle, and then abruptly change direction partway down to miss a second object.

Aside from the fact that these are mostly myths, there is a more serious problem with the basic idea. In every case, they depend on the feller staying at the stump as the tree falls, cutting the hinge in various ways during its descent to earth. This may account for the fact that none of these miracle workers seems to be around anymore.

All the techniques for freeing hung trees mentioned in this book are to be put into practice after the tree has settled into whatever direction it is going. Nothing written here should be taken as a recommendation to stick with a falling tree to try to guide it to where you want it. Once it starts to go, you start to go—away from the stump. You can always come back a minute or so later once things have settled down.

Statistics show that 80 percent of all fatal tree-felling accidents occur within a six-foot radius of the stump. Part of this may be because this circle is where most people are most of the time, just as highway accident statistics always tell us that most accidents occur within a few miles of home.

Within six feet of a falling tree, however, is a very dangerous place to be. Still, trees that are felled as described don't suddenly crash down without warning. They lean over, rather slowly at first, then tip and fall, gaining momentum as they go. The feller has time to assure himself that the tree is falling in the proper direction and then to walk away briskly. If the hinge should break, resulting in the tree falling in an unplanned direction, it is fairly easy to simply step to the opposite side of the stump and walk away that way. This is not so easy if you see the tree coming at you as you retreat.

As I said earlier, however, there is no need to run when felling a tree and surely no need to linger. I don't feel that procedures that require you to run to escape the consequences of your actions are fit to be described. The possible exception to this might be hanging May baskets, but people don't do that any more. Looking back on it, I probably should have just accepted being caught and kissed even then.

So what I've described is what I consider to be all there is to proper felling. The important points are the thickness of the hinge and the aiming of the notch. There are various techniques to felling "problem" and large-diameter trees, and we will discuss them, but they all have the results just mentioned as their goal.

You should leave stumps high enough so that you can work comfortably while felling. If you cut stumps too low, you risk running your saw into root outswelling and dirt. Besides, your work position at a low stump is awkward, and it's hard to do a good job. Low stumps are necessary if you are cutting valuable timber, but there's not much firewood in four inches of trunk. That extra height can make your work a lot easier.

There is a rule of thumb about stump heights. It says that the height of the stump should be one-quarter the diameter of the tree. Thus, a 16-inch-diameter trunk rates a four-inch stump. That sounds pretty good, but I wouldn't worry about being too exact. Naturally, if the stump is going to be in a roadway, you should cut it down further than that. If you are going to clear the land and push the stumps over with a dozer blade, it pays to leave the stumps high so that the blade can get some leverage.

If you are cutting firewood, it might pay to make your felling cuts the length of a chunk off the ground and then come back and cut the stump down, salvaging the chunk. This involves no more cutting than starting at the stump, and would be easier. Remember, if you plan to cut stumps down, don't put it off. If you wait, mud and sand may splash up on them and dull your saw.

Even if you have perfected the open-face method of felling, you are limited by natural factors in putting trees where you want them to go. Before felling any tree, you should examine not only that tree but the other trees in its vicinity. While it is not always possible to drop an individual tree where you want it to go, it is always possible to control the sequence in which you fell trees.

Your first goal in choosing a felling sequence must be to avoid hanging trees up in other trees. It is usually best to start felling away from the road and work toward the road. That way you are not encountering slash (tops and branches) on your way out; it's all behind you.

No matter how skilled you become, you are always going to hang up trees in other, standing trees. The main danger from hung trees is that they fall at unpredictable times. Safety manuals are pretty cagey when it comes to releasing hung trees. My manual, which is full of "dos" and "don'ts," labels the section on hung trees as "Some Suggestions." All manuals list two big don'ts, however, and OSHA backs them up in its new regulations. The big no-nos are: Don't try to release the hung tree by felling the tree holding it; and don't try to fell another tree onto the hung tree with the hope of dislodging it. OSHA groups these two practices under the term "domino felling," and prohibits it.

The usual advice that saw manuals give, after explaining several generally ineffective and impractical methods, is to leave the area and rely on heavy equipment to push the tree down. Large logging jobs furnish boundary-marking tape with the words "killer tree" printed on it. The feller ropes off an area equal to twice the estimated height of the hung tree, similar to how police rope off a crime scene. He then works outside the roped-off area while waiting for a skidder to push the tree down.

This all sounds pretty slick, and it does emphasize the dangers in working around hung-up trees, but it doesn't work for everyone. Probably it doesn't work for you.

The main point I would like to emphasize is that, if you hang up a tree, everything else becomes secondary. Just as a hunter has an obligation to pursue a wounded animal, the cutter has an obligation to deal with a hung tree. If a skidder happens to be operating nearby, and if the standing trees are far enough apart so it can get through, and if the ground is not littered with logs it can't drive over, then the problem is simple. That is rarely the case for us, however. Even on large logging jobs in my area, the skidding is often a separate operation, possibly even a separate contract. By the time the skidder arrives, the logging crew is often off on another job.

This is, in many cases, a safe way to operate. The literature is full of reports of skidders backing over workers on the ground and of fellers dropping trees on skidders. If nothing else, the presence of the two crews near each other is a distraction for both. In my case, I do both these jobs myself and don't even take the skidder to the job site when I am cutting. But if you are working with a farm tractor, as a lot of people do, your tractor is not designed to crawl over logs, nor is it safe to push trees over with a tractor. That pretty much obviates this whole discussion for the average person.

The prohibitions in the safety manuals seem to assume that it is okay to prohibit certain dangerous practices because there are other, safer methods available. That's not so in most cases. An elderly friend of mine told me that he was driving down into Florida in the 1920s. There were several roads shown on his map that led down into the state. He stopped at a filling station and asked the attendant which road he should take. The attendant looked at the map and said, "Whichever one you take, you'll wish you'd taken one of the others."

So it is with freeing hung trees. In reality, the choice is often between a bunch of dangerous practices, the most dangerous of which is often doing nothing. I am appalled at how many times I find myself back under a tree that I have hung up and left waiting for wind or warming by the sun to bring down. I find myself concentrating on what I am doing and forget all about the hanger. This is exactly how many loggers are killed and maimed. It's a case, I guess you could say, of not being able to see the trees for the forest.

So, in most cases, you've got to do something; you can't just walk away. Your options depend on a lot of things. What works for slender pine trees won't work for large hardwoods. Some books suggest using a "come-along" to drag the butt out. That's not a bad suggestion. The problem is that wood cutters are generally an optimistic lot and are unlikely to haul the come-along and sufficient cable to attach it to a nearby tree with them into the woods. If they have to go home to get this equipment, they will try a lot of other things first.

One of the things they will eventually try is felling another tree onto the first one, domino-style. Even though nobody—including me—suggests that anyone do this, it does work in special cases. Often, however, the weight of the second tree is not enough to force the first tree over. Then, you have two hung trees. Keep it up and your woods start to look like an Indian encampment with teepees made out of trees.

There are very good reasons why this dangerous operation is prohibited, and I agree with all of them. I don't, however, feel that denying people information is a good way to keep them from danger; thus, I will tell you what I have learned about domino felling.

In my experience, the least dangerous method is to fell the second tree straight onto the first. This way, both trunks should slide down together, the second right on top of the first. The danger here is that the butt of the second tree may be thrown up as the trees fall, so I stay well back. If my only shot is a second tree off at an angle from the first, then it becomes especially dangerous. If the second tree hits the trunk of the hanger at an angle, its butt may well fly into the air and the whole tree slide down the trunk at unpredictable angles. It may hit other trees on its way down or it may tip right over the trunk and slide off the other side. In all these cases, the tree is out of control. It's best not to be around when it starts its wild ride. I have minimized the chances of this happening by opening the notch on the second tree, in hopes of keeping it attached to its stump. I wouldn't bet my life on it, however. Even with a notch so wide that it never closes, if the trunk hits the hung tree so that its top hangs over, the weight of the top pivoted on the trunk may tear the hinge apart and allow the butt to fly up.

Often the second tree will not quite carry the hanger through. Then it becomes necessary to either fell yet another tree across the first two, or pull and pry them down. The pulling and prying can be as dangerous as the felling. All these actions can occur when the trees finally let go, just as they would have had the original tree carried on through when it fell. Now, of course, there is little chance to escape.

It should be obvious from this description why this sort of domino felling is prohibited. It will work sometimes with pine trees. However, neither it, nor any of the other techniques I described earlier, will do much good with hardwoods.

I don't have much experience logging valuable hardwoods, but because they are valuable, it probably pays to go to more elaborate means of freeing them, such as the come-along and cable. With pines and firewood, cutters are reluctant to spend a lot of time and effort on a single tree.

If the tree is in an open area, it might pay to put a cable on it as you fell it and pull it over with your truck. Again, though, be sure to allow plenty of cable. You see the tree foreshortened, and it could easily hit your truck when it goes over.

There are, no doubt, other tricks to felling trees in the open. I have no experience with this kind of felling, so I can't comment. I should add that I have had ample opportunity to gain this sort of experience. Because people know I am a logger, friends often ask me to take out troublesome or dead trees from their yards. Except in the case of very simple, straightforward jobs, I always beg off. I know my limitations when it comes to trees.

While I have little experience with valuable hardwoods, I have had a lot of experience with firewood, specifically scrub oaks. These present the same felling challenges as fine oaks, but because they are going for firewood, more options for dealing with felling problems are available.

If a firewood tree hangs up, I simply cut chunks off the butt until the tree slides down. I use a wedge to prevent the weight of the tree from closing the kerf and pinching the saw. I finish each cut from the underside and kick the chunks free as I go. That, in effect, takes the tree down 16 inches at a time. Sometimes the hung tree is too heavy, or standing up too straight for that, and I have to cut several chunks before they can be kicked free.

One hazard with this method is that the butt may smash your foot as you kick the chunks away. Also, if the tree is held tightly at the top, the butt may swing forward and out, dropping the top back on you. Those are real dangers if you're trying to cut logs, but by going 16 inches at a time, you can usually foresee and avoid problems.

Never forget: Whatever method of felling trees you use, you're doing the most lethal work in the woods. Go slowly, think ahead, and don't become stuck in a situation where you have no options.

● Special Cases ❦ ▲

MOST OF THE TECHNIQUES DISCUSSED IN THIS CHAPTER will involve "bore" or "plunge" cutting. This is a valuable technique that every chain-saw user should know about. Most, however, tend to shy away from using it because of the danger of kickback that it presents if improperly done. So the first order of business is to gain a thorough understanding of kickback: what it is and how to deal with it.

Actually, there are two forms of kickback. There is "rotational" kickback and a second form, which occurs when the bar is pushed out of a cut. This second type can occur if you are bucking a large log and the kerf starts to close as you cut beyond the center point of a log supported on both ends.

When this happens, the closing kerf squeezes the sides of the top, forward-cutting portion of the chain. This part of the chain pushes against the walls of the kerf and "walks" the chain right up and out of the top of the cut. Once free of the restraint presented by the wood, the saw revs up and comes out of the cut at a rapid rate. If you are in the way, it may cut you.

While dangerous, this form of kickback is not very common and doesn't happen with the lightning speed that rotational kickback does. Interestingly enough, it is the only type of kickback from which an inertial chain brake will protect you and a safety tip will not.

You may notice that the makers and sellers of safety tips always speak of rotational kickback when they tout the advantages of their product. They are not just being overly precise when they talk that way. They are, in fact, limiting the discussion to the type of kickback they can handle by subtly ruling out types they can't.

Rotational kickback (from here on, called simply "kickback") occurs when the forward motion of the chain is stopped momentarily by a tooth jamming in the wood. The force that was driving the chain into the wood is reversed, and now violently rotates the bar inside the chain in the opposite direction. This transfers the momentum of the chain to the saw itself, and the saw tends to rotate in the hands of the cutter, throwing it back at him. Fast.

There is no warning. The force is tremendous, the speed is blinding, and there is no time to react. The whole thing is over in less than a second. If the victim does recover his senses, his first instinct is to push the saw away. This often causes him to squeeze the handle, thus depressing the throttle and revving the saw. Some unfortunate souls actually have gutted themselves as the saw is pulled down through their chest and stomach.

Pretty scary. That, of course, is the ultimate in kickbacks, but it does happen. While I have never cut myself—or anyone else—I have had my saw kick back so hard that it numbed my arm. Even now, it's not uncommon to have my chain brake actuate several times a day to stop a kickback I never felt. When that happens, I always try and understand what it was that tripped the brake.

There is actually only a very small area of the bar where all the kickbacks originate: the upper quadrant of the tip, where the chain is starting to move around the end of the bar. It's probably no more than about 45 degrees out of the top of the tip that is involved. This is the area shielded by the safety tip.

Aside from the cumbersome and limiting safety-tip option, there are means to reduce this dangerous area of the bar. All modern bars have slender noses, thus reducing the area where kickback can occur. At one time, nonsymmetrical bars were sold. These were the so-called banana bars. They also reduced the kickback region, but they only worked one way and couldn't be reversed to equalize wear on the bar. You don't see them anymore.

As mentioned before, the raker portion of the cutter determines the depth to which the tooth will penetrate the wood. It does this because it sticks up in front of the cutting point of the tooth. As the chain goes around the curve of the bar tip, it no longer lies flat. Thus, as each tooth goes around, it tilts forward.

In the top quadrant of the bar, this tilting has the effect of lowering the raker, allowing the tooth to dig deeper into the wood. This can cause the tooth to jam into the wood, producing the reactions discussed earlier. It only takes one tooth to do it, and all the teeth are passing through this zone at a rapid rate.

Chain manufacturers have tried to design chain to minimize this phenomenon. They have added links to some chain designs in an attempt to hold the point of the tooth out of the wood for a longer period as it passes through the danger zone. This helps some. The chain I use has these "guard links."

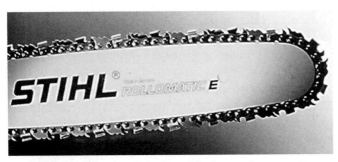

As the chain goes around the tip of the bar, each cutter tilts forward.

Nothing short of the safety tip completely eliminates the danger, however. All the remedies discussed just minimize the forces—and, hopefully, the consequences—of kickback. The trick is to make the saw as safe as possible without detracting too much from its performance. The critical link, of course, is an operator's caution.

All safety manuals stress the danger of cutting with the tip of the bar. They instruct users to cut as far back on the bar as possible. Because of the potential for kickback, it is dangerous to use the saw without both hands firmly gripping the handles. The force is strong enough to knock the saw right out of your hands if you don't have a firm grip, which means thumbs hooked around both handles at all times.

Bore cutting involves pushing the bar directly into the wood and, thus, cutting with the danger area of the bar. This can be done safely, but only if you keep the mechanics of kickback in mind at all times.

The basic trick in boring is to avoid cutting with the top of the tip until it is so far into the wood that, if it kicks, the force will be taken up in the cut and the saw will not come back at you. You can start a bore cut with either the top or the bottom of the bar. If you start with the bottom of the bar, any kickback will be out of the wood, back at you. If you start with the top of the bar, the kickback will actually be a "kick forward," into the wood, not back at you. I know this sounds counter to what many experts say, and I've tried to see it their way, but can't. It's not only theory, it's the way the saw feels to me when I'm cutting.

In spite of my own experience, all books I've read emphasize starting the bore with the bottom of the bar, so I will describe that method first, even though I almost always use the top.

I. Standard Bore Cut

When tree diameter is greater than bar length,
but less than two bar lengths.

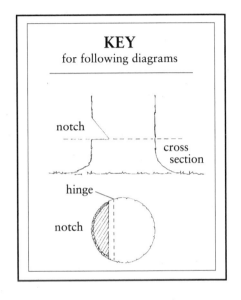

KEY

for following diagrams

notch

cross
section

hinge

notch

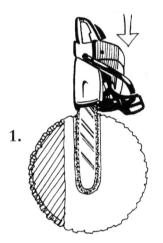

1.

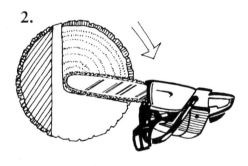

2.

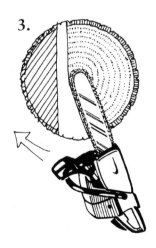

3.

Tree will fall somewhere
between steps 2 and 3.

II. Modified Bore Cut

When tree diameter is slightly greater than bar length.

1.

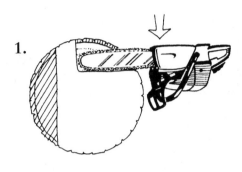

2.

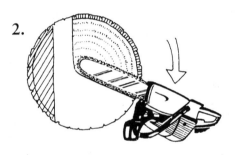

3.

Tree will fall somewhere between steps 2 and 3.

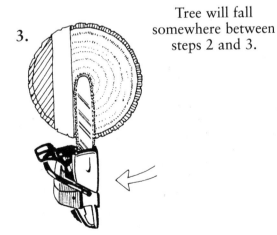

III. Maximum Bore Cut

When tree diameter is greater than two bar lengths.

1.   **2.**

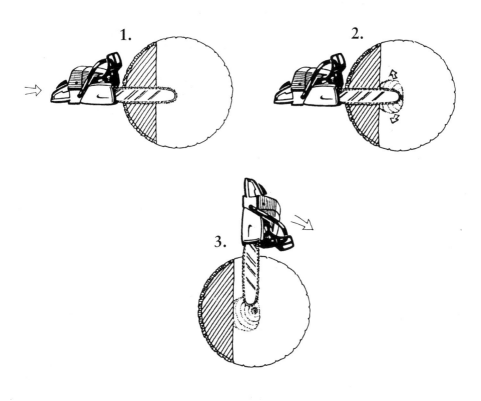

3.

Tree will fall
somewhere between
steps 4 and 5.

5.

4.

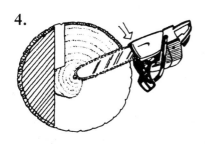

The best way to start the bore is to press the bottom of the bar against the trunk with the tip at the point where you want to start your bore. Start into the wood as if you were making a regular felling cut. When you are in far enough so that the tip disappears into the cut, gradually rotate the saw around until it is cutting with the tip only. Then, continue the bore by pushing the saw straight into the wood, tip first.

By not rotating the saw until the tip disappears into the cut, you have created a ridge in front of the tip that will absorb any kickback forces. Once the tip is in the cut, kickback is no problem. If you withdraw the saw from the bore, there is a danger point where the tip exits the cut. This is identical to the danger as the tip enters the cut. You can minimize this danger by not revving the saw as you pull it out.

If you start your bore with the top of the bar, the technique is the same. The difference is that any kicks will be into the wood rather than back at you. The big danger here is that, if you are careless, a kick could move the saw out of the cut and around the trunk, thereby coming back at you.

To me, entering with the top of the bar is at least as safe as entering with the bottom. In each case, the trick is to start with a cut flat into the trunk, and then to rotate the saw gradually until you are plunging it directly, tip first, into the wood.

As you grow more experienced with this type of cut, you will determine for yourself just how much of an angle you will need to safely rotate the bar into the tree. It probably won't be 90 degrees, as it is when you are starting the cut with the bar directly against the tree. Chances are it will be somewhat less than 90 degrees, but it's never wrong to do it that way. And it's a good place to start if you have little or no experience with this technique.

It takes some practice to get a feel for how hard you should push the saw into the wood. Because of the kicking forces in the bore, the saw sometimes tends to "chatter." You can avoid that by easing up when you push. Don't relax your grip just because the tip is in the wood. Kickback can push the saw right back out of the cut if you're not careful.

Don't ever back off the throttle while cutting. This is always a bad practice. As the tooth passes around the curve of the tip, it is more likely to snag and kick back if it is moving slowly than if it is moving fast. Saws should either run full throttle or idle with the chain stopped—nothing in between.

So, you may ask, why make a bore cut in the first place?

Usually, bore cuts are made to fell trees whose diameter is greater than the length of the bar. The bore cut is made just behind the notch, leaving about two inches of hinge wood between the notch point and the front of the bore. (It is wise to leave a little more hinge wood than normal because the act of boring cuts a bit off the hinge.) This is the difficult part. It is hard to hold the saw exactly parallel to the notch so that the hinge stays uniformly thick across its width. You have to align yourself directly behind the boring saw to see if you are boring straight ahead. Even then, it takes practice to get it right.

It's a good idea to practice on trees small enough so that the bar tip will pass clear through and out the opposite side. This way you can see if the bore is parallel to the hinge face. On bigger trees, the tip doesn't emerge from the wood, and so you can't easily tell if you have followed your line.

If the tree is less than two bar lengths wide, you can proceed to make your felling cut without removing your bar from the bore. The bore has established the hinge thickness, so all you have to do next is to "walk" the saw around the tree. You do this by pulling it back against the rear of the bore and sawing right around in a circle until you reach the point directly opposite the bore on the other side of the tree. At some point, as you approach the opposite side, the tree will start to fall.

As you move around the tree, you can insert a wedge, or your felling bar, at a point opposite the hinge face, about halfway around.

It is not easy to keep the felling cut horizontal so that it meets the hinge face on its level on the opposite side of the tree. If you just guide the saw around, it will probably move off the horizontal plane. The weight of the saw head tends to tilt the saw slightly as it moves along. I try to maintain a slight "up-and-back" pressure on the saw to counteract this weight. Even so, I don't always succeed. Since I usually start my bore with the top of the tip, my felling cut is made with the top of the bar leading. The weight of the saw thus tips my bar down toward the front, and I find my cuts diving down into the dirt as I come around if I'm not careful.

Often, if the tree is not much wider than the length of the bar, I use a modification of the bore cut. I start by placing the saw against the tree, perpendicular to the notch cut with the tip at the point where I want the hinge to begin. This is identical to the start of the bore cut. I then saw straight into the tree, keeping the nose perpendicular to the hinge face again, just as in the bore cut. Next, when I have cut deeply enough into the tree so that the remaining wood is less than the length of the bar, I don't bring the saw around toward the hinge to start a bore. Instead, I bring it around toward the back of the tree and continue on around—just as if I had made a bore.

Maybe you can understand this better if you think of it as two felling cuts. You can actually do it that way if you wish. Make your notch, then move to the side of the tree and make a cut perpendicular to the notch, keeping the tip back so as to leave the proper hinge thickness. When you have cut deeply enough so that the remaining wood is less than the length of the bar, remove your saw and make a normal felling cut with the bar tip extending into the first perpendicular cut.

This method eliminates two problems: You don't have to worry about trying to keep a bore cut parallel to the hinge face; and you can easily see if your tip is maintaining the proper hinge thickness. Finally, you don't have to worry about your cut remaining parallel as you move it around. That's because you don't move it around—you use a normal felling cut.

If you lead with the bottom of the bar, the chain will throw the sawdust out of the kerf as you move around. This makes for smooth cutting and leaves a clean kerf, which makes it easy to insert a wedge or felling bar.

If you lead with the top of the bar, the sawdust is not thrown out. It builds up in the kerf behind the saw. This can sometimes clog the chain and make cutting a bit jerky. It may also cause some difficulty in placing a wedge. Still, despite these drawbacks, leading with the top of the bar offers one positive feature, which, in my opinion, overrides the negatives. Because the chain does not throw the sawdust out, it fills in the kerf behind the bar. This accumulation is sufficient to prevent the tree from settling back on your bar, which means that, even if you have judged the lie wrong or a wind comes up, you can always withdraw your saw. You can see this pattern on the stump after the tree is down. Sawdust will lie on the stump in a swirling pattern, ending with a smooth area where the bar was withdrawn.

To me, anything that prevents the bar from pinching is worth a lot. Once your saw is stuck, you've pretty well had it. If I have access to my saw, on the other hand, there are all sorts of things I can do to salvage a bad situation. Some of them are listed in previous chapters.

If the tree is wider than two bar lengths, you can still safely fell it. Start by making your notch cut. (You will have to complete this cut by moving to the opposite side of the tree to finally remove the notch wood if the tree is that thick.) Next, move to a position directly in front of the notch and cut a bore into the center of the notch, removing as little hinge wood as possible. With your bar all the way in, rotate it to both sides, gouging out a fanlike opening in the center of the tree.

If you are careful in rotating the bar, you won't enlarge the opening in the hinge wood by very much. This is important, since you don't want to remove any sapwood from the hinge.

There is a special case, however, where you intentionally cut through the sapwood. This is called "cutting the corners." It is done to prevent a condition known as "side scarring." Because the sapwood is so strong, it will sometimes tear rather than break as the hinge breaks. This can pull fibers on either side of the log, possibly destroying valuable wood. To prevent this, loggers will cut into the corners of the hinge to sever the sapwood prior to making their felling cut.

Getting back to the technique for cutting trees wider than two bar lengths: once you have completed this operation, move around to the side of the tree, make a normal bore cut, and walk the saw around the tree in the usual manner. Insert a wedge, if necessary, as your bar passes the back of the felling cut. Continue on around until the tree starts to fall. The sapwood, being the strongest, should hold the hinge. It is probably a good idea to leave a slightly thicker than normal hinge to compensate for the heartwood you removed.

There is another special case in which a bore is used to fell a tree, even though the tree is not wider than the bar is long. This is the felling of a tree with a strong forward lean. If you attempt to fell a heavy leaner in the normal fashion, you may well end up with a "barber chair."

Barber chairs occur when the lean of the tree is so great that the weight of the top splits the trunk

A *"barber chair."*

vertically before you can complete the felling cut, severing the trunk horizontally. This can occur at any time during the felling cut, and it happens with some species, such as ash, more often than with others. Loggers believe that barber-chairing is most likely to occur in the winter, when the moisture in the tree is frozen.

The result of a barber chair is a half-cut butt that swings back at the cutter, and then flies up in the air to the point where the splitting trunk bends or breaks. The top ends up on the ground with the butt either falling off to one side or suspended from the split portion somewhere up the trunk. This is obviously a very dangerous situation and, like most woods hazards, happens fast, with no warning. Even if you escape without getting hurt, you will have destroyed a possibly valuable log and will be faced with the problem of completing the felling.

Old-timers were well aware of this hazard. They dealt with it by wrapping the trunk with a logging chain. It was felt that the chain would hold the splitting trunk together until it fell in the normal manner. I guess it would, but it wouldn't prevent the trunk from splitting. It would simply hold the split together as it fell.

The only relatively modern use of chains I've ever seen was when lumberjacks used to top huge West Coast trees to prevent them from splitting when they hit the ground. These guys were in danger of either being squeezed to death or dropped to the ground if the trunk split as they cut off the top. In old pictures I've seen, they wrapped the trunk portion with chain to guard against this.

Obviously, though, it is better to prevent the trunk from splitting at all, rather than trying to hold it together when it splits. With modern saws and techniques, this is easy to do. If you can complete the felling cut before the weight of the top splits the trunk, you have a winner. Most loggers know this, and some of the untrained ones will try and make the felling cut fast enough to sever the trunk before it has time to split. This is a foolish and dangerous procedure.

The correct approach is to make your notch, then bore through the trunk the proper distance behind the notch to leave a hinge of normal thickness. Next, pull your bar directly back, making the felling cut from the front to the back. The tree will not split, because the uncut wood at the back of the felling cut will hold it.

When you have about a hinge thickness of wood at the back, you can either pull the bar right on through, or remove the bar from the cut and sever the remaining bit from outside the kerf. Either way, the tree will fall when you sever the final bit. Because the tree is overbalanced and would have fallen long ago had you cut it normally, it will fall rapidly, but not unexpectedly. You have complete control; the hinge will guide it down, and it won't go anywhere until you make the final cut. Remember, it will fall rapidly, so be prepared to retreat quickly.

If you are logging, splitting of the trunk is a serious mistake, since it can damage valuable timber. One sure way to split a trunk is to fell a tree with a forked trunk so that one side of the fork hits the ground before the other. You can avoid this by felling such trees so that both sides of the fork hit the ground at about the same time. You must use your directional felling skills to do this. It should be one of the things you consider as you evaluate the tree prior to felling.

Sometimes when a tree hits the ground, it tears the hinge wood and, in the process, pulls fibers out of the log. Known as "stump pull," these fibers stick up from the stump and can degrade the butt log. This can be serious business if you are cutting valuable timber. The butt log is usually the most valuable log, and timber buyers check for stump pull. It occurs when the hinge wood is too thick and/or the notch is not open enough. It can be avoided by avoiding the conditions that cause it.

All the previous discussion assumes that the felling is being done on reasonably level ground. That is not always the case, however. If you are working on hills, special cautions apply. If you are working on a side hill, it makes sense to complete your felling cut so that you and your saw are on the uphill side of the tree when it starts to fall. You also want your retreat path to be uphill. Unfortunately, it is usually easier to do everything from the down-hill side. It takes less bending that way.

"Stump pull" can damage a valuable sawlog.

If you are felling trees straight up and down a hill, the safest way is to drop the trees so that they fall with their tops pointing down the hill, with you retreating up the hill. Gravity is, of course, the main factor in both these cases.

These are two of the rare times where the safest way is not the easiest way. If you are stacking pulpwood or small logs, it is a lot easier to drag the upper logs downhill to make a pile with the butt log, than it is to either drag the butt log downhill to pile with the upper logs or to carry the upper logs up to the butt log.

It is therefore easier, in this case, to fell the trees the more dangerous way, that is, with their tops pointed up the hill. This is more dangerous because a trunk is more likely to buck back off the stump at you as gravity works to move it in your direction. You could make this method somewhat safer by widening your notch, to make it more likely that the hinge will hold after the tree is down. But you can't be sure it will work every time.

In this case, you will have to decide for yourself what is best. For me, if the trees are small and the hill is not steep, I fell uphill to make the stacking easier. If, however, the trees are big or the hill is steep, I fell down-hill and try to bunch the logs as best I can without moving wood uphill.

Sometimes I just accept that I can't do much bunching and leave individual sticks where they lie for the forwarder to pick up one at a time. If I decide to fell uphill, I try not to forget that it is a dangerous procedure and that extra care is required.

Any work with wind-thrown and downed timber is dangerous. It is hard to evaluate the stresses in wood felled by nature. This is especially true if the trees have been tipped so that large root masses are sticking up. Sometimes, if you sever the trunk of an uprooted tree, the weight of the root mass will tip back, taking the stump portion—and possibly your saw—with it. Naturally downed timber also introduces all kinds of opportunities for "spring poles," a hazard we will be discussing when we talk about bucking.

● Benching ◂◆◂

BENCHING IS A TECHNIQUE FOR EASY AND SAFE limbing and bucking.
It consists of felling trees over obstacles, which keep the trunk up off the
ground at a height that makes limbing easy.

Before Søren Eriksson introduced this method to my area of the country, cutters would fell trees directly onto the ground, and then straddle
them as they moved up the trunk limbing. To avoid bending too low, these
guys would typically use long bars on their saws. A lot still do it that way.

The Swedes actually designed and built a portable bench that they used
in felling small trees. This was a strong, lightweight affair that resembled a
sawhorse, except that the top consisted of a fiberglass roller. It stood about
a meter high. The cutter would place the bench out from the tree he was
felling and fell the tree onto it. This would keep the trunk off the ground
for easy limbing. When he finished his limbing, he severed the top and then,
using his pulphooks, he could pull the trunk back along the roller, bucking
off pulpsticks as he went.

In a modification of the bench, the roller was mounted on a tracked
vehicle that resembled a pallet jack. This device was used just like the
bench, only when the cutter pulled the pulpsticks back and bucked them,
they fell onto the bunk of the vehicle. When he got a load, he started the
engine and guided the device out to the road where he dumped his load.

These gadgets never caught on here, but they are typical of the inven-
tions the Swedes have come up with. Logging in Sweden must be done on
a very small scale, and wood must be very valuable. I saw these devices

demonstrated by Eriksson in one of his first appearances in this part of the world. They were novelties, and he quickly stopped using them. For one thing, there was only one of each of them on the continent, and they were expensive to import. The bench, for example, cost $500 in 1985.

While I never seriously considered using these gadgets, I bought into the principles they were designed to employ wholeheartedly. I started to make my pulp piles where I could fell trees onto them, and I left logs where they lay until they were no longer close enough to act as benches. This is a simple concept, and it requires no special felling techniques to utilize it. Yet the idea of keeping the trunk off the ground revolutionized my work. And you will notice that this philosophy dictates much of what you will read about in the following chapters.

A "benched" stem is much easier to limb and buck.

About all you have to do at this point, though, is to keep the basic ideas in mind and then adapt your felling and piling to take advantage of them. You can, for example, fell a tree across the area where you will be felling others, and then use this tree as a bench to fell others across. As you proceed, the trees you fell later will end up further off the ground than the first tree, and you can, by varying your aim a bit, utilize these as benches for even more trees. How far you can carry this depends on the trees available, but, if you are clever, you can continue on out for quite a distance.

In some cases, it will pay to fell a tree over an obstacle using a wide notch, so that the trunk stays attached to the stump. This can cantilever the trunk out beyond its fulcrum and keep it up off the ground. Then, later, when you have gleaned as much use out of it as possible as a bench for other trees, you can come back and sever the hinge.

There are some unique hazards involved in this type of felling. A tree hitting an obstacle is more apt to fly around if the hinge breaks than one landing smack on the ground. You can avoid some of the danger by using wide notches so that the hinge doesn't break when the tree falls, and then cut the hinge after the tree is down. Even if you do this, the hinge may tear, or the butt may fly up when you sever the hinge, so be extremely careful.

Cantilevering is an attractive method, and one that I would like to use more than I do. The big problem with it is the hinge. Just how thick a hinge you need to hold without tearing is a function of many things, including the type of tree, the season, the height of the bench, the distance of the bench from the stump, the weight of the top portion, the angle of the notch, and the diameter of the tree. Underestimate any one of these variables and you will end up with a torn-apart hinge that can tear way up into the log.

This isn't serious with pulpwood, but in timber it can cost you in the form of butt-log degrade. Even if all these things work out, often the tree will hang up partway down, and I find that I have to cut partway through the hinge to enable me to twist it free with my lever. This defeats the can-tilever, since the hinge will then break when the tree hits the bench. It's much easier to fell across two benches, or simply to let the hinge break as it hits a single bench and depend on the counterweight of the butt to hold the top portion up out of the dirt.

Carried to an extreme, benching can also lead to a pretty cluttered work-place and involve dragging limbs and tops off piles and logs. This creates extra work, which in turn introduces its own hazards.

While there is some benefit in bucking and piling, or "bunching" in bench-felling, the main benefit is in limbing. Perhaps surprisingly, limbing is one of the most dangerous tasks in the woods. Most saw cuts are sus-tained while limbing, so we will devote some time to it.

It's not unusual for me to trip and fall while I am working, especially while I am limbing. When this happens, I try not to let go of my saw in an attempt to break my fall. I keep both hands tightly gripping the handles, forcing the saw away from my body—even at the expense of rolling on the ground. This is harder than you might think. It is human nature to put a hand out to protect yourself from a fall, and it can be difficult to overcome that natural instinct.

I can't overemphasize how benching eases the work. Often if I miss an obstacle with a falling tree, or spot something on the ground I didn't see when I was felling, I will stick a hook into the butt of the fallen tree and move it one way or the other to lift it up onto the obstacle. This is surpris-ingly easy to do with a long, skinny tree. There's not a lot of weight on the butts of such trees.

A guy I know says, "If you are strong enough, everything is portable." That's true, I suppose, but nobody is strong enough to lift everything in the woods. Up to a point, you can substitute strong for smart, but not in all cases, and not indefinitely. I started out with a lot of strong and not much smart. I've spent most of my logging lifetime trying to reverse these percentages.

I attended a woodland owner's conference recently where one of the speakers talked about safety in the woods. He started his presentation by asking how many of the two hundred or so attendees had ever been hurt working in the woods. A few hands went up. "No sprains, pulled muscles, or back injuries?" he asked. A lot more hands went up, including mine.

Somehow I had never considered these common problems as "getting hurt in the woods." Apparently, a lot of the other people present didn't either. Yet, as I read back over my *Swedish Forestry Institute Safety Manual,* I realized that it devotes at least as much space to back injuries as it does to saw and tree-felling safety.

I would guess that, if you looked at workers' compensation records for woods workers, you would find more claims for back problems than for any other type of injury. I think the reason we don't hear more about back injuries is that they are common to all types of work and are not covered in chain-saw safety manuals, nor in many of the logger training programs.

I brag that no one has ever been hurt in my woods, but that's not true. In fact, I would guess that the opposite is true. Everyone who has worked in my woods has been hurt if you accept this definition of "getting hurt in the woods." We've all had pulled muscles and sore backs.

The experts say that you should lift with your legs and not your back. I try to do that, but I find it really awkward, and, before I know it, I've "backslid" into my old habits.

Having looked at the posters showing proper lifting techniques, I wonder how in the world anyone can lift anything this way: Back completely straight and vertical; squat straight down; maintain your back rigidly straight (about this time I would topple over sideways!); lift by straightening the knees. That might be easy on the back, but how about the knees? They give out, too. (I mentioned this to a physical therapist once, and she said that you can replace knees, but not backs. I don't take a great deal of comfort from that.)

There seems to be some sort of movement afoot now to encourage people to wear back braces whenever lifting is involved. This is not a new idea. My dad hurt his back years ago and had to wear a brace for several years. Back then they were called "corsets," and people who had to wear them wore them under their clothes. Now it's fashionable to wear them on the outside.

I have no experience with these braces, but I have always thought that if you wear any sort of brace for a long period, the muscles being braced would weaken and you would then have to wear the brace essentially all the time—sort of like a staked tomato plant. If this were not a problem— if simply wearing the brace while doing heavy work would reduce the numerous back pains and strains that seem inevitable—then I would be all in favor of them.

Unfortunately this doesn't seem to be the case. The National Institute of Occupational Safety and Health (NIOSH) has released a study concluding that these belts not only don't prevent back injuries, they may actually cause some because they encourage wearers to exceed their abilities. NIOSH says that the only way to reduce back injuries is by redesigning tasks and by physical conditioning. That's a large part of what this book is intended to do.

| *Patient to Doctor:* | It hurts when I do that. |
| *Doctor to Patient*: | Then don't do that. |

13

● Limbing ◀▬

THE TERM "LIMBING," AS USED HERE, means cutting off branches on tree trunks—either standing or fallen—to present a clear trunk. It does not include the lopping of big limbs for firewood. That will be covered in Chapter 17, which deals with firewood.

Cutting branches, or branch stubs, from standing trees is called "prelimbing." The techniques and hazards involved are identical to those encountered during pruning with a chain saw. In both cases, the biggest danger is that you might strike the trunk with the tip of the bar, causing the saw to kick back. This is especially dangerous in these cases because the saw is often being held at—at least—shoulder height.

Most books tell you never to operate a saw above shoulder height, and that is good advice. When you are prelimbing, however, it is tempting to reach just a bit higher than you should, to get one last ring of branches. With pruning, it is also a temptation to get one last limb rather than have to get a ladder, or saw it off with a bow saw.

The higher off the ground you hold the saw, the more difficult it is to handle kickback. You can protect yourself to a certain degree by always keeping your left arm straight out, with your elbow locked, and cutting with the saw end of the bar rather than the tip. The biggest danger occurs, however, while you are moving the running saw from branch to branch. That is where you are most likely to strike the trunk with the tip of the bar.

The only safe way to do this work is to position yourself so that you are never directly behind the saw. This is not as hard to do as it sounds. You can do it efficiently by cleaning the trunk in four steps, moving around as you go and always cutting with the inside of the bar against the trunk. This simple technique keeps the saw off to your right side. All it takes is a bit of practice to make it seem like second-nature.

If the limbs are heavy, you must always cut downward on them to keep the saw from binding. If you start on the higher limbs, you can safely reach and cut down through the succeeding ones. This way, you won't have to pull the saw away, just let its weight bring it down as you cut. It's both safe and easy.

Limbing the stem prior to felling.

If you are cutting dead limbs and stubs, it is possible to cut them from below with the top of the bar. You can then alternate your cutting as you move around the tree. If you start your first cut from below, you will make your fourth and final cut from the top, which will end with the saw down, ready to move on to the next tree, or to your notch cut.

Both the operations just described are done by gunning the saw at each branch. That is the safest way. If, however, you are dealing with trees such as spruce or fir—as opposed to pine—this isn't practical, since there are apt to be a myriad of small branches and twigs with no definite rounds of branches. The only good way to deal with these is to "sweep" the trunk with a speeding chain. This is inherently more dangerous than easing off on the trigger between branches, but the same cautions apply.

Cut hanging limbs from above.

You may not be able to accomplish the task in four stations, but you should still cut with the inside of the bar against the trunk, and position yourself so that your body—especially your head and neck—are not behind the saw.

In logging, most limbing is done on fallen trunks. Here is where benching really pays off. It is considerably easier to limb a trunk that is supported at waistheight than it is to limb one lying flat on the

Cut compressed (bottom) limbs from below.

ground. Not only is constant bending tough on your back, it is also hard on the saw, because it is difficult to sever the bottom branches without sticking your bar tip into the ground. Finally, since fatigue is one of the biggest causes of accidents, it is also safer. Bench the stem up and these problems are minimized. A further benefit to benching is that the logs and limbs fall to the ground as you sever them.

It is easy to spot any limbs you overlooked by observing the log as it falls. You can also check for overlooked limbs by rolling the log with your foot. If a limb remains, the log won't roll.

The safest way to limb is to work from one side of the trunk with the saw always on the other side. That's not really practical, though, since you would have to go up and then back down the length of the trunk to finish the job. Few loggers would be willing to do that. You can do it all safely from one side, however, by following a simple routine.

Start at the base of the trunk. Rest the flat part of the sawhead, just ahead of the muffler, on the trunk and slide it along to the first branch on the opposite side of the trunk from where you are standing. Using the trunk as a fulcrum, lever the top of the bar up and cut off the branch. Next, tip the saw 90 degrees so that the inside of the bar rests on the top of the trunk, against the top branch. You can do this without lifting the saw off the trunk, just rotate it around the base of the bar. Cut off this branch using the top of the bar.

Next, slide the saw off the trunk on your side of the trunk so that the bottom of the bar rests against the next branch and the outside of the bar rests against the trunk. Use downward pressure on this branch to cut it off.

Finally, move the saw up to the underside of the trunk with the top of the bar against the bottom branch, the inside of the bar against the trunk, and your elbows resting on your knees. Pry forward to sever this branch.

Put the saw back up on the top of the trunk and slide it forward to the next round of branches and repeat the process.

That is the pure sequence for easy and safe limbing. It seldom works quite that way in the woods. Sometimes there are a lot more branches than the four I have described. Sometimes there are fewer. Sometimes some of these branches are bent against the ground, forcing you to cut them from the bottom side to avoid binding the saw. Sometimes you may wish to leave some of the bottom branches until last, because they are holding the trunk up off the ground.

The main points here are: Always work from one side of the trunk (usually the right side), and don't straddle it or jump from one side to the other; rest the weight of the saw on the trunk wherever possible, and use the trunk as a fulcrum to lever the saw; use your right knee as a fulcrum while cutting limbs on your side and the bottom.

Using these techniques requires that you change the position of your left hand on the front handle. This should become easy after a while. You should practice sliding your hand around on the handle. Sometimes I trigger the saw with my thumb in such cases. It goes without saying that you should keep your thumb under the handle at all times when cutting.

There are variations to this limbing procedure as well. For example, when moving up the trunk to the next branch or set of branches, you can set the saw down on the trunk and use the chain to move it forward by gunning the engine slightly to scoot it along the top of the trunk. (This is the only case I can think of where it is okay to operate the saw at less than full throttle.) Sometimes it is easier to cut a branch on your side from the bottom with the top of the bar, using your knee as a fulcrum.

By staying on one side of the trunk, your measuring tape will reel straight out and not snarl up. If you have someone running a stick for you, you can buck off eight-foot logs as you move up the trunk. Usually I don't do that. If the trunk is suspended on both ends, bucking off a stick will cause it to drop down and make the work harder. Even if the butt log is suspended back from whatever is supporting the trunk, cutting it off will cause the weight to shift to the remaining portion of the trunk, and the top will sag. If you leave it attached, it will act as a counterweight and cause the top portion to tip up off the ground.

Even if you have had to drop the tree right onto the ground and it appears to be lying flat, the normal lumps and bumps in the ground will hold it up in places. You lose what little advantage you have by bucking as you go. Even though it involves walking back along the trunk to buck, it usually pays off.

If the tree falls flat on the ground, it is tempting to straddle it as you limb. This puts the saw between your legs. Whenever I have asked male loggers why it is dangerous to cut with the saw between your legs, they all come up with an answer right away, and they are right, but there are several other reasons as well. The femoral arteries that supply blood to the legs run down the inside and back of the thighs. Cut one of those and you will bleed to death in less than a minute. To make matters worse, the pads on safety pants rarely extend around to the backs of the thighs.

If you don't buck as you go, you have to mark as you go. You can do this quickly and easily if you learn a simple stroke that will mark the stem with the saw. It pays to make your mark as far around the trunk as is practical. Often when you sever the top, the trunk will roll, putting your marks on the bottom where you can't easily see them. One way to get the mark well around the trunk is to make it in two cuts, one with the bottom of the bar across the top, the other on your side of the tree using the top of the bar, so that the two marks meet.

It is easier, quicker, and more professional to do this in one move by starting on the side near you with the top of the bar and running this cut up and over and down the other side. This is a lot safer and easier than it sounds. It also ends up with your saw in position to lay it on the trunk and slide it forward with the bar safely on the other side of the trunk. The danger of kickback is nil because you are cutting with the top quadrant of the tip away from you, so that any kick will be forward, away from you. With a little practice, you will find that the saw moves smoothly up and over the trunk with little more than gentle guidance from you.

Sometimes, as you limb, branches will fall down on the trunk ahead of you, and you will have to reach up and push them aside. This puts your wrist in a position where, if the saw were to kick forward, you could cut yourself in about the worst possible place. When I need to do this, I hold the saw resting on the trunk and wait until it has coasted down before I reach out.

"Spring poles" are dangerous and should be cut with extreme caution.

With a tool like a chain saw it is often easier to simply cut through limbs and branches rather than trying to drag them out of the way. That seems strange at first, because your normal instinct is to pull things clear. Usually that's the hard way.

If there are large limbs in the tree, it often pays to avoid severing the bottom ones as you move up the trunk. As noted earlier, these limbs can be useful in holding the trunk up off the ground. Also, since they are usually compressed by the weight of the trunk and awkward to reach, it is often easier to pass them by. When the top is cut off, these limbs will frequently roll the trunk over, exposing themselves so that they are easy to cut off.

If you have felled the tree over a pulp pile, there will, no doubt, be branches left on the pile, which will interfere with piling and forwarding. With a little practice, you can clean these piles off as you go by kicking the branches away as you limb and, finally, by "wading" over the pile, kicking as you go. If the top has fallen over a pile, you should cut it in two so that the top portion falls off the pile, and then drag the bottom portion back off the pile.

If you are working in an area where there are small trees, some of these may be bent over and held down under part of a felled tree. These are called "spring poles" and can be very dangerous. Since they are under stress, they can fly back toward you either when you cut them or when you cut a limb that is holding them down.

It is best to cut any saplings that will be in the falling path before you start, but you always miss a few. They must be dealt with individually and should command some respect.

You can release a spring pole by carefully cutting into the stem at the point of greatest tension, which is the top of the curve. Stand as far back as you can beside the pole and sever the stem by making a series of small cuts across the top of the curve, using the tip of the bar. Each cut will sever a few strands and release some of the tension. Nevertheless, the final cut will probably still cause the severed end to fly back, so you must be alert for it. The main danger is that it may swing the saw back at you.

Some safety experts recommend releasing a spring pole by cutting fibers on the *underside* of the top of the curve. This way, when the pole is released and flies up, it won't take your saw with it. If you do it this way, you will have to be alert so as not to bind your saw in the collapsing fibers.

Evaluate each situation carefully, and take your time.

● Bucking and Bunching ◖▲▲

IF YOU ARE WORKING WITH VALUABLE TIMBER, bucking can make or break you. The main goal of bucking is to concentrate as many defects as possible into the smallest number of the shortest logs. To do this, the bucker must have a good knowledge of the log rules and a good eye. This "good eye" should start when the tree is upright. Defects such as "sweep" (long curves in a trunk) can best be seen while the tree is standing. In spite of this, some contractors pull all their trees out full length and buck on the landing. Sometimes this is because they don't trust their fellers to buck properly. They feel it is better to let one trained person make all these decisions, possibly the contractor himself.

There is no one secret to proper bucking. The rules change with the markets and prices. There is often a difference between bucking for maximum yield and maximum profit. Sometimes it pays to try and get as many logs as possible out of a trunk; other times it may pay to cut only the longest and biggest logs, letting the other portion go for pulp or firewood.

Variables that must be considered—and that can change daily—include prices, specs, and markets for such diverse products as pulpwood, firewood, log-cabin logs, and sawlogs, as well as the possible yield of these products from the tract you are working in.

In Wisconsin, where I live and work, pine log-cabin logs are normally eight-foot logs. There are two markets, one for logs down to eight inches in diameter, the other to ten inches on the small end. The ten-inch logs are worth more per cord than the eight-inchers. Sawlogs bring less than cabin logs, but they only have to be six inches at their smallest diameter. This market won't accept eight-or ten-foot logs, however, only 12- and 16-footers.

Pulpwood brings the lowest price of all, but the limit on pulpsticks is four inches. Finally, there is a market for utility poles. This is the highest-paying market of all for red pine logs, but the specs are very tight.

Note that I have given the nominal length for these products. In practice, some trim, usually four inches in extra length and sometimes more, must be left on each log. Failure to do this will likely result in the log being downgraded by two feet, or rejected altogether.

Prices, markets, and specs for these products change from time to time, so you have to keep on top of them and lock them in as much as possible before you start to buck. Large contractors can combine logs from various jobs to make full loads. A small producer can't do that. Thus, before you start, you must decide, for example, if there

Plastic "go/no-go" gauge for determining where the sawlogs end and the pulpwood begins.

are going to be enough ten-inch logs to make a load, or whether you should buck down to eight inches. Would it pay to try and take two cabin logs per tree, or should you take one cabin log and then saw logs and pulpwood? It is not unheard of for a logger to have to cut off and waste four feet from a number of 12-foot logs to get them down eight feet so they will sell for pulpwood. That's discouraging work.

In addition to all these considerations, the more varied your mix, the more difficult it is to sort and pile the various products. Because forwarders and skidders can't just bounce over logs in the woods, you can't haul out one product from the entire tract and then go back and get another. You must do it all at once, either by running in and picking up all of one kind you can reach and then doing that with the next type, etc., or by mixing them all up on the forwarder and separating them out at the landing. Either way, it's a lot of work.

If you sort on the landing, you need lots of room, and you will have to run the forwarder from pile to pile as it unloads the various sorts. Finally, you have to end the job with almost full loads from each sort or you may end up eating some of your logs.

Faced with this, you may decide that it doesn't pay to sort for grade and just let it all go for pulpwood, even though that means putting some nice logs in the pulp pile. If you don't do your own work, you should at least understand what the contractor needs to keep in mind when he bids your job.

So much for bucking theory. Now to the practice.

Anyone who has sawed any sort of lumber with a handsaw knows that one of the big problems is caused by the saw pinching in the kerf. Chain saws are no

Logs sorted in piles at the landing before loading for shipment to the mill.

different. The solution, obviously, is to support the work so that the kerf opens rather than closing up as the work progresses. That's fairly easy with a board, but not so easy with a log.

In all cases, success boils down to sawing into wood under tension rather than under compression. There are a few problems with this. Sometimes it is not obvious which stress you are cutting into, and sometimes the stresses change as you cut. It is also sometimes possible—and easier—to simply bull your way through a limb under compression rather than move around and cut it the proper way.

Since logs are too heavy to move around very much you must deal with the forces as you find them. Basically this comes down to cutting from the top of the log down on logs that are suspended from points other than the ends, so that the weight of the log tends to open the kerf as the cut proceeds, and to sawing from the bottom up on logs that are suspended by their ends so that they will tend to bend down and open the kerf as the cut proceeds into the wood.

You have to be careful, however, that the weight of the severed log isn't so great that it splits as it falls off. You can avoid this by starting with a shallow cut on the side of the log under compression, being careful to withdraw your saw before the kerf starts to close. Sometimes, rather than switching from top to bottom, it is easier to insert a wedge in the kerf after the saw has passed to keep the kerf open all the way.

Whether you wedge or cut from both sides, you must act before the saw binds. You can see this as it begins to happen, and you can feel the action on the bar if you move the bar back and forth as you saw. The minute it starts to squeeze, withdraw the saw.

Lopping the top is the final act of the delimbing process.

If you cut off a heavy, unsupported log, it will sometimes carry the saw down with it as it drops. You can avoid this by making your final cut slightly offset from the undercut, or by cutting on a slight angle, top to bottom.

When it comes time to "lop the top," I often use a stroke that resembles paddling a canoe. I reach forward and, cutting with the top of the bar, pull back across the stem, severing the top. Sometimes, I take a step forward and brace the saw against the inside of my right knee for additional leverage. This works well, but don't ever step so far forward that the bar ends up between your legs.

As you sever logs from the trunk, the forces on the trunk change, and it may roll unexpectedly. In addition, the log may roll as it falls free. This is why it makes sense to buck from the uphill side of the log on hillsides.

Even though bucking is a comparatively safe operation, some of the worst kickback accidents happen to people who are bucking logs. These occur when the upper quadrant of the bar hits either a stump or the end of a previously cut log. The forces generated from these encounters are stronger than those caused by jamming the tip into a log from the side. Apparently the end grain resists the tooth more than the long-side grain and throws the saw back with greater force.

Whether you start bucking from the top or the bottom of the trunk is your choice. Don't automatically buck all of the logs right away, however.

Make piles in the woods as tall and narrow as you can.

If you have benched the tree, the trunk may be resting on a pivot point, so that by either waiting to buck, or by selective bucking, you can balance the trunk at some point and swing it around to a more favorable position, or roll it on logs lying on the ground. It is always easier to roll a log on other logs than it is to roll it on the ground. (Remember, logs taper. If you roll them, the big end always "wins.") This can often save you work when it comes to bunching logs or piling pulpwood.

If you are piling several logs from a single tree, it seems natural to bring all the upper logs to the butt log. This is not the most efficient way, however. It makes more sense to make your pile around the second log. The second log is often almost as heavy as the butt, and it doesn't pay to try to move it. Either you can pile small logs from other trees with it, or you can just leave it by itself for the forwarder to pick up.

Make your piles as tall and narrow as you can. They should be pyramids with narrow bases. You want each pile as tall as you can get it with a given number of logs. Don't make them too big. Keep the base as narrow as possible. Broad bases take sticks that should be used to increase height. They also tend to collect more branches than narrow piles.

Piling is the hardest work you do so, so it doesn't pay to leave it until the end of the day. On the other hand, it doesn't pay to pile too soon. Often by waiting, logs from other trees will fall nearby, and you can form piles with less walking and carrying or dragging. There is a downside to waiting, however. If you wait too long, tops will fall on logs lying on the ground, and you will have to drag them off to pile. Also, if more than one log falls across a pile, you will have to move all but one off before you can add to the pile.

Try to make your piles across the path of falling trees and fell the trees over them. If you make your piles parallel to the direction of falling, they are harder to hit, and, if you do hit them, the falling tree tends to scatter the pile. Try to hit near the center of the piles. If you hit too close to the ends, the sticks will fly up and scatter. Always watch for trunks suspended across several piles, and don't buck them if they are situated so that they can act as benches for further trunks.

All this thinking and planning pays off in the long run. Finally, don't "marry" any one method or technique. Be flexible in your approach, ready to change methods if conditions change, or if you just need a break.

15

● Economics ❦ ♠

WHAT IS A PINE TREE ACTUALLY WORTH? That seems an obvious question, yet it doesn't lend itself to a simple answer. I tried to come up with some answers a while ago. Since then, the value of wood "on the stump" has about doubled. I haven't changed the numbers accordingly, because we are talking about relative value, and that hasn't changed much.

My trees are about 25 years old. They will usually yield three sticks: typically, a four-inch (diameter), a five-inch, and a six-inch stick. These are worth to the landowner, standing, 12 cents, 19 cents, and 28 cents, respectively, for a total value of 59 cents—say 60 cents per tree. (Based on a stumpage value of $15 per cord. In 1997 this rose to more than $30).

Since I have my calculator out, how does the value of a six-inch stick change as it progresses to its ultimate fate? Again, this is all based on average central Wisconsin scales as I know them. Our stick is worth 28 cents as the butt log of the standing tree. It is worth 48 cents felled, bucked, and trimmed. Stacking it in a pile in the woods brings it to 55 cents. Piling it in a large deck at a landing, accessible to a pulp truck, brings it to 72 cents.

(These figures, too, have been changing. Stumpage prices have risen faster than prices at the mills, thus narrowing the gap that you can fill by doing it yourself.)

This is the point at which I have to stop if the stick goes for pulp, since the price at the mill depends not only on where you are, but who you are. If you were to haul it to the mill yourself, and if you were less than 30 miles from the mill, and if the mill would buy it when you got it there, it would be worth 85 cents. On the other hand, if you have your own small sawmill and saw the stick into two rough, green, 2 x 4 studs, it is ultimately worth $2.50.

It might be interesting to speculate on how much each of these steps would cost you were you to do them yourself. Growing the tree for 25 years to get the first 28 cents is a highly variable cost, so I'll start my analysis with the tree standing there. In order to fell, buck, and trim the log, you would need a good chain saw plus clothing, gas, oil, etc. for an investment of about $800. This adds 20 cents to the value of each stick. To stack, all you need is a strong back, although pulphooks make life much easier—let's say zero investment to add the next seven cents.

Now, how to get from the woods to the landing? Here's where the bucks start adding up. There are many ways to do this. I would guess that I've considered essentially all of them and tried a lot of them.

If you plan to log more than a few acres, the only reasonable method is the use of a hydraulic loader and trailer. If you have a four-wheel-drive tractor of 35 horsepower or more, you can get a trailer with a knuckle-boom loader for about $10,000. There are other options. For instance, you can get a loader that fits onto your tractor, and then use any sturdy trailer you have. At any rate, it isn't going to be cheap.

I don't believe it is feasible for anybody to buy a pulp truck to simply haul his own pulp to the mill, so I'll just skip that option.

The small sawmill option is interesting, though. I bought a Mobile Dimension sawmill for about $12,000 complete, and I use it to saw lumber out of small-diameter logs from my plantations. I've been doing this for some years now, and, even in rough times, I've shown a small profit. The economic considerations involved are rather complex, and I'm not sure that I have a good handle on them. Suffice it to say that operating costs include the interest on $12,000 and a few gallons of gas.

Obviously, we're playing a numbers game here, which taken alone tells you almost nothing. The main reason people invest in forwarding equipment is not to add $7 a cord to the price of their wood, but rather because often you can't sell pulp stacked in the woods. It's difficult to find anyone who will buy it where it lies. You have a much better chance of finding truckers who will buy it (or haul it) if it is piled alongside a road. In the wood business, you need everything going for you that you can arrange.

In years of trying to get wood out with inadequate equipment, I've learned the wisdom of the phrase, "You're not out of the woods yet!" I also learned what it means to be "stumped."

I may also have discovered a "Law of Do-It-Yourself Logging," which is: "The weight of an individual log is independent of the total number of logs." Simply stated, this means that, just because there aren't very many, doesn't make them any easier to handle.

Of Pizzas and Pulpsticks

I often attend forestry field days. Sometimes these events include a pulp-cutting demonstration. I listen to the comments of the people around me, and, invariably, someone comments on the waste involved in the "large" tops left lying in the rows.

I used to feel that way too until I started cutting pulpwood myself. The pulp mill specs call for at least a four-inch top diameter, but everyone knows that, if the average is good, the mill won't dock you if you go down to a three-inch small-end diameter. I don't do that though. I hold the line at four inches.

There is a lot of taper in the top eight feet of a pine tree—especially a big pine tree—so tops may look large when you view the thick end, but eight feet up they often taper off to almost nothing. Unfortunately, it is the butt of that last stick—not the top end—that landowners look at.

My neighbor had a contractor thin a red pine stand right next to mine. I was thinning my stand when his contractor finished up. My neighbor came over, and I asked him if he was happy with the job. He said that it was "okay," but that he felt that the cutter had left too many big tops. I went over with him and looked, and it seemed to me that maybe he was right. He had a chain saw, so I told him that if he wanted to he could trim up these tops and I would scale what he had and add it to my pulp pile. He thought that was a good idea and the next day I heard his saw. I heard it the day after that, also. After that, I didn't hear it anymore.

I got curious and walked over to see how he was doing. What I saw were two small piles with what seemed like hundreds of skinny sticks in each. The total was probably less than half a cord. He never came over to see me, and I guess he felt a bit sheepish.

It was a good lesson for me. Many times I've stood with my saw idling, peering up through the limbs in the top trying to decide whether it was worth taking another stick. Often I would start limbing only to find that, after having trimmed a few feet, it was obvious that I wouldn't get another stick.

This is no small matter in a day's work. I would guess that about 50 percent of the work in limbing goes to the top stick, where most of the branches are located. Thus, 50 percent of my time, 50 percent of my energy, and 50 percent of my saw gas is dedicated to the top stick. And for what? Not much, that's what!

Even so, isn't it a real waste to leave that stick in the woods? That depends on who is keeping the books. To the forest, the real waste is in the material being removed, not what is left. Anything left will rot down and return to the soil. From a ecological point of view, the best thinning would cut the trees required to thin the stand and simply leave them lying there.

Since all pulpsticks are the same length, you can forget about length and compare them as if they were circles. The area of a circle is equal to pi (a transcendental number written as π and approximately equal to 3.14) times the radius squared. (You would have learned that if you had paid attention in school, but had you paid attention in school you probably wouldn't be cutting pulpwood in the first place, so I'm not going to nag.)

This formula is well known, and it is the basis of many dreaded "story problems." I can't recall that I ever actually worked a problem using this formula outside school, but the implications of it for forestry work are many.

Since we are only interested in comparing circles rather than finding exact areas, our task is pretty simple. We can, for instance, use diameters rather than radii. We can also eliminate pi, since we are not interested in numbers, only comparisons. Doing this, we can say that the areas of circles vary as the squares of their diameters. Thus, with equal lengths, the volumes of logs vary as the squares of their diameters. This is something we can work with.

Let's compare the volume of a four-inch pulpstick to that of an eight-inch stick. Since an eight-inch stick is twice as big, you might assume that it contains twice as much wood. You wouldn't assume that, though, if you knew about the actual relationship. You would square the diameters of the two logs and use those squares to determine the ratio. Doing that, we find that the difference is the ratio of 8 squared to 4 squared or, 8 x 8 = 64 to 4 x 4 = 16. From this we can see that the ratio of the volumes of the two logs is 64:16, or simplified, 4 to 1. Thus, an eight-inch log contains not twice as much wood as a four-inch log, but four times as much!

The bottom line is that, if a given log is twice as thick as another log, it contains four times the volume.

That's obviously good stuff for a sawmiller to know, but there's more. We can also compare the circumference of logs and thus get an approximation of how slab varies with diameter. Again, comparing circles, the circumference equals pi times the diameter—not the square of the diameter, just the diameter. This means that doubling the diameter doubles the circumference at the same time that it increases the volume by four times! So, roughly you get four times the lumber for two times the slab. No wonder sawmills like big logs. More lumber, less waste.

Getting back to my neighbor's problem, we see that four-inch sticks cord up at a ratio of 16:9 over three-inch sticks. Almost twice as much in that one-inch difference! In fact, it takes an average of 217 three-inch sticks to make a cord, compared to 125 four-inch sticks. That's a lot of sticks. Going a step further, it takes only 54 six-inch sticks.

Figuring pulpwood stumpage at $20 per cord, that makes the three-inch stick worth about 9 cents, the four-inch about 16 cents, and the six-inch about 37 cents. For the cutter, who makes about $15 to cut and stack, the numbers are 6 cents, 12 cents, and 23 cents.

There's a real limit to how much work you can expect a cutter to do for 6 cents, especially since it only costs you 3 cents to leave him alone (9 – 6 = 3 cents).

My table goes on to list the approximate number of trees per cord based on diameter breast height (DBH). For example, it takes 91 five-inch DBH trees to make a cord compared to only nine trees with nine-inch DBH.

There are many formulas involved in forestry, Site Index and Basal Area, to name two, but it seems to me none of them is as important as the simple $A = \pi r^2$. An understanding of this ratio explains everything from board feet calculations to the logic in letting stands grow to maturity.

Oh yeah, about those pizzas: Same old formula. A twelve-inch pizza contains four times the goodies of a six-inch pizza. If it costs less than four times as much, it's a better buy.

True, a calculator can really help in doing this arithmetic, but it won't do you any good unless you know the formula. If you have cut and stacked much pulpwood, you know it instinctively, which is probably the best way to know anything. But now you know why. That's good, too.

16

● Selling Your Wood ◂▴▴

PROBABLY FEW PEOPLE READING THIS BOOK will do all their timber harvesting themselves. Some will do none. There's nothing wrong with that. It brings up a whole new set of problems, however. When times are good, it is hard to get people to do small jobs. When times are bad, there are lots of people willing to do small jobs, but you probably will have no more luck than they do marketing the products. That's why times are bad.

As timber harvesting becomes more mechanized, it is increasingly difficult to get contractors to do just part of the job. Most of them have the machinery to efficiently do the whole operation, and they are reluctant to, essentially, subcontract out part of the job to you while their machines sit idle. Doing that is also inefficient.

It is cost-effective for most loggers to load logs and pulpsticks directly onto trucks from the woods. This takes a lot of organization—so much that it is unlikely that they can fit it all into their overall operation with you doing the cutting and skidding. Usually this results in wood being piled on the ground and then onto trucks. Twice the work.

Mechanization, furthermore, has narrowed the spread between what contractors will pay for timber on the stump and timber stacked alongside the road. Competitive bidding has driven stumpage prices up, while the prices the mills pay have not kept pace.

In many cases, if you subtract the stumpage price from the price anywhere further down the road, you find that your return for the work you plan on doing doesn't produce much income. You are, increasingly, better off to just sell it on the stump and devote your time to keeping an eye on the contractor you hire.

In spite of this, I do my own cutting and skidding because it supports my way of life, which I am not willing to give up. If you hire contractors, you will possibly harvest your woodlot once or twice in your lifetime. That's not much involvement. Do it yourself and you can produce a steady income, year after year. Certainly there is a lot of satisfaction in seeing your woodlot properly maintained regardless of how you do it, but, for my money, the greatest satisfaction lies in doing it myself.

The old logging adage holds true: "If you don't have a load, you don't have zip."

No matter how you plan on doing it, however, don't rush right out and dive right in. Be as sure as possible before you start that markets exist and that you have a way to move the wood to the market. Pine pulpwood will quickly lose its value if cut in the summer and left out in the woods too long. Hardwood pulpwood will not degrade appreciably under those same circumstances. Sawlogs of both types, on the other hand, require more care. Some hardwoods, such as maple, will stain if cut and left in the woods during the warm months. White pine logs will quickly become so stained and full of wormholes as to become worthless for anything but pulpwood. If you are cutting sawlogs of any kind during the warm season, it is a good idea to expedite their sale and shipment to the market. Also, if you sell either logs or pulpwood by weight, leaving them stacked for any length of time in the summer will cost you money as they dry and lose weight.

Assuming you are going to sell your timber on the stump, you have essentially only two options: lump sum or mill scale. Sometimes the decision is beyond your control. In some areas of the country, all bids are lump sum. In others, all are by mill scale. There are advantages to both methods, and there are disadvantages.

A lump-sum sale offers the landowner the major advantage of being able to directly compare all bids. These contracts normally require full payment in advance of any machinery moving onto the property, which means you are protected financially. This method works well if you can convince people to bid this way. In effect, you are shifting all the risk to the bidder. You get yours up-front, and he tries to get his after the work is done. Any damage he does to the timber—a barber-chaired veneer log, for example—is his problem.

This works well as long as you receive multiple bids. Never agree to a lump-sum price from a guy who simply shows up at your door with a bundle of bills in his hand. Often these operators will tell you that they are just finishing a job nearby and can give you top dollar because their machinery is in the area. This, they say, is a once-in-a-lifetime chance because they won't be back your way again. They will typically quote you prices, by the board foot or cord, well beyond the going rate in your area. That would be great if you knew how many board feet or cords of timber there are in your woods. You don't, but he does.

If neither of you know, or if you don't trust his estimate, you can sell your timber by the thousand board feet or by the cord. This is a pay-as-you-cut arrangement, often with 10 or 20 percent down. While you can't directly compare total price this way, you can compare unit prices.

The problems with this method are obvious. Since he doesn't have to pay until the wood is gone, he may not pay at all. To support his payment to you, he may furnish you with the scaling slips from the mill, but will he furnish you all the scaling slips? Even if he does furnish you all of them, did a log or two fall off each load in his yard on the way to the mill? If he scales the logs in your presence, what scale is he using?

There are, unfortunately, various log scales. In the past, attempts have been made to settle on a single scale for all parts of the country, but it's never happened. One problem with agreeing on a single scale is that all scales benefit someone at the expense of someone else. While all the scales attempt to fairly determine how much lumber is contained in individual logs, assumptions have to be made in these estimates, and these assumptions vary widely. There are "sawmiller's scales" and there are "logger's scales," depending on who is thought to benefit from the scale in question.

The scales were developed by estimating how many board feet of one-inch thick boards a given log would yield. The variations arise from differences in logs. A scale that is accurate with large-diameter logs may be wildly inaccurate with small-diameter logs, and vice versa. Deductions are also made for defects, and these also vary.

The three best-known log scales are Doyle, Scribner, and International. Big differences exist between these three, especially with small-diameter logs. For example, a 16-foot, eight-inch-diameter log will scale, in the order above as: 16, 32, and 40 board feet. At the other extreme, a 16-foot log 30 inches in diameter will scale 676, 657, and 675 board feet in the same order. Notice that the estimates draw closer together as size increases.

There is no "legal" scale in any area, but there are scales that are "usually" used. A good way to check on this is to find out which scale is being used by government agencies in your state. Then be sure that is the scale your buyer is using. Log-scaling tapes are available in each of the three main scales, and it's easy for the buyer to carry all three in his pickup. Make sure he uses the one you have agreed on.

Finally, with a "mill-scale" arrangement, what's his incentive to strive for maximum value from your timber? Wasted, miscut timber hurts you, not him.

These problems are exacerbated by the distrust of all concerned (which, I'm afraid, I may have just added to). Everyone hears all sorts of horror stories about "timber thieves." A lot of these stories, unfortunately, come from the very people doing the bidding. In our area, the bidding is so fierce and the profit margins so thin that about the only recourse the contractors feel they have is to paint all the other bidders as crooks. I suppose that, in the short run, this sort of thing pays off for some people, but in the long run, it hurts every one involved. Even landowners who are completely satisfied with a job quickly become dissatisfied if they talk to enough people who insist that they should have received more.

Aside from the type of bid, the main concern of landowners is that the contractor cuts only what should be cut, and all of that. Often this means cutting all the trees the contractor would rather not cut and leaving those he wants. This either involves a large degree of self-discipline on the part of the contractor, or some means to identify what should be cut. In both cases, a further method of determining if these rules were followed is a good idea.

In this regard, consider that the guy who paid a lump sum is, essentially, cutting his timber, while a guy who pays by scale is cutting *your* trees.

A lump-sum buyer would like to cut all he can, since it costs him little more to do that. A scale buyer, on the other hand, would like to take only the most valuable and easiest-to-get timber, since he only pays for what he takes. One is tempted to take too much, the other to leave too much.

The scale cutter may leave low-grade wood either standing or lying in the woods. The lump-sum logger might reach over the fence a bit to get some valuable trees, while the scale guy might not bother to log the few trees in the swamp.

There are various ways to indicate, for the contractor's benefit, which trees to take and which ones to leave. If you have a mixed forest, you can specify certain species to be left or cut. If you have a mixed-age stand, you can specify a "diameter-limit cut." If you want to thin the stand by removing the smaller trees to put maximum growth on the big trees, you can specify that everything up to a certain diameter be cut, leaving the best. If you want to harvest mature trees to release the younger trees, you can specify that every thing down to a specific diameter be taken.

If your woodlot is a plantation, you can either specify the rows to be taken out or the number of trees to be removed—every other tree in the row, for example—or you can specify a basal area you wish to leave. ("Basal area" is simply an estimate of the volume of trees growing in an area. It is expressed in square feet per acre. Thus, a typical basal area before thinning a pine plantation is about 160. This means that there are 160 square feet of pine tree stem cross-sections growing on an acre. This says nothing about the diameter of the trees. It can indicate a few big trees or lots of little ones.)

You can simply trust the contractor to carry out your wishes, or you can mark the trees you want cut yourself, or you can hire a forester to do the marking for you.

In some areas, there is yet another option. You can sign up in a "Tree Farm Family" program operated by a pulp company or large sawmill. These organizations will, if you wish, simply manage your woods for you, sending you a check when they cut on your land. Naturally, they will take into account their needs as well as yours, but many people are happy with this approach.

You can hire a consulting forester to set up a timber sale, mark the trees, supervise the work, and handle the finances. Consulting foresters generally base their fees on a percentage of the sale price. They are therefore subject to the same financial incentives as the contractors to cut as much as possible. This generates maximum income for all parties, but it may not be the best thing for the forest in the long run.

Usually, both consulting foresters and loggers live pretty much where they work, and, thus, reputation is important to them. The landowner should inquire before he chooses either one. It pays to be cautious, but not paranoid. There are plenty of good, ethical people in both categories.

If your woodlot is a mixed forest that contains valuable timber, it probably would pay to hire a forester for his technical knowledge. If, however, the work consists of simple thinning of a plantation, a respectable contractor has sufficient knowledge to do the job right without benefit of a middleman. Some contractors, in fact, employ foresters as part of their team.

Marking the stem as well as the stump is a good way to ensure that the right trees have been cut.

No matter who decides what is to be cut, bear in mind that the cut must be large enough and contain enough value to attract bidders. This means that at least some valuable trees must be cut in every harvest. You can't expect a contractor to weed your garden and pay you for the privilege.

Even if the contractor is known to be reliable, it is good practice to mark the trees you want cut, both on the trunk at eye level for him to easily see, and on the stump where you can see it after the tree is gone. Once the trees are cut, all the stumps look pretty much the same. If the trees are very valuable, foresters sometimes also mark the most valuable ones, indicating that they are to be protected and not damaged during the logging operation.

Make an effort to mark the trees on the side the logger will see most easily, or make the marks visible from all sides. It costs money if cutters have to walk around each tree to see if they are marked. It really costs if the cutting is being done by machine. You might want to talk to the logger before you mark.

If you have special requirements, spell them out in the contract. You should expect the logger not to "bark up" the remaining stand of trees and take care not to tear up your roads, but normally he won't cut the remaining tops down to ground level, for example, unless you specify it in the contract. If you do have special requirements that will cost the logger time and money, take that into account when you prepare the bid invitations.

Sometimes, for example, there are insect concerns or ground conditions that make it undesirable to harvest timber during certain periods. Other times, the owner and his friends want to hunt his land and don't want work going on during hunting season. These are reasonable requirements, but they interfere with the logger's scheduling, so they must be clearly understood and agreed to by both parties.

Naturally, it makes sense to have a written contract before cutting begins, but even more important than a contract is the reputation of the logger. There is no contract that will protect you like dealing with an honest man. Ask around, and ask the logger to provide references and check them out. Ask other landowners and local foresters. State foresters are a good source of information, but take any lists of "reliable" contractors they may give you with a grain of salt. There are legal implications to these lists. State officials can face lawsuits if they refuse to list a contractor or remove someone from their "approved" lists.

I've had timber harvested on my land several times when I was out of the country. I just got a check and a bunch of scaling slips when the job was done. I had the same logger each time and never had a contract with him. I just trusted him.

The contractor not only has to be honest, he has to be competent. You also have to be realistic about the appearance of the woods after the work is done. Logs don't come in velvet boxes. Logging is an act of violence to your woods, and it will probably reflect that for sometime after the job is done. To the uninformed, a good logging job looks a lot like a bad one. Don't be too quick to judge. Time heals many wounds.

Marking your own timber for cutting is an appealing idea. I tried it once and found I couldn't do it. I do okay when Marcia and I select trees as we go along when we do the cutting, but when I tried to mark them for a contractor, I was reluctant to let any good trees be cut. I marked so few that the guy refused to start the job because, he said, he couldn't make any money at it. I finally just told him to do what was best and went away. He did a fine job—much better than I could have directed.

If you do have a contract with a logger, be sure you set a time limit with a penalty if he hasn't finished by the agreed-upon date. This is especially important if the bidding has been highly competitive. The high bidder may have based his bid on his guess that prices will go up. If that is the case, he will be tempted to wait as long as possible to cut, using his time to cut jobs that cost less, first. If prices don't rise as he anticipated, he may not want to cut your wood at all. If prices go down, he may have to cut your wood at a loss to fulfill the contract.

That's the breaks, I guess. Even so, it may be worthwhile to consider sharing some of the pain by lowering your price a bit rather than going through the legal hassle to either get him to do the work at the bid price or to recover the penalty. Even if you win, you will then have to rebid the job. Other loggers may be reluctant to bid if you were exceptionally tough on the first guy. Word gets around.

17

Managing for Firewood

OVER THE YEARS, I HAVE USUALLY FOLLOWED the advice given to me by the Wisconsin Department of Natural Resources (DNR) foresters, and usually that advice has proved to be correct. Usually, but not always.

The DNR people have always been negative toward scrub oak; their advice has been to get rid of the oak and convert the land to pine. In the past, girdling or poison injection for small stands or aerial spraying to kill large stands was advised. Now, they seem to favor selling it on the stump to be clear-cut by wholesale firewood operators.

I'm sure the statistics bear out the wisdom of this approach. Given the slow growth of oak, the stunted forms of the oaks doing the growing, and the stumpage prices for oak pulpwood and firewood, owning scrub oak land is bound to compare unfavorably with pine plantations in the long run. In fact, it probably compares unfavorably with almost any investment you can name.

Still, I didn't kill off my oaks, and I'm glad that I didn't. A portion of my annual income comes from my oak woods, as well as a large degree of pleasure in maintaining them. Not all scrub oaks are the same, but scrub oak land in my area has several things in common. First of all, there's not a sawlog in 40 acres worth skidding out. True, there are a few trees that contain logs which are straight and which appear sound enough to produce lumber, but they are so scattered that it is not worthwhile to recover them. Even if you do get them out, more than half of them usually contain enough rot to render the whole log useless. So forget logging and forget traditional Timber Stand Improvement (TSI). You don't have a timber stand. You have scrub oak, and no efforts on your part will change that.

Secondly, even though all the oaks are scrub oaks, they vary considerably in shape, size, and vigor. While they may all be losers when viewed from a timber standpoint, they are not all equally bad.

A typical central Wisconsin scrub oak stand with a pine understory.

Thirdly, firewood economics are such that, even though the trees are losers, the wood derived from them is a winner. The oak from these trees makes some of the best firewood available and commands the highest prices when sold at urban retail markets.

Finally, almost all the value of firewood is in labor and transportation. A face cord of oak firewood brings about $3 on the stump in central Wisconsin and about $55 delivered to a home in Milwaukee, about 200 miles away. That's more than a 1,800 percent markup. For that, you must cut it, split it, age it, and deliver it.

With this kind of markup, one can assume that all the value of firewood is in labor and transportation, with the standing trees being worthless. Still, if you don't have the trees, you have nothing to labor over and to transport. So, the trees do have value.

I don't know if you've ever seen a clear-cut oak stand but it's not a pretty sight. Large stumps abound, making replanting difficult. Mainly brush and useless sprouts remain. That's no way to treat a woods.

By contrast, I have been thinning my oak stands for several years and have removed hundreds of cords of firewood. The stands look better now than when I started. They not only *look* better, they *are* better, since the remaining trees are healthy and of fairly good form. From a distance a thinned stand looks as if someone had used a tree straightener. The remaining trunks are all reasonably straight and tall.

I am very selective in the trees I cut. I leave the best of a bad lot, and I try to leave about half. While I would like to leave all straight trees with no crotches or big limbs, I look more for vigor than form. If a tree has a healthy look, I'll leave it, even if it crotches low, and especially if taking it would leave a large, open space. If a snag looks like it is a den tree—a home to wildlife—I leave it.

I don't mark the trees in advance. Often, the felling of a tree alters the picture in ways I couldn't have foreseen, so I select as I go. Sometimes I fell "good" trees to avoid hang-ups or to make roads as I attempt to get my truck in close.

One exception to this is dead trees. If I'm going to work in an area in the winter, I mark the dead or dying trees in the summer. With their leaves off in the winter, you can't tell which ones are dead.

Given a choice, I favor white oaks over red and black oak varieties, since white oaks are resistant to oak wilt. I don't cut oaks from April through August, since this is the time oak wilt spreads most rapidly. Also, I try to avoid scarring living trees, since this leaves an opening for the oak wilt spores to enter.

If a tree has a shelf fungus or "conk" on it, I take it. The presence of a conk indicates rot at that point, and it will eventually cause the tree to break off in the wind, especially if you take other trees from the immediate vicinity.

Much to my surprise, few of my trees have extensive rot in them. Almost all of them have some, but since the goal for firewood is 16-inch chunks, it is easy to skip over the rotted parts. Thus, a tree that is useless for lumber will produce a lot of good firewood. A trunk length with rot in the center, if left lying, will hollow out and make a snug home for skunks, or a drumming log for prairie chickens. Brush piles from the tops are ideal places for a rabbit to hide from an owl.

In some areas I have white pine scattered among the oaks. Even if these pines are distorted from rubbing against oak limbs or from tip weevil attacks, I try to clear the oaks around them, hoping the pines will act as seed trees. If they do, I will cut a few more oaks where the seedlings are sprouting to bring in a little more light.

Naturally I try to fell the oaks in a way that avoids breaking off the pines, but I don't always succeed. Even if I break a pine, I leave it, since it still may send up a new leader and become a source of seed.

"Conks" on a doomed oak tree.

When I finish a first thinning in my oak tracts, I plan to repeat the process, and again take about half the trees. Even if I never get to the second cutting though, I will have improved the stand. If I want to sell it later, it should be worth more than if I had done nothing.

In the meantime, I've never had any trouble selling all the wood I cut. I deliver some of it locally, and some people come and pick it up on their own. I sell most of it to semi-truckers from Milwaukee.

While the DNR foresters may be right in the long run, we live in the short run, and viewed from that perspective, scrub oak makes me a good dollar. I can produce $30 worth of firewood in two hours, expenses deducted. Fifteen dollars per hour is not a bad wage where I live.

Also, in many ways it is a lot more interesting cutting oak than thinning pine plantations, and doing it can reward the owner with a steady source of income and the satisfaction of seeing the woods improve year after year. You can't ask for much more than that.

Cutting and Selling Firewood

Unlike other timber harvesting on a tree farm, cutting firewood can be done without using expensive equipment. A chain saw, safety

Carrying firewood chunks with Swedish log tongs.

clothing, splitting maul, plastic wedge, and a pickup truck or farm tractor and trailer are all that's needed. That's less than most deer hunters spend on their equipment. And wood cutters seldom come home empty-handed.

I use a 2.7-cubic-inch chain saw with a 16-inch bar, a K Mart splitting maul, and my 1975 pickup. Starting with standing trees, it takes me about 30 minutes to fell and block slightly more than a face cord of wood into 16-inch lengths. This is typically two or three trees. It takes another 20 minutes to split these blocks into chunks, splitting them right where they fell, and another 20 minutes to throw the chunks into my pickup. If I can't get my truck close enough, I use my Swedish tongs to carry the chunks to the truck, adding about 10 minutes to my task.

I've often thought that people from cities who own oak woods in our area and who come to the country could pay for their trips by getting small, two-wheel trailers and taking loads of wood back with them each time they return home. I have a small trailer that holds one and a quarter face cords. In Milwaukee that would be worth about $60. If they're going to the city anyway, their only transportation costs would be additional gasoline, and that wouldn't amount to much.

Still, I don't know anyone who does this. Quite possibly, people are intimidated by the cutting and splitting involved. Granted, you're not going to do a face cord in an hour and a half at first, but you will soon learn how to work more efficiently and build up your physical strength, and there's a lot of satisfaction in that.

If you want to sell wood in bulk, several problems must be solved. First, how do you load it into a semitrailer? The only practical way to do this, in my opinion, is with a conveyor. I have a 40-foot hay elevator that I bought used for $600. I drive it with my tractor PTO. One time, four of us loaded a truck in two hours with this setup. That was a record, though. More likely, it would take closer to three hours.

Farm elevators are not designed to handle chunks of firewood. The major problem I had with them is that chunks got caught crosswise between the "flites," jammed up and broke the chain. Fixing a broken chain is a big job with cold hands. You can eliminate a lot of this problem by removing every other flite. ("Flites" are the crosspieces that carry the product along the conveyor).

I then tried another type of conveyor. This one was made with a wide rubber belt, to which flites were bolted. I bought it from a farmer who used it to move potatoes. Since it was solid, there was no way for the chunks to jam up. There was a problem, however. When you threw the chunks onto the belt, a lot of them bounced right back off again. I guess I should have thought of that, but I didn't.

Finding people who want to buy semi-loads of wood is not a problem. Dealing with these potential customers, however, can create problems. Some of these difficulties include determining what the price per cord will be, who will furnish what land or labor, how the wood will be paid for, and how much wood the truck holds (how many cords, in other words, you will be paid for).

As to the labor, usually I furnish myself and one other worker. The truck driver and one other person come with the truck. If the driver comes alone, I will furnish an extra worker for $20.

Many people in our area have had trouble with bad checks from wood buyers. I think we all eventually got our money, but only after some worry and hassle. A wise practice is to demand cash before loading. This should be easy, but sometimes, after you have sold wood to the same buyer many times with no problem, you tend to become lax and don't insist on either cash or payment in advance. That's when you get stuck.

Any time I've been beaten, it's been by someone I thought I knew. The problem is compounded by the apparent fact that everyone who sells wood retail depends on answering machines. Thus, if they don't choose to pick up the phone, you can't confront them directly. All you can do is leave a message on their machine and hope they respond.

The only accurate way to measure firewood on a truck bed is by stacking it.

Officials in the state of Maine, in response to constant controversy about how much wood a truck will hold, threw a number of measured cords of 16-inch pieces randomly into measured bins. They came up with a figure of 180 cubic feet of loosely thrown wood to a full cord, or 60 cubic feet for a face cord. That compares to 128 cubic feet and 42 cubic feet for stacked wood. Thus, a 40-foot semitrailer measuring 39 feet long, by 7 feet 6 inches wide, by 4 feet high, would contain about 20 face cords loaded flush to the top. If the driver heaps it up (like they always seem to do), you would probably end up with about 24 face cords. This when the wood is thrown in loosely. If the driver stays up in the trailer and throws the chunks around as they come off the elevator, he is, in effect, stacking it in, so he gets more in the same space (a heaped-up load in a standard pickup box consists of between one and a quarter and one and a third 16-inch face cords).

In the final analysis, only the buyers know how much they get on the truck, and all the sellers can do is negotiate their best deal. Even if the wood has been carefully stacked on the ground, it will have settled while curing and will not measure four feet high if that's how high it was originally piled. Also, the wood itself shrinks as it dries and the bark comes off, so no matter how it is done, it's not an exact science. I've settled for anywhere from 20 to 24 face cords on the same-size truck.

If you don't feel you can cut and split wood yourself, it can still be profitable if you find someone to do it for you. Quite often people who live in rural areas enjoy working in the woods and are pretty conscientious about doing a good job, once you take the time to explain what it is you are try-ing to do.

Years ago I paid a man $14 a face cord for wood that he split and stacked in my yard. I allowed him to use my tractor and trailer to bring it in. Using his own saw, he made about $7 an hour.

He did a good job. He worked irregularly, usually a day or two a week and sometimes not for several weeks at a time. But since I only paid for wood delivered, I really didn't care. That made for a good working relationship. These days, of course, you want to carefully consider the implications of liability on your part, since a person in this situation could well be considered your employee, leaving you with all the legal responsi-bilities involved in that relationship.

Not everyone wants the same thing out of their firewood. A young, nice-looking guy showed up one day wanting to buy a trunkload of fire-wood. He said he didn't want the seasoned oak I had advertised. What he wanted was dry pine. He said he wasn't interested in Btus or long-burning wood.

He lived in a condo in Chicago and had a fireplace in his bedroom. What he wanted was some wood that would catch quickly and burn brightly. He said that he sometimes took girls up there, and he didn't want to spend any time trying to get a fire going nor did he care how long it burned after he got it blazing. So I sold him pine slab.

Blocking

Bucking trees into firewood is called "blocking," and the unsplit result is known as "blockwood." Blocking is simpler than bucking, but is still skilled work. Since all blocks are the same length, your considerations are limited to safety and efficiency, but there is enough in these two items to provide plenty of challenge.

Once you have a tree down, you need to decide whether to start block-ing at the stump or up in the top. Where you start will be determined by how the tree landed. Since you are at the stump end, this is a logical place to start, but only if the trunk is off the ground. Usually the butt of the tree will be resting on the ground or on the stump, in which case the top is the place to start.

Sometimes, however, the branch structure, shape of the trunk, or objects on the ground will hold the butt free. In this case, the butt end is the place to start.

Most firewood is blocked to a nominal 16-inch length. Stove manufac-turers say that your wood should be four inches shorter than your firebox, but this is only a guideline. Some people prefer 20-inch or even 24-inch wood. If you choose to cut your wood longer, bear in mind that the longer it is, the harder it is to split.

Sixteen inches works out fine for me because my firewood bar is 16 inches long, and I use it to measure the

blocks. If you have a different length bar or prefer a different length of wood, you can locate or mark a spot on your saw to allow you to "saw-measure" as well.

Before starting your cut, just lay your saw along the trunk and note the length required; then turn the saw 90 degrees and start cutting. I only do this now when I'm cutting large blocks, where a mistake will affect many chunks, and otherwise only occasionally to be sure I'm not losing my eye for the 16-inch length. To me, nominal means plus or minus one inch, and I can usually eyeball measurements within an inch.

If the butt of a firewood log is off the ground, take your first cut 16 inches from the end.

Blocking requires only the basic felling tools: the saw and the plastic wedge. This is very important, since a lot of time can be wasted carrying and locating tools. It's easy to lose things in the woods. I spray-paint my tools electric blue, since nothing that color occurs naturally in my woods. Even blaze orange can sometimes disappear in the midst of autumn leaves. Still, even with the electric blue, I sometimes lose tools in the woods.

The Swedes did a study of color visibility, which found that electric blue shows up better in the woods than blaze orange. They did this by stationing observers in a wooded area and then having a group of people dressed in either orange or blue walk in a line toward them. The observers spotted the people dressed in blue sooner than they did the ones in orange.

So, if the butt is off the ground, take your first cut 16 inches from the end. Just cut straight through—there's no need to undercut. Take each block the same way; don't stop and clear anything, and let the blocks fall where they may. Be alert for any movement in the tree. Each time you cut something off the tree, it changes the forces on it and can cause it to move. This is more important when working in the top, but it pays to consider it down at the butt end as well.

Try to cut your blocks off with flat, square ends. When it comes time to split, blocks cut at an angle will topple over, thus adding work and annoyance to the splitting phase. (If I'm working on a hillside, it sometimes occurs to me that I could cut off chunks with the same angle as the slope of the hill and have them stand straight when it came time to split. I never really tried it though.)

If your cuts are angling, the problem is sometimes due to poor chain sharpening or a worn bar. For a full discussion of sharpening and bar care, see Chapter 8.

Continue cutting blocks off the trunk as long as it is convenient. Even with the trunk resting lightly on the ground, you can cut, as long as you don't run your chain into the dirt. This is a good time to start using your plastic wedge, however. After starting each cut, insert the wedge behind the saw and tap it home with the heel of your hand. This will keep the kerf open, even if the trunk is touching the ground. When you have finished your cut, just leave the wedge there until you need it for the next block; then move it over.

Whether you are working from the butt toward the top or starting in the top, don't cut large limbs off at the trunk. This is a very common mistake made by amateur cutters, and it is the source of all sorts of problems, as well as increasing the work involved. Pick a limb that is essentially horizontal and, at a convenient height, move out to the tip of it and work your way in toward the trunk, lopping off 16-inch pieces as you go. How far out should you start? That depends. Most cutters will take limbs out to about three inches in diameter. If you have a small stove you may want to take even smaller pieces.

I usually start my cutting at about three inches, but that depends on a number of things. If I'm going to have to drag the slash, I'll go a lot lower than if I can just walk away when I'm finished. If the limb is clean, I'll start where it first branches off, so I don't have to lop off a lot of small branches to get a clean piece. When starting at a point where a limb branches, I leave a much neater job when I cut both branches just above the crotch rather than doing it with a single cut below the crotch. The two branches are easier to drag and will end up lying closer to the ground if you leave them.

As you work your way down toward the trunk, be aware of the effect that your cutting is having on the tree. As you remove weight the tree may roll, usually away from you. Branches that were once on the ground can come swooping up and knock you and your saw about.

If the tree rolls, reevaluate the situation. The butt may be rolled free of the ground, in which case you can start blocking there. Or, other limbs may now be in convenient positions. Always be alert; always think.

Don't cut all the limbs and then saw the trunk as a log. Logs roll around and are hard to buck, and sawing a log on the ground is a lot more work than sawing one suspended at a convenient height. This is an example of applying the benching theories to situations where actual benching usually doesn't apply. Do it right, and you will have no need for any log-lifting devices.

Leave some limbs in place to hold the log up off the ground. If you have to block the trunk on the ground, make cuts every 16 inches almost through; then, when you reach a point where you can cut through without running your saw into the dirt, cut through, roll the log, and finish your cuts from the top.

Be wary of sawing into crotches. Often they contain sand and even stones brought there, I suppose, by squirrels. Better to cut just below the crotch and then split it with your maul.

Do all your trimming with your saw, before severing the piece. This includes twigs. It's easier using a saw than an axe or maul for this job. And it's a pain to work with a cut-off piece that's lying in the dirt. Freeing the pieces from the stem should be the last thing you do.

Many firewood trees contain rot, but few are all rotten. A tree may be rotted at the base but sound a few feet up. The only way to tell is to just keep blocking until you reach sound wood. If it is rotten, just move up 16 inches and try again.

If you must cut large limbs at the trunk, do so very carefully. It is hard to tell which way the tension is working in a downed limb. A limb that is under tension when you start cutting will often twist as you cut, binding your saw. Then you have real problems. Sometimes, the only solution is to disconnect the bar and leave it and the chain stuck in the tree, until you can fit your saw with a spare bar and chain and cut the stuck one out. That can easily eat up half a day.

If I have to cut off a big limb, I cut with the tip of my bar and proceed very slowly, always ready to pull the bar out if the limb starts to twist. If the limb is thick enough, I get a wedge in behind the bar as soon as I can. Still, this should be avoided if possible. Even if you succeed in cutting the limb off, it will fall to the ground, and you'll have to bend over and saw in the dirt to block it. A much better approach is to work from tip to trunk.

No-Bend Woodsplitting

Splitting wood by hand has a certain appeal for those who don't do it very often. Years ago I remember seeing promotional photographs of prize-fighters splitting wood in their training camps, and then there was President Reagan busting them up on his ranch. Have you ever noticed how they do it? They set a chunk of wood up on a block, hit it with a mighty blow with an axe, and watch the pieces fly. That may be fine for them, but unless you have training camp hustlers or Secret Service men to chase the pieces, it's not for you. You won't get in a winter's supply of wood using photo opportunity methods.

I used to do it the same, picture-perfect way: Standing up a chunk of wood and splitting it, often with one blow. The pieces would go flying. I'd set them back up and split them again. I used to count the number of blows it took to split a given number of pieces. Like most people, I felt that the striking of the blows was the hard part, and that the fewer it took, the better I was doing. I would split until I had enough wood for an armload, then gather the pieces up and load them onto the truck or trailer. That not only provided some relief from splitting, but it also kept things picked up and made for a neat workplace.

As time went on, however, I found, that while splitting was hard work, the constant bending to set up the chunks and pieces was just as tiring. I noticed that if I split the wood where the tree fell, I didn't need a splitting block—I could split the blocks right where they fell. Then I began to notice that, whenever a piece of wood flew up against a chunk or another piece and leaned against it, I didn't have to bend over to stand it on end again.

As I thought about that, I realized that the number of times I got lucky was in direct proportion to the number of pieces lying around. And, that realization led to the basic principle of no-bend woodsplitting: Clutter is your friend.

Don't pick up the pieces as you split. Leave them lying around. The more pieces there are, the more chances a piece that's being split will end up leaning against another and thus not have to be set up for resplitting. This simple concept is probably the most important feature of no-bend woodsplitting.

Once I started using the split pieces this way, it confirmed my suspicion that bending is, in fact, the hardest part of the splitting process. I began counting the number of times I bent over to produce a given amount of split wood, instead of counting the number of blows it took to split it. No longer did I simply hope that pieces would land in the right place; I used my foot and my maul to nudge them up against other pieces and to stand up chunks for initial splitting. That worked pretty well, and it was a lot less tiring. I found, however, that I was pretty clumsy and spent too much time pawing chunks with the maul, trying to get them to stand. Often, I could tip them up, but then I'd have to bend down and grab them before they fell.

The modified maul.

I practiced moving wood with the maul until I got about as good as I was going to get, which wasn't very good. It soon became obvious that the maul just wasn't designed to do what I needed. How could I modify it so that it would do the job? Simple. I sawed about an inch and a half off the tip of a baling hook, sharpened it, pounded the end over to make a slight hook, and welded it to the flat end of the maul's head.

Then I really had something. I could tip up chunks and pieces. I could

When splitting firewood, messy is good.

roll big blocks out of line and tip them up. I could swing logs around. All with the maul. After a little practice, I found that I could split an entire tree's worth of wood without bending over once. I could work for a longer period of time, because I wasn't tiring as quickly.

After I worked out the wrinkles of the maul design, I went on to develop other techniques for making splitting easier. I no longer tried to split a chunk or a piece with a single blow, which usually resulted in my using too much force and driving the maul into the ground. The key to all manual work is to use "appropriate force"—just enough to do the job. Swinging hard on the first blow will probably split most pieces, but how much of that blow is wasted? Splitting with one blow is like paying the first price asked. It's better to dicker a little to see if you can get by for less.

Try a light blow on the first swing and observe how the wood reacts. If it opens a wide crack, a light second blow may take it through. If it resists the first blow, make the second one harder, and so on. If you hit roughly in the same line each time, the effect of the blows is cumulative, so no swing, however light, is wasted. Even if you give up on one line and try another, the damage done by the first strike will pay off after the initial split.

The most accurate way to deliver blows is by raising the maul directly overhead and bringing it straight down. Both the aim and the force applied can be controlled in this manner. Roundhouse swings are only good for impressing girls at the carnival.

Another reason for light blows is that you are more able to control the splitting so that pieces don't fly off to the side or topple over. With a little practice, you can split a chunk into four or more pieces, keeping them standing and held lightly together until a final blow knocks them apart. If you do it right, the pieces on the ground will be almost completely severed, enabling you to separate them with light blows as they lie flat. Of course, with enough pieces lying around, they probably won't end up flat, but leaning against another piece. So much the better.

When you stand a chunk up against another piece for support, the natural thing to do is to split it by hitting perpendicular to the supporting piece, causing both pieces of the standing chunk to fall when you split it. However, if further splitting is required, you'll have to stand the pieces back up. Instead, try hitting the chunk so that the split is parallel to the supporting piece, allowing the split piece nearest the support to lean back against it. Then split this piece again, this time perpendicular to the support. When you've finished splitting it, hook the other half of the chunk and flip it up against the support.

Always think a step ahead and try to influence things so that each step benefits the following one. I walk around a lot now. I don't try to bring things to me if I can go to them. If a chunk is standing up, I will walk over and split it rather than bring it to me. It's my back that gives out, not my legs.

There are exceptions to the walk-up-to-it rule. The easiest way to move wood in the splitting area is to roll blocks. This is much easier than picking up pieces or moving logs. So, if hauling is made easier by moving wood prior to splitting, use the maul point to roll blocks to wherever you want them. If you need to rotate a large block, hit it hard enough to stick the maul in it; then use the maul as a lever to turn it. That's what's known as "getting a handle on the problem."

One good reason to move blocks before splitting is to avoid interference from overhead branches. Even small pine boughs will deflect your swing. It's easy to break these branches off with your maul, but if for some reason you can't or don't want to do that, move the blocks to a clear area. Nothing makes me madder than having a well-aimed swing deflected by a branch.

Another reason for rolling blocks is to get rid of the inevitable unsplittable chunk. My first rule for these is, "Always try." Often you will be pleasantly surprised. Don't make quick judgments on what will split and what won't. As long as I've been at it, I can't tell by looking. I try several blows from various angles, and, if I have no luck, I flip it over—which is easy to do with the maul—and try from the other end. Always do that; it's amazing how often a chunk will split from one end but not the other. I tell guys I hire to make wood for me that I don't object to "unsplittable" blocks being left in the woods, but that I'd better see several maul marks in each end.

Some people believe that it's better to split from the "top" end of blocks, while others think it's best from the "bottom." I've never found any consistent pattern. My only advice is to attack the piece from the end away from a problem area, such as a large branch stub. This way the maul will usually penetrate, where as in a true cross-grain it will simply bounce off. If the block of wood is large, I try to take slabs off the outside first, then move toward the center as the block gets smaller. When you can't split off any more, just roll the chunk aside and leave it.

Don't let pride or stubbornness keep you pounding away. Again, the key is "appropriate force." If you keep pounding, you may eventually split the block, but how much effort will you have invested in those few pieces? If you are splitting where the tree fell, you have little invested in each piece. Just let it return to the soil with the leaves and branches. Don't fool around with splitting wedges or "super" mauls.

If small blocks or pieces are harder than usual to split, leave them unsplit and compensate by splitting easy pieces finer. What you want is a mix of large and small chunks.

If you run across blocks that are rotten in the middle, it's still possible to salvage something by splitting slabs off the outside. Don't ever drive your maul into a rotten center. It won't split, and, if the rot is firm, your maul will get stuck. If the center is really rotten, the maul head will zip right through and the handle will hit the sound outer wood and break.

Try to take advantage of natural conditions to make splitting easier. Deep snow, while causing a lot of problems, will also keep pieces from falling over when they lean into it. Slash will support pieces of wood. Don't be in a big hurry to clean up your work area. The worst situation for no-bend woodsplitting is a bare, flat surface. It's wise to stop occasionally and load some pieces, in order to break up the work, but don't take those pieces that are near where you are working or will be working. The same goes for day's end: don't pick up all the wood. Leave enough so that you don't have to start with a bare workplace the next time.

Don't let your maul fall over. Always lean it against something. It saves bending. At day's end, drive the maul into the ground. That prevents the handle wood from drying out and loosening the head.

The maul I use is a standard discount store model with an eight-pound head and a wooden handle. I've had it for years and have gone through numerous handles. I don't do anything special to protect them. I consider handles to be consumables, like saw chains. They're not something to be handed down to the grandchildren. They cost about five dollars apiece and will last several seasons. I always keep a spare, though, since they break at unpredictable times. Don't make your own handles. It's not worth the effort, and you tend to get attached to them and baby them.

An eight-pound head is rather light for a maul, but since I don't care about splitting with one blow, I don't see any sense in swinging extra weight. Since I've put the point on, I'm especially glad that the maul isn't any heavier than it is. When you use it as a pick, the weight acts against you, making the maul harder to manipulate.

These are simple tools and methods for a simple job. It's a lot like cross-country skiing. You pit yourself and your equipment against a natural task. Physical conditioning and skill in using and caring for your equipment increase as you practice. In other words, you get better, accomplishing more and enjoying the work more.

By using these methods I have increased my output of stove-ready fuel by about 20 percent, but even if I hadn't increased output at all, I increased my enjoyment of the task, and that, in the long run, is what it's all about for me.

I don't see any advantage to buying or renting a hydraulic splitter unless you are dealing with truly unsplittable wood, such as that from some elm trees. Whether you bring the splitter out into the woods or haul the blocks home for splitting, you end up moving a lot of heavy blocks, either by having to load them into the truck or by having to carry them over to the splitter. Then, you have to load them onto the splitter and off the splitter onto the truck. That's a lot of extra work. All I ever handle in the woods is split chunks, and I only handle them once.

There are still some people who use PTO-operated "buzz saws" to block logs into firewood. As far as I'm concerned, chain saws made these things obsolete. It's beyond me why anyone would wrestle logs up onto a platform to be cut when you can do it right where they landed with your chain saw. Not only is this a lot of work, but buzz saws are also about the most dangerous gadgets imaginable.

Don't try to split with an axe. Because of their thin wedge shapes, axes usually end up stuck in the wood. They are for cutting, not splitting. For the same reason, don't ever sharpen a splitting maul. They are meant to break their way through the wood, not cut their way through. Sharpening just makes them more axe-like, and you will end up sticking them almost as often as the axe. To me the axe has no function anymore. Like the two-man "misery whip" saw, it is a relic of the colorful past.

How do you get what's left of a broken handle out of a maul head? Some people resort to drilling and pounding, often with little effect. One way is to simply cut the remains of the handle off near the base of the head and throw it (the head) into a wood stove or other fire. You can throw the broken handle in the fire too, if you like. After about 10 or 15 minutes, fish the maul head out with a wire or poker, and toss it into a bucket of water. No harm comes to the maul head, and, as soon as it cools down, you're ready to fit a new handle and head back out to work.

Note: A *face cord* generally means any stack of wood measuring 4 feet by 8 feet on its face. For cordwood cut into 16-inch lengths, one face cord equals approximately one-third of a *standard cord* (which is a stack measuring 4 feet by 8 feet by 8 feet). So my trailer loaded with one and one-quarter face cords would equal a little less than half a standard cord of wood.

18

Wood Burning

EVERY FALL WE HEAR CAUTIONARY TALES about the harmful effects of buying and burning wet (or "green," unseasoned) firewood. These warnings generally focus on creosote buildup and the economics of burning wet wood. Both are serious concerns, but they are often given only superficial treatment.

Creosote buildup in chimneys is a direct result of incomplete combustion, regardless of the source. It can, and does occur, in chimneys in the homes of people who burn only seasoned, dry wood. Any time you regulate airflow you affect combustion. Restrict it too much, and the air-starved fire will produce creosote-laden smoke. If your chimney system is as hot as it would be in an insulated chimney or one that rises through the interior of your house, the smoke will pass up and out without condensing, carrying the creosote-forming compounds with it in their gaseous state.

If, on the other hand, your chimney is cool, as it will be if it is located outside or if it is cooled by a poor fire, the smoke produced will condense on the cool chimney surfaces, and creosote will form inside the chimney. Just where it accumulates will depend on the temperatures that exist inside the chimney. If you insulate your chimney, you may simply push the creosote-forming area up without actually pushing it out, thus solving nothing.

One of the best ways to deal with creosote, regardless of your chimney situation, is to always burn a small, hot fire rather than overloading the stove and restricting the air inlet to control combustion. This, unfortunately, cancels out a lot of the benefits of modern airtight stoves, which are designed for precise air control and long, slow burns.

One way around this is to use your wood to heat water in a boiler. With a boiler, you can fire wide-open, packing the heat into the water or steam in the boiler and then, through the use of flow controls, release the heat from the water or steam into your house in a controlled manner as you need it.

Outside heating systems use this approach. Through circulation systems, they provide a controlled flow of hot water to your home heating system. They do not depend on controlling combustion. They are fired wide-open, and intermittently. They have their share of creosote problems too, however. When the water in the boiler attains the specified temperature, an inlet damper closes, starving the fire of all air. In the process of shutting down, the wood—which was burning—smolders, and the smoke formed condenses in the cool firebox and stovepipe, form-

An outside wood-fired boiler.

ing creosote. If the boiler is operated and designed correctly, the next cycle should burn the creosote out. If not, you've got problems.

Burning wet or green wood contributes to creosote problems. In order to understand why introducing wet wood into your stove causes such an immediate and dramatic effect, it is necessary to understand a little about the nature of heat.

There are two types of heat: sensible and latent. *Sensible heat* is just that, heat which we can sense. Things which contain more sensible heat are hotter, because introducing sensible heat causes temperatures to rise. *Latent heat* is just as real as sensible heat, and its effects are just as real. Latent heat does not raise temperatures, however. Instead, latent heat is absorbed or released during changes of state. The latent heat we are most concerned with here is the latent heat of vaporization. This is the heat required to change a liquid—in this case, water—to a gas—in this case, steam.

Water brought into a stove in wood exits the chimney as steam, carrying with it all the heat it absorbed in its odyssey from cold water entering the firebox to steam at 212 degrees. Much of the white cloud leaving your chimney is actually steam, not smoke.

In our English system of measurement, heat is measured in British thermal units or Btus. A Btu is the amount of heat required to raise the temperature of one pound of water one degree Fahrenheit. The actual scientific definition is slightly more limiting, but the simpler definition is generally accepted and sufficient for our purposes.

The metric equivalent of the Btu is the calorie. This is the amount of heat needed to raise the temperature of one liter of water one degree Celsius. Were it not for some historical quirk, we could well be measuring firewood in calories and ice cream sundaes in Btus!

So, let's construct a scenario to find out how much heat we actually lose with wet wood. Let's say that a stove user brings a load of wood into the house from his outside woodshed, and that this armload of wood contains a pound of water as moisture in the wood. The homeowner puts it into his stove and burns it. For our purposes it doesn't matter whether he burned wet wood or dry wood. Water is water, and that is all we are concerned with at this point.

Let's assume that the outside temperature is right at freezing, so the temperature of the wood and the water is 32 degrees F. To raise this pound of water from 32 to 212 degrees F requires 180 Btus (212 – 32 ÷ 180).

This is all sensible heat, since no change of state has taken place. All we have done is heated the water. Now, to change from water at 212 degrees to steam at 212 degrees, we have to add the latent heat of vaporization. This takes a whopping 970 Btus, and that is where our big loss of heat takes place: boiling the water. Changing the 212-degree water to 212-degree steam requires more than five times the heat it took to raise the temperature from 32 to 212 degrees!

The person who said that a watched pot never boils had probably experienced the long wait for a pot of hot water to actually boil. There is a big difference between bringing water to a boil and actually boiling it—970 Btus per pound difference to be exact!

So, to bring our pound of water to 212 degrees F and then boil it, we have to use 1,150 Btus (180 + 970 = 1,150). If we had assumed that the water in the wood actually existed as ice, we would have had to add another 144 Btus, which is the latent heat required to melt the ice (that is, to change ice at 32 degrees F to water at 32 degrees F).

This heat can only come from one place: the fire itself. And so it does. Water in the wood not only doesn't contribute to the stove's performance, it actually removes heat from the fire and sends it up the chimney. This explains why, when you add wet wood to a fire, the stove cools down as heat is extracted from it. If you have a stack thermometer you can see it very clearly. The stack temperature drops and doesn't recover until the water is gone.

Removing heat from the fire will not only cool it down, it may actually put it out. This is because the heat of the stove may fall below the combustion temperature, at which point combustion can no longer be supported and the fire goes out.

All firewood contains some water; the question is, how much? Moisture content is the technical term used to describe the amount of water contained in wood. It relates the weight of the wood being tested to the weight of the same wood minus all water. This is determined by weighing a sample, then drying it in an oven and weighing it again. The two weights are compared and the result expressed in "percent moisture."

Freshly cut wood can easily contain moisture as high as 100 percent. In some cases, the weight of the water in the wood can actually exceed the weight of the wood fiber, resulting in a moisture content in excess of 100 percent. Wood dried outside, under a roof through a summer will typically have a moisture content of around 20 percent. Quite a difference!

Tables I have seen vary as to the usable Btus available from wood at different degrees of moisture content. Values for wood at a 20 percent moisture content are usually given as about 6,000 Btus per pound; wood with a 60 percent moisture content comes in at around 4,000 Btus. That's about a one-third loss in heat due solely to moisture.

If all wood contained the same amount of moisture, you could compare heating values of the various species simply by comparing their weights. The heating values of all woods have been tested and found to average out at about 6,400 Btus per pound. The difference in heating value per cord is thus almost entirely due to the density of the wood. Dense wood has more pounds per cord and thus more Btus. In actual practice, density comes down to weight, so we can say that, for wood of equal moisture content, the heavier the better. The catch here, of course, is the phrase "equal moisture content."

About the only way I know of assuring yourself that your wood is dry, is to buy it early and dry it yourself. Even then, there are variables. Split wood dries faster than wood with the bark left on. Wood stacked loosely where sun and wind can reach it, and covered with a roof, dries much faster than wood treated otherwise. Wood simply cut and left lying on the ground doesn't dry much.

You find people who want all "body wood"—that is, wood split from large blocks. They feel that it burns better than limb wood. If it does, it's because split wood dries faster than wood with the bark on, such as limb wood. Thus, body wood may be drier. Wood cut from dead trees is apt to be drier than wood cut from living trees, but not necessarily. It depends on how long the tree has been dead and where it has been. If it fell and was lying on the ground, it may contain more moisture than "live wood."

Some people think you can tell if wood is dry by looking at it. Some think that you can tell by banging two chunks together or by smelling it. Not so. You can't even tell by weight, unless you happen to have a wet and dry chunk of the same size to compare. Even then, I doubt it.

There is a plus side to buying your wood early and drying it yourself. You can usually get it cheaper and you have ample time to get it stacked up right. Of course, you tie up your money and space for that much longer, but in my opinion, it's worth it.

If you stack your wood outside on snow, stack it along a north-south axis. If you stack it east-west, it will topple over in the spring. The snow under the wood turns to ice. Then, when the sun hits it in the spring, the ice on the south side melts fastest, tipping the pile over toward the south. If you stack against a tree, pick a big one. Small trees sway in the wind and will tip your pile over.

If you build a woodshed, it pays to build one that is open on more than one side. If you have a single door to load and remove wood, you will have problems. If you load your shed over a period of time, you will end up with the driest wood at the back of the shed and the green wood up front. Even if you load all at once, and you don't use all the wood that winter, it ends up being covered up by the new wood you put in next year, unless you carry it all to the front. I load my shed from the back and fuel my stove from the front. This eliminates the first problem, but I still have some wood that has occupied the back of the shed for several years.

Firewood is almost always sold by volume, often in units. The only "official" unit generally recognized is the "cord" sometimes called the "full cord." This is a stack of wood encompassing 128 cubic feet. For loggers, a cord usually consists of eight-foot logs stacked four feet high by four feet wide.

Sometimes you can buy a load of logs for firewood from a pulp contractor. These are logs destined for the pulp mill, which he will sell to you either at a higher price than the mills pay or, possibly, for the same price if he can save on transportation. Pulp logs are cut eight feet, four inches long, and thus a "pulp cord" contains 4 percent more wood than a full cord.

These are useful measurements for large quantities of wood, but most wood is sold stove-length. Thus, we have the "face cord." A face cord consists of a stack of wood four feet high by eight feet long by the length of the chunks. This is a useful measurement, but only if the length of the chunks is specified, so people talk of "16-inch face cords" or "12-inch face cords."

The usual length of chunks is 16 inches, which means there are three face cords to a full cord. Four 12-inch face cords equals one full cord.

Some people—mainly men—feel that asking for prices in full cords shows a degree of sophistication that face cords lack. When I quote them the price of a full cord, they invariably ask, "How much is that a face cord?" These same guys always ask me how much a "thousand" I charge for lumber, then come right back and ask, "How much does that come to for an eight-foot 2 x 4?" Women generally just ask the price of what they want to buy.

A woodshed should be open on more than one side.

There are other terms used locally, such as "ricks" and "units," and, I'm sure, still others. If I were buying wood in one of these measurements, I would wonder why people who price things this way don't stick to the usual terms, and I would be a bit suspicious.

Stacking wood solely to measure it is a lot of work, so sometimes wood is delivered thrown loosely in a truck. Sometimes, also, the wood has been stacked but is delivered to you thrown in. This saves stacking it twice, but it also makes it difficult to see how much wood is actually on the truck.

I deliver wood with my ¾-ton pickup truck. If I throw the split wood in until it is heaped up in the center, it stacks up at between one and a quarter and one and a third 16-inch face cords. For more on calculating and comparing the volumes of "throw-on" versus stacked wood, see Chapter 17, page 154.

People wonder if you get more wood if it is split fine rather than left in bigger chunks. The answer to that is that you get the most with a mixture, so that the small wood fills in the gaps left between the larger chunks. After all is said and done, though, the really important thing is dry wood. Everything else is minor by comparison.

● Wood Stoves ❧ ◆

WE HEATED OUR 90-YEAR-OLD WISCONSIN FARMHOUSE for 12 years with just parlor stoves, and recently a gas-fired backup unit. It's reassuring to know that the backup is there, but it really bothers me to use it. I am a pretty sound sleeper, but if I'm in bed asleep and the thermostat kicks the gas on, it wakes me right up and I go down and stoke my stove. That's really sort of silly, since the price of my letting the gas do that one task is minimal, but it's the principle of the thing. I heat my house with wood; I don't heat it with gas. I'm even defensive about my backup and go out of my way to let people know that I only installed it so I could go away overnight occasionally.

This year I am installing an outside boiler and doing away with the two parlor stoves. Good riddance! No more ashes on the rug and bark on the floor. No more drafty floors. No more uneven heat. No more creosote-stained chimney walls upstairs. No more smoky-smelling clothes. No more worrying about chimney fires, and no more climbing up on the roof to clean and inspect the chimneys. I'm really glad to see them go!

And yet, I'm not really sure I'm doing the right thing. I'm going to miss those stoves and the comforting rituals that went with them. When I come in from the cold, there isn't going to be anyplace really hot where I can warm up instantly. There aren't going to be any potatoes and squash baking all day long on the stove. There isn't going to be any iron pot steaming away with instant hot water for coffee or cocoa.

Firing parlor stoves is an art, and it took me many winters to learn how to fire mine. My dad heated his office almost all his life with a Round Oak stove. When he retired he gave us the stove, and we hooked it up in our living room. He came to visit us sometimes in the winter when we had that stove going. Nobody ever mentioned it, but when Dad showed up, the stove duties reverted to him. Without even realizing it he would poke the fire, throw in wood, and fiddle with the dampers. It was second nature to him, and I'm afraid it has become that way with me.

Somebody told me once that men back up to a wood stove and warm their hands behind them, while women face the stove and warm their hands over it. I never really noticed any difference. Dad was a fur buyer, and not many women were trappers, so not many showed up in his office. With our friends, the stove stance seems about equal.

Dad always fired strictly by "feel." I don't do that. I rely on stack thermometers. With these thermometers, I can anticipate changes in room temperature by seeing what's going on inside the stove, thereby keeping things more even.

By saying that I "rely on" stack thermometers, I mean that I use them to tell me the stack temperature. I don't pay any attention to their "helpful" wording. If I did, I would freeze.

My thermometer calls temperatures from 32 to 210 degrees F "creosote range." I don't argue with that, but I do disagree with the implication that this is the only range in which creosote buildup is a problem. Unfortunately, it ain't that simple!

The range from 210 to 380 degrees F is labeled "best operation." That is pretty arbitrary—it all depends on stove design. It's not a big thing in any event.

What I really quarrel with is the labeling of anything above 380 degrees F as "overheated." If I never operated my stove in the "overheated" range, I would end up with my chimney full of creosote and probably a chimney fire to boot. The way I keep a clean chimney and avoid chimney fires is to fire way up into the "overheated" range every morning. If any creosote has accumulated during the previous 24 hours, I burn it out with what is actually a small, controlled, daily chimney fire. This works out well, because first thing in the morning is when I really want a good hot fire to drive away the overnight chill and get the coffee water boiling quickly.

Dad always controlled his stove with a stack damper. That's another place where we disagree. I took my stack dampers off and control strictly with the stove air inlets. This way, there is usually a slight vacuum in the stove, and any leakage is air into the stove rather than smoke into the room. Because of this, I get rather sloppy about maintaining my door gaskets. Since the stove always needs air, it doesn't bother me that a little sneaks in around the doors. I realize, though, that to let it go too far would be dangerous, since the first line of defense if a chimney fire should occur is to starve it by cutting off its air supply. You need a tight stove to do that.

Sometimes during a long winter I would start to feel sorry for myself and get after my wife and children for sticking me with all of the stove duties. "You're cold?" I would say, "Why don't you put some wood in the stove?" Even as I said it, though, I knew that I really didn't want them to put wood in the stove—or do anything else with it, for that matter. I knew they could never do it to my satisfaction. Worse yet, they might do it very well without any art at all. Just throw in a chunk and open the inlet damper. Surely I couldn't tolerate that. I was the fire-giver, the one who warmed the hearth for the women and children. That was a deep part of me and I couldn't let go.

Now, of course, I am letting go, but not really, I'm just moving outside, but it won't be the same. I can use really big wood now, so I won't have to do much splitting, and my boiler has enough capacity that I will only have to fire once or twice a day. I can certainly see the advantages in this system, but it seems so damned impersonal. Simply tending a machine! I can't believe that I will ever form any attachment to this boiler as I did to my parlor stoves.

I won't have that early morning time alone, sitting with my coffee, watching the stack temperature rise as my new charge of wood takes hold, seeing the glow through the stove's windows, switching on the blower and feeling that hot blast warming the chilly room. I won't be coming downstairs not knowing whether the house will seem warm or cold; not knowing whether the coals lasted overnight, so that all I will have to do is put in some chunks and open the dampers, or whether I will have to start from scratch.

The coals usually last. I let the fire burn down over the evening, then, just before I go to bed, I spread the coals out as evenly as possible. Then I take two split chunks and lay them flat-side-down over the coals. I place them so they don't touch. I don't want them to burn, just to cover the coals and keep them alive until morning. I shut my dampers down tightly. I can sleep well then, knowing no heat is being drawn up the chimney through open dampers and there is no fire in the house. In the morning, I roll the chunks over, exposing the coals. All I have to do then is add wood and open the dampers. If my coals die out during the night, I still have two bone-dry chunks to start out with.

I don't use kindling, nor do I "lay" a fire in the usual sense. I used to do that, but often the paper-and-kindling fire wouldn't spread to the chunks, and I would end up having to pull the charred chunks and black paper ashes out and start over. It wasn't bad enough that the fire failed to catch. What was really irritating was that the whole thing would collapse so that you couldn't put any more paper in under the remaining kindling. That and the hassle of having to deal with kindling led me to develop a better way.

This method only works with stoves that are loaded with the wood straight in. I have another stove in which the wood lies crosswise, fireplace-fashion. This is much harder to light, and I usually end up carrying a scuttle full of coals from my big stove in to get it started.

What I do is to load the stove with regular chunks. I roll up a newspaper to make a torch and hold the torch against the ends of the chunks until they catch. When the torch burns down, I push it into the stove and light another from it. Usually I can get the chunks burning with one torch, but occasionally it takes two. Once the fire has caught, I partially close the doors so that a draft is created—but not too strong a draft, or it will blow the flame out. I leave the doors partially open until the fire is roaring, adjusting them as needed to encourage the fire. I don't fully close the doors and set the dampers until I have a fire that is really pushing up the stack temperatures. This is actually the only time I can see "secondary combustion" in my stove's windows. The flames burn the windows clean of soot, and it's easy to observe.

I read somewhere that "secondary combustion seldom occurs in wood stoves." That has been my experience. I bought my stove because I was impressed with the full-color diagrams in the brochure showing primary and secondary combustion in reds and greens, with arrows showing heat going everywhere except out the chimney. Well, it's a good stove, probably as good as they get, and yet I don't see much secondary combustion during normal operation. The only way I ever see it is when I am firing full-bore in the morning. After that, nothing. It doesn't bother me, though. I doubt if other stoves do much better. It serves me well. At least, it used to.

Most of this will now be taken care of by the pump and forced draft controls on the boiler. A big improvement for sure! I just wish I felt better about it.

I don't keep close track of how much wood I burn in a year. The shed I use is the one that was here when I bought the farm, so it is a good indication of how much wood the original owners planned for when they built the house and shed in 1906.

I burn about a half a shedful every year. It's true that the previous owners cooked with wood and I don't, but the biggest difference is that I insulated the house. It's a two-story house, and there is no fireblocking in the walls. I simply poured cellulose by the bagful into the tops of the walls in the attic, and it ran right down to the foundation. Thus, I was able to insulate all the walls except under the windows. When I finished, I poured six inches of insulation in the attic and have been nice and warm ever since.

Some of the children of the original owners have come to visit. We always welcome their visits because they add to our knowledge of the farm and the people who farmed here until the Depression and drought hit, and they let the farm go to the county for back taxes. My father-in-law bought the place in 1947 for $2,500—290 acres and all the buildings!

The children, who are now old themselves, tell us of winter nights when Pa would sleep on a cot downstairs by the stove so he could get up and put wood in every few hours. I doubt that Wisconsin winters were any colder then than they are now, yet I don't do that. I go to bed and usually sleep right through the night.

I wonder why they never insulated the house. They did the barn. The room with the stanchions for the cattle had sawdust insulation in all the walls and was right below the haymow, so it must have been nice and warm. They say that if a cow died during the winter, the farmer had to get another one to replace it, since only body heat warmed the barn, and the loss of one cow could jeopardize the whole herd.

I have asked people why the old-timers didn't insulate their houses. Most people have no idea, but some have told me that it was because they feared rodent and insect infestation if they poured in sawdust. That may be, but cellulose is basically newsprint. It's strange that some enterprising person didn't produce insulation. Maybe they did, and the builders of my house simply elected not to spend the money for it. Farmers are notorious for taking better care of their cows than their families.

People in this part of the country say that it takes about a week of labor to get enough wood to heat through a winter. They say this is true whether they cut the wood themselves or work at their regular job that week and buy it. That sounds about right to me. It comes pretty easy to me, but it must have been a real chore years ago when all they had were crosscut saws and teams to haul it home on sleighs. From the old pictures, it seems as if they cut their wood in the winter when there was less farm work than in other seasons. Still, they had lots of continuing chores that had to be done in the winter. Just pumping and hauling water for the livestock must have eaten up a lot of time.

The well and pump are closer to the barn than to the house. That was an annoyance to us until we got plumbing in, but I'm sure the cows needed more water than the family, so it makes sense that it should be that way. They also kept hogs and chickens and sheep and, of course, horses. All these animals had to be watered, and this situation was further complicated by the layout of the farmstead.

All these buildings are separate, and, while they are arranged in a sort of circle, they are quite a ways apart from each other. That must have made for lots of snow shoveling. I am told that they separated the buildings so that, if there were a fire, it wouldn't take them all. Well, no fire took them all, but the county did!

I admit that I don't know much about farming and almost nothing about how farming was done in the old days. I stand in awe of the work those people were able to do with the tools they had, but sometimes it seems to me that, while they clearly were hard workers, they weren't all that swift. Principles of heat transfer and combustion have been known for centuries, and yet the folks here didn't insulate their houses, nor did they use airtight stoves. They just threw in more wood.

Hindsight is keen however, and I wonder what people will say about us in a hundred years or so. I'll bet my farmhouse will still be standing, although sometimes I think it may revert to the county once again.

There is a footnote to all this. Since I completed this chapter, I got my outside wood burner and used it for several heating seasons as well as two summers to heat my domestic hot water. It did everything I asked of it. I shut my electric water heater off and my electric bill went down by about $20 per month—this by burning about two chunks of wood a day, plus all my burnable trash in the summer. I operated it, filled it with antifreeze, and shut it down for a month when I was away in the winter with no ill effects. Then, it started leaking.

Because I had filled the boiler with antifreeze, there was no internal corrosion, but it developed a leak right at the top of the firebox. It was still under warranty, so I called the factory. They said that all carbon-steel boilers would eventually leak. It was just a question of time. They stood by their warranty, offering me the choice of replacement with another carbon-steel model with the warranty to continue on the new stove, or an upgrade to a stainless-steel model with a ten-year warranty at about $1,500 extra. That was the option I took. (I guess it wouldn't hurt to identify the make of stove. I didn't hesitate to name the saw manufacturers, so why not the stove builders? My stove was a Heatmor manufactured by Reed Metal Works Inc., Warroad, Minnesota.) They did right by me.

There is a footnote to this footnote. For several years my knees started bothering me every fall. I thought this was just a function of age plus cold weather. I tried wearing knee warmers, but they didn't help. Recently I began to notice that I didn't seem to have the problem. I didn't understand why the pain should have gone away. I was just thankful for small favors.

As I thought about it, however, I realized that one thing that had changed in my life that could have affected my knees was the outside wood burner. When I had the parlor stoves, I was an obsessive poker and stirrer. With the two stoves going, I must have done 20 or 30 deep knee bends a day, often with chunks in my arms. That's not a good way to treat aging knees. With the outside stove, I simply throw in the wood and take out the ashes from the waist-high fire door. I don't do any knee bends.

20

● Vehicles ◆◆

IF YOU ARE GOING TO DO ANY SORT OF MEANINGFUL WORK in your woodlot, you need vehicles. Unfortunately, there is essentially no limit to the variety of vehicles you could put to use. Because you will probably attempt the whole range of operations that the big guys do, you could easily use all of the machinery they have, from ATV's to Cat dozers. It's a sad truth that, just because you aren't going to do much logging work, it doesn't make what you are going to do any easier. Individual logs, as I have said in earlier chapters, weigh what they weigh regardless of how many there are.

Most woodland owners I know start out with a used farm tractor and a beater pickup truck. Those two will actually take you a long way.

My truck is a 1976 Ford F250, 3/4-ton pickup. I tried a standard 1/2-ton pickup, but it lacked the clearance I need to drive on my stumpy roads. It is not a four-wheel drive, and sometimes I wish it were-—but, overall, it is a good choice. People who own 4WD trucks and use them in the woods tend to tear them up pretty badly. If you have a 4WD truck, you should use the 4WD feature only to get you out of trouble, not to get you into trouble. Always operate in two-wheel drive unless you need the extra traction to get you out of a bad spot. The truck will last longer that way.

Those "high-rise" trucks you sometimes see have no useful function in the woods. Even with oversized tires, they don't buy you much clearance, and it's a lot more work to load wood—or anything else for that matter—into a high truck bed.

In addition to my pickup, I have a one-ton flatbed dump truck, which I use for delivering firewood. I can stack seven face cords of 16-inch wood on it and dump it off in the customer's yard. I always offer to let the customer scale the wood before I dump it since it's easy to do at that time and impossible afterwards. Nobody ever takes me up on this, but I offer.

Nice wood is not always handled by nice equipment.

If you use a dump truck, be sure that you are on level ground when you raise the bed. It's possible to tip a truck over sideways if you raise the bed on a sideslope.

Even though real junker trucks are often advertised as "good wood haulers," it pays to buy a pretty good truck—but not too good. If you live any distance at all from your woods, you probably need a truck that has sufficient lights and brakes to be street-legal. I ran my old truck unlicensed for a year or so, but it turned out to be a real hassle. I ended up sneaking along back roads with an illegal truck. On the other hand, if you get too nice a truck, you may be reluctant to use it as it needs to be used in the woods.

Maybe, then, you need two trucks—or think you do. Chances are that you will only be operating your woods truck over short distances. Because of this, fuel economy counts for very little. Reliability is everything. It doesn't really matter if it burns oil, as long as it starts.

I hired a guy to haul some logs for me once. He had mounted a loader on the back of an old truck and smashed out the rear window so he could operate it by turning around and kneeling on the seat. I rode with him to the sawmill where we were delivering the logs. He had a case of oil sitting on the seat and a flexible tube sticking up through the floorboards. After we had gone about 20 miles, he pulled a rag out of the tube and poured a quart of oil down it into the engine. As he did this, he kept right on talking as if this was something everyone did. It was a first for me.

Power brakes aren't of any real value in the woods, but power steering is. You do a lot of steering in the woods. Also, I can't imagine operating an automatic transmission truck in the woods. The reason is, you need to be able to select the gear you need to be in before you actually need it. An automatic transmission waits until you are in trouble and then reacts.

Snow tires are a definite plus and should be left on the truck year-round. Several years ago, I bought a set of chains for my truck. They had to be ordered specially and I never really got the knack of putting them on right. They would loosen and then fly off, and I would be stuck lying in the snow trying to get them back on. This would usually happen on a town road when I was going reasonably fast. I never tried them again after that winter. Wood ashes work really well for getting traction in snow and ice. I always carry two full buckets in winter.

The key to traction is weight over the rear tires. That's fine, but there isn't much money in simply hauling the same wood into and out of the woods. To make any economic sense at all, you have to go in empty and come out loaded. Knowing this, you can reasonably back into places where you would have trouble getting out, if you know that you are going to load up and thus will have better traction going out. You have to be careful when doing this, however. Weight in the rear will settle the truck down on its springs and sink the tires into the ground. This combination can cause you to hang up on stumps you cleared easily on your way in. You can literally end up "stumped."

On soft ground and in snow, it is the corners that get you, especially corners on an uphill grade. You have to slow down or you may spin out, yet when you slow down, you lose traction. Sometimes, if you do it often enough, you will wear grooves for the tires in the road, and you can then get around faster without slowing. Often, however, driving on woods roads makes them worse rather than better. Each trip in and out is a new experience. The fact that you have made it before is no guarantee that you will make it again. Just the opposite may be true.

Even if your truck is a beater, you have to make some accommodations for it. You can't just go crashing through the brush like it was a tank. Don't ever think that everything that can be torn off already is. There are always brake and fuel lines, which must stay intact to even move the truck, even if all of the electrical wires are gone. You won't go far with a punctured radiator, and you won't easily find anyone willing or able to repair old radiators anymore.

Tires passing over branches lying on the ground will often push one end of them up and into wiring and tubing on the truck undercarriage. You have to clear these off before driving the truck in the area. You can eliminate a lot of this hassle by starting your work at the far side of the woods you are working in. Then, by using your felling skills, you can fell all the trees you cut away from the truck. Do this, and you will always be working, walking, and driving over relatively clear ground.

Still, eventually you will do damage to your truck. One problem I have is tearing off front bumpers. I concentrate on what's behind me when I'm backing and sometimes cramp the wheel sharply, hooking the bumper on a tree. Of course, I have torn off or badly bent all outside mirrors. I've also punctured several radiators and torn off countless mufflers and tailpipes.

Most beater pickups I see in my area lack tailgates. This is a real problem if you are hauling wood. Try to avoid damaging your tailgate by never backing up with it down. Having the gate down not only makes the truck longer than you are used to, but it is also so low you can't see it. A tailgate bends easily, and it doesn't take much bending before it won't close. If you hit something with the gate up, the bumper takes the hit, which is, after all, what it is designed for.

Some people customize their woods trucks by replacing the bumpers with four-inch pipes and putting screens across their grills. These are good ideas if you are able to do the work yourself.

Regardless of the hassle, I always work with my truck close by. When I'm loading firewood, I'll get in and back the truck as little as four or five feet to get it up close to the wood. I throw the chunks in with the tailgate down until I get to where they are falling out the back; then I close the gate and heap up the load. My limit is never weight, even with green oak. My truck will haul all I can throw in.

I also depend on my truck to take me and my equipment in and out of the woods when I'm logging. Before I start work, I always turn the truck around so that it is facing out of the woods. I leave the keys in it and never fell anything across its path. If it is stuck, I free it up before I start working. If I find that I have moved away from the truck, I move it when I refuel my saw to keep it close (although not so close that I have to worry about hitting it with a tree).

I think having a clear "retreat" path out of the woods at all times is as important as having a retreat path away from a falling tree. I assume that, if Marcia or I got hurt, the other would be rattled and shouldn't have to maneuver the truck any more than is necessary.

This is an example of "before-need planning," and it should become a part of your daily routine. It takes no longer to turn the truck around before you start than it does on your way out, and it just might save your life. We are also well aware of where the nearest hospital is located and the fastest way to get there. You don't have to spend your day worrying about injuries, but it pays to think and talk these things through and keep them in the back of your mind.

We don't carry a first-aid kit in the truck, even though we should. What I do have, however, is a four-inch compression bandage tucked up inside the webbing of my hardhat. It's been there for a long time, and I hope it stays there a lot longer. It is there rather than in the truck because, if I ever needed it, I would need it immediately. The blood from even a bad cut will gradually clot if given a chance. That is what the bandage is for. Wrapped tightly over a wound, it should slow the blood flow down to allow clotting to take place. I hope that, if I ever need it, I will remember it is there.

When I cut firewood, I work alone. That, of course, carries with it a whole list of dangers, especially in winter, when exposure and hypothermia become a problem if you are, for example, pinned under a tree.

People caution against working alone in the woods, and rightly so, but these same people tell you that felling trees is a one-person job, so take your pick. The OSHA regulations specify that, except in special cases, felling is a one-person job.

Still, aside from firewood, Marcia and I work together. We feel this is the safest way for us. It may not be for you. Marcia not only does her share of the work, she also provides a second opinion on hazards that arise. She is by nature more cautious than I am and balances out the work. She often sees hazards I don't see, or sees things we both see in a different light. Even if she doesn't say anything, just the fact that she is there, watching, tempers my recklessness.

The agencies that make up these worker safety rules usually seek input from the industries they are regulating. In this case, OSHA took comments from the timber industry. The people commenting represented companies that employ woods workers, not the workers themselves. It is entirely understandable that employers are not keen on regulations that would require them to essentially double their workforce. Thus, don't expect to see any studies or regulations that would favor making felling a two-person operation.

This is not to say, however, that working alone is a bad or dangerous practice. In most cases, it is not, but there are some cases where teamwork pays off. It does for us. You have to decide whether it does for you.

There is no really safe way to work in the woods. All you can do is minimize the hazards, and then take your pick among those that remain. One obvious precaution you should take when working alone is to let someone know where you will be and what you will be doing. From long experience, Marcia knows about when I should be back. That offers some assurance, but sometimes it works the other way when I hurry to try and get back at the usual time and take shortcuts that I might not take if no one were waiting for me.

Cellular phones are an option we haven't explored, but like CB radios before them, they aren't practical things to keep right with you. And they won't do you much good back in the truck if you are pinned by a tree. There are devices that detect motion and sound an alarm if no motion is sensed for a certain interval. All I know about them is that they exist.

I've known guys who go out with a saw in a toboggan or sled, or on skis or snowshoes to work in the winter. I wouldn't do that. I did work one winter out of a snowmobile. It worked okay, but I wasn't very good at operating it, and there were no trails and lots of hidden brush. It was an old model with a reverse gear, which helped. Even at that, it seemed unrealistic to think that I could pull the starter cord and drive it out if I was hurt. Some people do it, though. I knew a guy who cut firewood all winter using a snowmobile. He hauled the wood out behind the snowmobile in a car hood, which he used as a sled. Another guy I know cuts two slim poles, and he and his wife use them as a "stretcher" to carry chunks out to the road.

All this is a lot easier if you have good roads. If you are just starting out planting what will someday be a forest, the thing to do is to plan your roads in advance and don't plant trees in them. If you have to cut trees to make a road, you end up with stumps. If the trees you cut sprout from the stump, like oaks and aspens do, you will be fighting them forever.

In our pine plantations, stumps bond with the root systems of the living trees and remain "alive" forever. I'm still bouncing over the stumps of trees I cut 20 years ago, and will be 20 years from now. They are as sharp as ever and are all black from rubber scraped off the tires of the various vehicles they have abused over the years. They stick up higher now than they did originally because the soil around them has been packed down. They are so full of sand and grit that I can't cut them down without ruining any chain I use.

Personally, I like straight roads. Some people prefer winding roads. Either way, they have to be wide to accommodate large equipment and to act as fire lanes. If you are laying out roads before planting, it's hard to imagine that they have to be as wide as they should be. In fact, you should make them about 30 feet wide. That seems like a huge bite to take out of your woods, but it fills in fast once your trees start to branch out. Fire lanes actually serve two purposes: (1) to act as a fire break and (2) to allow access to firefighting equipment. Good roads not only increase your enjoyment of your woods and make working in them easier, but they are also an important safety consideration.

Tractors

Of all the vehicles we've owned and used around our farm, we've only named one, our old Ford 9N tractor.

"Trusty" was the first vehicle we bought specifically for use in the woods. We've used him to drag logs out, to "skid" pulpwood with a front-end loader, and to plow our roads. He has pulled stumps and hauled firewood. There is something about the squat shape and friendly "chug-chug" of an old farm tractor that endears itself to its owner.

It's hard to remember that this cheerful vehicle is a real killer, especially when used in the woods. Farm tractors are designed for use in flat fields. They were never meant to operate in hilly or rough terrain, and they certainly were not designed to work in the woods.

One obvious hazard is rollover, either sideways or by flipping over backwards. Modern tractors are equipped with rollover protection systems (ROPS), consisting mainly of a steel framework which, if the operator is not thrown out, should prevent the weight of the overturned machine from crushing him. Obviously, this will only work if the operator wears a seat belt. If you don't, and you are thrown out, the ROPS is just one more thing to land on you. Tractors are designed to carry just one person, the operator. There are no belts or seats for anyone else, and no one else should be there. Especially, no children.

Generally speaking, tractors are more stable back-to-front than they are side-to-side. If you have to climb a grade such as a ditch with your tractor, it is best to climb it head on, saving any turning until you are on level ground. If the slope is really severe, the safest way is to back up it.

One of the most frequent causes of rollover accidents with tractors is improper hitching of loads. All tractors have hitching points. It is extremely important that you hitch all loads to these points and nowhere else.

Hitching points are designed so that, when pulling a load, the pulling force is applied to the tractor at a point below the rear axle. Pulling force applied here will act to rotate the tractor body around the rear axle, forward, onto the front wheels. This is a very safe, stable situation.

If you hitch loads anywhere but these points, force may be applied above the rear axle. In this situation, the force will tend to rotate the tractor body backwards, flipping it over onto its back. Even if the load is light and seems to present no danger, any force applied in this manner destabilizes the tractor. If you were to hit a rock or stump with the front wheels, especially at high speed, that little extra might be enough to flip the tractor back onto you.

Any weight that acts to hold the front wheels down exerts a stabilizing influence; thus, a tractor with a front loader is more stable than one without (provided that the loader is not extended upward).

There have been cases where tractor rear wheels have been frozen to the ground, and, in an effort to free them, an operator has raced the engine and popped the clutch. Since the wheels couldn't rotate, the torque was absorbed by the tractor body, which flipped backwards, killing the driver. You could get the same effect trying to power your way out of a mudhole or jamming the rear wheels on stumps or in sand. The further the rear wheels sink down, the more hazardous the situation becomes.

A technique used by some people to free a tractor stuck in the mud is to lash a small log to both tires, and then try and drive out using the log for traction. If you do this, lash the log to the top of the tires so that you will be backing out. This way, if it flies off, it won't come up and hit you.

Another source of serious accidents is the power takeoff shaft or PTO. It is used to power equipment from the tractor. Woodland owners often use it to power brush cutters and snow blowers. I also use mine to operate a conveyor to load firewood into semis.

One of the big dangers with PTOs is that they don't appear to be all that dangerous—simply a short, slowly turning shaft. Don't be fooled. My neighbor got his nylon shoelace wrapped up in his PTO shaft and it was slowly squeezing him to death, breaking all his ribs, until it tore off his foot, releasing him and saving his life.

All PTOs should have protective covers, which shield the entire shaft when it is not in use. Lots of old tractors are missing these covers. If you don't have one, you can make one out of a small can or piece of pipe. Don't depend on the "engage" lever to keep the PTO in neutral; mine constantly slips into gear for no apparent reason. If you have to do any work around the shaft or any machinery driven by it, again, don't rely on the gears to keep you safe—shut the tractor off before getting down from the seat.

I know that this is easy advice to give but tough to carry out. After all, all you're going to do is to pull that stick out of the wheel and then get right back on. It started hard this morning and might not start at all if you shut it off now. Remember my neighbor? That's what he was going to do.

Our current tractor is a 35 hp four-wheel-drive SAME diesel. When I first bought it, about 15 years ago, I also bought a "cart skidder," which is a special trailer fitted with a knuckleboom loader that I used to "skid" pulpwood out of my plantations and stack it alongside the road for pick-up. Since then I have bought a regular forwarder and use the SAME now for tree planting and snow blowing.

The snow blower works fine on our driveway, but it doesn't work anywhere else, such as around my sawmill or in the woods. Even in the driveway, I have to be sure I get all the larger sticks out of its way before it snows, or it will shear off pins every time it hits one. That rules it out as a practical machine to use anywhere but the driveway.

The forwarder is built like a tank. The driver's area is surrounded with heavy mesh, the floor is steel deck plating, and the entire belly is covered with steel sheets. It is roofed over with I-beams and plates. What a difference from a farm tractor! This is a machine that is truly designed to go in harm's way. It has both ROPS and FOPS (falling object protection system).

For years, Marcia did all our skidding with the cart, and then with the forwarder. The controls are all hydraulic, and so there is no reason why women can't operate them as well as men. This is also true of the harvesting machines that have taken over much of plantation thinning. When these machines were first introduced in our area, quite a few contractors hired women to operate them. This seemed to work out well. The contractors said that the output per day for the

An expensive forwarder with full ROPS and FOPS protection.

women operators was slightly less than their male counterparts, but overall the women's output was higher because they were less rough on the machines and so had fewer breakdowns.

The newer machines had heated and air-conditioned cabs and were equipped with radios and tape players. In spite of all this, I don't know of any women who stayed with it. I don't know why. Operators that I know of now are all men.

Forwarders are not practical machines for the average woodland owner. And yet, many woodland owners do with small tractors exactly what I do with my forwarder. The only difference is that they do less of it. This is one of the dilemmas of "hobby farming." You need to do the same work as the professionals, but you can't afford the equipment they use. Compromise is thus necessary.

While you do need to do the same work as the pros, you don't have to do as much of it, and you should be under no pressure to do it rapidly. You can drag logs out one at a time; you can carry pulpsticks and firewood on a trailer or in the bucket of a front loader. You can substitute time and patience for power and efficiency. At least, up to a point you can. The hazards the forwarder is designed to deal with are real, however, and are all there regardless of how you do the job.

One very real hazard involves dead trees and dead limbs. These "widow-makers" present a major threat to chain-saw operators, but are just as dangerous for equipment operators. They are the reason for the I-beam roof on the forwarder.

Anytime you bump into a tree you place yourself in a dangerous position. Sometimes, I have intentionally pushed over dead trees with my forwarder. Like a tractor, the point at which I contact the tree is pretty low to the ground. Thus, the tree hardly ever simply falls forward as I push. Often, it will break in the middle, with the top tipping backwards onto the roof of the machine as I drive through and under it.

Sometimes the trunk breaks with the initial impact, with the bottom portion falling forward under the machine and the top coming straight down onto the roof. These things scare me when I'm in the cab of my forwarder. They might very well kill you on your tractor. Striking even a living tree with the tractor or the load, as you might if you are turning while pulling a load, can easily break large limbs free, which can fall and strike you.

So much for hazards from above. Even more threats are in store from beneath, in this case, spearing.

"Spring poles" are tough, limber saplings that will bend under load rather than breaking off. As discussed in Chapter 13, they present a hazard in timber felling when they become bent under a fallen tree. They have to be cut carefully to keep them from snapping up when released, possibly striking the cutter or his saw, with predictable results. They are also a hazard to equipment operators. If you have a lot of undergrowth in your woods, you probably have a lot of potential spring poles.

One of the benefits of using tractors in the woods is that, unlike cars or trucks, you ordinarily don't have to clear roads. You can simply push over pretty good-sized saplings as you go along, thus making your work a lot easier and avoiding the sharp stubs you would leave if you cut them off with your saw.

There's nothing wrong with that. The problem arises when you turn around and drive back out of the woods in the opposite direction on the same path. Now, a few of the saplings you pushed over on the way in are pointed right at you like spears. Tractors afford no protection against this form of hazard.

On my tractor, a spear could come in right over the front axle and be guided up and into my lap. Bad enough if you are alone, but tragic if you are giving a child a ride in the woods! What's worse is that the pressure of the spear would probably push your foot off the clutch, causing the tractor to leap forward, pushing the spear into your body.

This is not a farfetched scenario. Over the years I have read articles about people injured in these situations. A man killed by a falling limb was found sitting on his tractor, which was against a tree, out of gas. Another man took a spear clear through his body, which he was somehow able to cut off. Then he drove himself to a hospital with the rest of the stick still in him. Imagine doing that.

Tractors can be reinforced to lessen these dangers, but it is, at best, a cobble-up job, trying to make a machine do work it was never designed to do. I believe that in this, as in many safety problems, knowledge is the best defense. Take the time to think things through. Be aware that what you are doing is not what your machinery was designed to do and, thus, it is probably more hazardous than it appears.

I have found that, if you plan to do something you haven't done before, it pays to discuss your ideas with some other person first. Your confidant may not be at all knowledgeable about what you plan to do, but just the mental exercise required to explain your plan, so that it makes sense to another person, forces you to think the task through more clearly than if you had just gone ahead with it. Better to feel a bit sheepish than a bit dead.

Finally, tractors are noisy and ear protection is cheap. Hearing damage is cumulative and irreversible. As I sit typing this, I hear a constant ringing in my ears—the result of a lot of low-level noise over a period of years. I'll hear it for the rest of my life, and it won't get any better. I can only hope it won't get worse.

At our place, Trusty the tractor doesn't work in the woods anymore; he is semiretired. He moves sawdust around the sawmill and plows a little snow. His place has been taken by more modern machines that whine and snarl rather than chug-chug along. They are more efficient and safer to use than Trusty, since they are either designed or modified to work in the woods. They have no names.

I'm not about to advise anyone to avoid using farm tractors for woods work. After all, that's probably why most woodland owners buy them. I will, however, urge everyone to weigh the risks carefully before operating farm tractors in the woods.

Tractors are basically machines for pulling things, not carrying things. Luckily, my tractor fenders are flat across the top, and I can hold my saw on there with a rubber cord. If you are not that lucky, you may want to consider making a saw scabbard out of wood and attaching it to your tractor (see Chapter 4, page 40).

Unless you plan on attending antique tractor shows, it doesn't pay to buy a tractor that's too old, and it certainly doesn't pay to buy the old style with the narrow front wheels. Any tractor you buy should have "live" hydraulics and a three-point hitching arrangement. Starting sometime in the 1950s, all tractors began to have these.

Hitching gear is classified by "categories." These are only related to size, ranging from 00 up to 3. "Live" hydraulic systems utilize hydraulic pumps, which are driven directly by the engine and thus run constantly when the engine is running. Older tractors' hydraulic pumps only run when the clutch is engaged.

A front loader is almost a necessity for woods work. You can buy loaders for four-wheel-drive tractors, but, because of their large front wheels, loaders for them are expensive and not available for all models. That's really too bad because, by going to four-wheel drive, you can do almost everything with a tractor of around 30 to 35 horsepower. Two-wheel-drive tractors of the same horsepower won't do nearly as much. If you put a loader on your tractor, you'll need a counterweight on the back if you want to lift much of anything.

If you are going to drive in the woods with your tractor, it won't be long before you shear off an air valve stem on a tire. This is inevitable if you don't protect them. The best way to protect stems is to weld pipe nipples over them and screw on pipe caps. Unfortunately, you can't weld on the rim with the tire on or you will melt the rubber. So, you can either do the wheels one at a time as the stems shear off, or you can take all the tires off and get it all done at once. It's up to you. Being an optimist, I did them one at a time as they sheared off. Either way, you'll end up doing them all eventually. This, of course, is also true of trailers used in the woods.

I haul all my firewood with a trailer. I used to use my truck, but since my hauls are short, I find it is easier with a trailer. My trailer is made from an old car frame and is long and fairly narrow. It's a flatbed with stakes on the ends. I can stack three rows of 16-inch wood on it. It's a lot easier to load and unload than the truck, or a trailer with sides, would be.

You would think that, with all the practice I get, I would be good at backing my trailer. Not so. The only advice I can give on that score is to concentrate either on the tongue or the tail end of the trailer. Don't glance back and forth. That is confusing.

Several times over the years I have considered buying a Norse- or Farmi-style winch for my tractor. These devices

A 35-horsepower, 4WD tractor with firewood trailer.

essentially convert your tractor into a cable skidder. They attach to your tractor hitch and have prongs that stick into the ground when you lower them. A cable runs out on a winch drum operated by your PTO. You can use it to winch logs up to the tractor, and then, using the tractor hydraulics through the three-point hitch, you can raise the ends of the logs up off the ground and drag them out.

Having one of these winches would enable me to salvage logs that are currently inaccessible. In

Norse skidding winch driven by tractor PTO.

my case, however, these are not valuable logs, and I'm probably ahead of the game by just leaving them. I don't have to intensively manage every square yard of my woods; I can just leave some to grow undisturbed.

If you have valuable timber that is not accessible with a tractor alone, you may want to look into one of these winches, but consider this: In order for me to sell logs roadside, I have to stack them up. I can't just leave individual logs lying on the ground. You can't pile logs with one of these winches. All you can do is to drag them out and leave them on the ground. If your timber is valuable, truckers might be willing to pick up individual logs; also, some log buyers may require that the logs be laid out individually for scaling. If not, you will need some means to stack logs up at your landing.

For me, the answer was a "cart skidder." The one I bought cost about $10,000 and consisted of a trailer with a knuckleboom loader attached. There are other models where the boom is mounted on the tractor and the cart is separate.

To operate these loaders, you need a separate hydraulic pump driven by your tractor's PTO, as well as a separate oil reservoir. I used mine for several years to "skid" pulpwood. It was a rugged machine and did all I asked of it. I could easily haul more than a cord per trip. For tires it had used 16-ply airplane tires, which never went flat.

It was not a really high-production combination. To operate the loader I had to get down off the tractor and stand on a platform built onto the tongue of the trailer. I also had to put the stabilizing "feet" down every time or the trailer would tip over. I could deck logs with it, but it didn't have enough reach to load trucks.

The reason I sold it, however, was not that it didn't work well. Under certain conditions, I just couldn't pull it. This was not because my tractor lacked power, but rather because I was operating in sand, and all four of my tractor wheels would simply dig holes when I tried to move with a load.

The main reason for this was that, with a trailer, the load provides resistance to moving, but because the weight is not over the tractor wheels, it does nothing to promote traction. With my current forwarder, on the other hand, the bunk is directly over the rear wheels, and I can't imagine it ever getting stuck. So far, it never has.

Forwarders and skidders are expensive—even old used ones. The purchase of our forwarder committed us to harvesting timber for a living. You can't justify an investment of more than $25,000 for a single machine on a part-time, hobby basis. If, however, buying that machine enables you to earn a living, then it's not such a big investment.

I should explain that forwarders haul the logs in a "bunk," where they are placed with a knuckleboom loader. Skidders drag logs on the ground. They either drag them with a cable or with a grapple attached to the skidder. They don't have loaders, which means they can't deck logs or load trucks.

Our forwarder not only hauls out all our logs and pulpwood, it also loads the deck on our sawmill and hauls away the slabwood. It has become indispensable.

If you want to cut and stack your own wood but can't justify the purchase of a big machine, you may be able to contract out the skidding. Be sure and check, however, before you start. When we started out, it was hard to sell pulpwood, and stacking it along side the road opened markets for us. There are a lot of trucks in our area that have loaders and can pick up roadside wood. There are far fewer forwarders around, and their owners were reluctant to move them to the job site to haul the few loads we were producing. We bought the forwarder to open up markets for us rather than to simply increase the price of the product.

Logging machines, generally, have plenty of brute strength, but unfortunately they have no instinct for self-preservation. They will use their strength to destroy themselves if you don't watch them. The engines are geared way down to where there is almost nothing they can't bend or break, sometimes so smoothly you don't even realize it is happening. It seems silly, but, because they are so strong, you have to be gentle with them.

Like most mechanical things, forwarders are a jumble of compromises. You want them to have a high wheelbase so that they don't hang up on stumps, but, at the same time, you want a low center of gravity so they don't tip easily. You want them to haul a big payload, but you also want them narrow enough so they can pass between trees in the woods. The result is a useful machine, but one that is unstable on side hills. Most people I know who have operated a forwarder for any length of time have tipped one at least once, and that includes me.

My forwarder is 7 feet, 10 inches wide, and the rows in my plantations after the first thinning average 12 feet. That's more than two feet of clearance on a side. You would think that would be more than enough, but I still bark trees. The tops of the stakes on the bunk are about 12 feet off the ground. With that height, it doesn't take much of an obstacle on the ground to tip the machine enough to eat up the two-foot side clearance, and so I bark trees driving in a straight line in rows. I can often feel the slight hesitation when a stake bites into a tree. It's almost as painful to me as scraping the skin off my nose would be.

Unreviewed Safety Questions

A friend of mine from Florida says that the most frightening sight that state has to offer is an old guy driving a new Winnebago. I thought that was pretty funny since I don't own a Winnebago and—at least when it comes to senior-citizen discounts—I'm not yet considered an old guy. Still, the more I thought about it, the more I realized that the logic behind the humor does, in fact, apply to me, and possibly to you as well. Let me give you a couple of examples.

When I decided to go into custom tree planting, I planned to use the one-ton flat-bed dump truck that I bought for delivering firewood to transport my planting equipment. I figured I could drive my tractor, with the planter attached, onto the bed, chain it down, and drive from site to site. For a ramp I used two 12-foot oak 2 x 10 planks. I drilled holes in the ends so I could bolt the tops of these planks onto the rear of the truck bed.

When it came time to drive up this ramp for the first time, I double-checked everything, and even though the bed looked awfully high and the planks looked awfully skinny, I slowly started up. All went well until I got almost to the top. At this point, the truck bed tipped up, dumping me, the tractor, and the planks onto the ground. Luckily, the front wheels had not reached the truck bed, so the tractor fell straight down and no real harm was done, but it was close.

What I didn't know then was that dump truck beds are not held down. They are pivoted toward the rear. Other than that, they simply lie on the truck frame. Putting weight on the back with none on the front causes them to tip like a teeter-totter. After that initial scare, I chained the front of the bed to the frame, and now I drive up without incident.

My second example involves my pulpwood forwarder.

The guy I bought it from delivered it on a semitrailer and drove it off the trailer into my yard. I paid him, and he left. The next morning, I started it up and drove out my driveway. At the end of the driveway, I had to turn right onto the road. When I got to the turn, I took my foot off the accelerator, pushed in the clutch and tried to turn the steering wheel right. The wheel wouldn't turn. The forwarder went across the road, into a ditch, hit a culvert, and almost turned over. The engine died, and there I was, hung up on the culvert, until I recovered enough poise to restart the engine and back off.

After some experimenting, I determined that the engine had to be turning over fairly fast for the steering to work. I should have raced the engine as I pushed in the clutch. When I did this, all went well.

The steering uses hydraulic rams. The rams require high oil pressure and flow to work. The hydraulic oil pump, which is driven by the engine, creates the oil pressure and flow. An idling engine does not deliver oil at high enough pressure and flow to make steering possible.

Again, once I understood the problem, avoiding trouble was simple.

Thinking about these incidents, I tried to see where I went wrong and to identify some method or principle that I could apply to similar situations to avoid dangers. I bought the equipment used, so I had no owner's manuals. I doubt the previous owners would have pointed these hazards out, even if I had asked them if there was anything that I should know.

The old guy with the Winnebago can only practice so much in his driveway. Eventually he's going to be out on the interstate, bopping along at 60 to 70 miles per hour. Likewise, I had to actually attempt my schemes before I exposed the pitfalls.

Nothing in my two years of operating my truck to deliver firewood exposed the hazard awaiting me when I used it for something new. Nothing in a lifetime of driving indicated that racing the engine while pushing in the clutch was the proper way to turn a corner.

I spent a good portion of my life working in nuclear power plants. If some new operation was planned, we had to determine if any "unreviewed safety questions" existed before we started. These were not obviously dangerous things; they were simply things that were new to us, and thus might contain hazards we hadn't considered. If it was determined that "unreviewed" questions did exist, they had to be reviewed and resolved before we could proceed.

This is probably a good procedure to follow in any operation. When you depart from standard procedures, ask yourself if what you want to do includes things you've never done before. If so, consider any unreviewed safety questions, which should be resolved before you begin.

Preventive Maintenance and Troubleshooting

In a way, preventive maintenance and troubleshooting are interchangeable activities, in that the less preventive maintenance you do, the greater opportunity you will have to troubleshoot.

There really isn't much to be said about preventive maintenance. Everyone knows it pays off in the long run, but it's often a messy business and easy to put off. Grease, however, is cheaper than steel, and a lot easier to apply. If you sell wood and buy iron, you are at a disadvantage in any event, and having to repair that iron just makes it worse.

There are a lot of grease fittings on my forwarder and almost none of them are easy to get at. Some of them depend on stopping the forwarder just right or you can't reach them at all. Most require me to either climb up on the boom, or lie on my back in the dirt or snow. It's not hard for me to put something like that off.

When I do delay greasing, I sometimes use the excuse to myself that it's bad to overgrease. I know when I say it that it only applies to bearings, and not all of them. Most of what I grease are bushings. You can't overgrease a bushing.

There are two, seemingly contradictory, points that can be made about greasing. They are:

1. Just because you can't grease all the fittings is no excuse for not greasing the ones you can; and,
2. If you fail to grease a fitting, greasing the others doesn't help the one you missed.

This brings us to troubleshooting. There are a few principles that you can apply in almost all problem investigations. First and foremost is to keep an open mind. Most of us tend to start with a pretty good idea of what the problem is. These ideas are often not the result of anything concrete. Instead they are ideas we have because of things we have experienced in the past. It's sort of like lawyers looking for precedents. This kind of thinking can quickly pull you down false trails. You will tend to view all the evidence as supporting what you thought in the first place, regardless of whether it actually does or not.

Often, very early in your investigation, you will have to choose between checking things which are the most likely to be the problem, versus things which are not apt to be involved, but that are easy to check. There's no strictly right way here; it's all tradeoffs. If the engine won't turn over, it's not likely that a broken fan belt is the problem, but it might somehow be involved, and it costs nothing to check. On the other hand, it doesn't make much sense to check the tire pressures in this case, and it's not as easy as looking at the belts.

At the other extreme, even though it may seem likely that the starter motor is seized, it wouldn't make sense to pull it out without first checking to see if the battery cables are connected.

If the problem is electrical, try squirting all the wires and components you can with WD-40. WD-40 will draw moisture out of wiring. Wait five to ten minutes, then try it again.

When troubleshooting a problem, it pays to move from the general to the specific, and to progress from large to small. You can often rule out entire systems early on. If the noise only occurs when the vehicle is moving, it's probably not the engine causing it. That narrows the search down quite a bit.

When you do start checking out a system, always start as far out from the source as you can. With ignition-system problems, for example, start at the plugs. If you have spark there, you have, in effect, checked out the entire system up to that point. If you don't get a spark, start moving back from there. That's a lot easier than starting back at the generator and moving out toward the plugs.

Always do only one thing at a time. Even though two things don't seem to be related, they can mask the effects of each other. Failure to follow this rule can cost you the whole ballgame, since you will not only miss the problem if one masks the other, you won't find it later either, since you will assume that you have checked it already.

Stick to your task. Don't become distracted by things along the way. Don't, for instance, make minor repairs on seemingly unrelated items as you go along. It's tempting to do this. Sometimes you may, for instance, have the belly pan off, and figure it's easy to tighten a few fittings since you already have it open. Doing this can lead to the problem in the preceding paragraph.

Try to determine an initiating condition. Something must have caused the breakdown. Try to remember anything that might have led up to the failure.

Finally, here's a specific technique for finding the source of sounds that in turn identify mechanical problems.

Sound is transmitted almost undiminished through metal. Because of this, it is usually futile to try to locate, for example, a knock in an engine by the usual method, which involves putting your ear on the handle of a screwdriver, pressing the point against the engine block at various points, and trying to determine where the sound is loudest. It will sound almost the same everywhere.

Instead, try this technique: Take a rubber hose and put one end in your ear. Without touching the engine, move the other end over the block. Because you are not touching metal to metal, the sound you hear will be transmitted through the air and will not travel as easily as it does through metal. This makes it much easier to isolate the source.

You can increase the sound-gathering efficiency of this arrangement if you attach a funnel to the end of the hose, as long as you don't touch the engine with it. A further refinement requires two people. The person listening turns away from the engine so he can't see where the funnel is placed. The second person moves the funnel back and forth over the engine. The listener then indicates whether the sound is increasing or decreasing, sort of like an acoustic "pin the tail on the donkey." This method works almost every time.

21

Should You Buy a Sawmill?

THERE'S A SAYING AMONG WOOD PRODUCERS, "Take your wood as far as you can." That's an appealing idea, especially when you see the numbers involved. Here is an example of pine pulpwood values: $16 per cord on the stump; $32 stacked in the woods; $40 piled along the road; and $52 delivered to the mill. Here's another for white pine sawlog values: $80 per thousand board feet on the stump; $95 felled and bucked; $110 piled along the road; $150 delivered to a sawmill; $280 rough-sawn and green; $325 air-dried; $425 kiln-dried; $550 planed.

These are rough estimates, but they illustrate why there's a temptation to keep moving through the process. The problem is that each step costs money for equipment. Each step also involves a different type of work, and thus determines how you spend your time. If you want to spend time in the woods, you won't be happy running a sawmill.

The largest value increase for the least outlay lies in felling, bucking, and stacking pulpwood. With just a chain saw and some safety equipment, you can significantly increase the value of your trees. That's an investment of less than $1,000.

Taking the wood out to the road and piling it adds another eight dollars per cord. This requires a forwarder, which, if bought new, will cost in excess of $100,000.

Regardless of the numbers, there are some steps in these processes that have a strong appeal to woodland owners, and others that have little, if any, appeal. Cutting and stacking pulpwood is an unappealing prospect to most people I talk to, but operating a small sawmill is a dream shared by many.

Woodland owners almost always approach the sawmill idea backwards. They envision their sawmill producing something they would like to produce, rather than something someone might like to buy. The prospect of increasing the value of their wood attracts many people. I can make two 2 x 4s that sell for $1.25 each out of a pulpstick that is worth about 50 cents in the pulp pile. Not a bad markup: 50 cents to $2.50; this 500 percent increase sounds pretty good. Stroll through your woods thinking like that and it looks like Fat City. Wouldn't it be a shame to see all those nice logs ground up for pulpwood?

Is it a good idea, then, to buy a small sawmill? Maybe. A lot of mills are available. Pick up any country living magazine and you see ads for all kinds of them: Foley-Belsaw, MinMax, Wood-Mizer, Mobile Dimension, and many others—mainly small—band mills. Prices start as low as several thousand dollars. That's not much of an investment to produce a 500 percent increase in profits.

A Mobile Dimension portable circular sawmill with a vertical edger.

The place to start when deciding whether to buy a sawmill is not in your woodlot, but in the city. What markets are there? Can you break into them without cutting your prices so low that you work for nothing?

The fact that you own your own trees is almost irrelevant. Most successful sawmills buy all their logs, and you could too. In some instances, I don't bother to sort my logs. I put them all in the pulp pile and then buy almost identical logs for my sawmill. I have only so much time and energy and I have to use it efficiently. Sometimes that involves hiring someone else to do work, like sorting out pulpwood, that I'm capable of doing myself.

When I bought my mill a few years ago, I thought that I could simply saw some lumber, run ads in the local papers, and sell my products to farmers, who always need lumber. I still do that, but sales are small and have actually fallen off in the years I've been here. Very few people today build things with boards. Pole buildings go up cheaply and quickly and are free of many of the problems of wooden structures. Even sawmills use metal buildings. And anybody (including me) who builds anything with wood that will be exposed to the atmosphere uses treated lumber.

The farm market is gone. "Roof boards" are actually plywood, and so is most sheeting on wooden structures. If you watch for sales, and builders do, it's pretty easy to pick up eight-foot studs for 99 cents each and often as low as 79 cents. True, these are economy studs. By definition, they contain knots, splits, and dry rot. But the studs you produce are, by definition, rough and green. People fear green lumber and don't like the look and feel of rough surfaces.

Even if a lot of these economy studs aren't much good, enough are so that it's a pretty good deal for most people. They are kiln-dried, planed, and cut to exact length. Rough studs are none of the above.

Discount houses often stock rough fencing boards. I thought there might be a market there, but when I actually examined these boards, every one of them had some little quirk I couldn't produce. Sometimes this was as small a thing as rounded edges on their tops. I couldn't do that, so I couldn't supply that market.

What market there is for local sales consists mainly of odd sizes, which you can't afford to stock. Eighteen-foot oak 3 x 8s are popular for hay wagons, but I can't afford to saw up 18-foot oak logs in hopes that someone may want them before they warp and twist their way into the wood stove.

If you try to stock many different sizes, you'll need a lot of space just to store logs and lumber. People say of my local competitor, "Fred has 40 acres of lumber, two feet deep."

You need a steady demand so that you can plan your work. The problem with this is not so much in finding this kind of market, but in finding a portion of it that you can supply. I know a market for red pine eight-foot 3 x 3s that sounds perfect. I have lots of pulpsticks that make good 3 x 3s. But I can't sell to this market. I tried it, and it didn't work out.

In many instances, the reason you can't take orders is sheer volume. You simply can't produce enough to even consider bidding. In this case, I was able to produce enough, but still couldn't make it. I had to deliver every Friday to the buyer's plant. I could do that. My one-ton flatbed truck seemed ideal.

Then the problems started. The lumber had to be bundled and banded.

Banders cost almost $1,000, and even if I got a bander, I had no way to put the bundles on the truck. I had a loader with forks on my tractor, but it wouldn't pick up the size bundle the customer wanted. The bundles had to be loaded so that he could pick them off with his forklift, so I couldn't band them on the truck, which is what I thought of next. So I needed a forklift, and a big one.

I tried taking the 3 x 3s right off the saw and bundling them immediately. This was in the summer, and by the time I got a load, the wood in the first bundles was black and green and dripping foul juices. I needed to sticker and stack my output to keep it from staining while I finished the load. That involved an extra big step, plus stopping and cutting and air-drying a lot of one-inch stickers for piling.

I met my first month's quota, returned all my borrowed equipment, and went back to pulp cutting, telling myself that that's really what I wanted to do: lead a simple life and work in my woods. Sawmilling seemed to rule out both of these.

Even though small sawmills vary considerably, they have many things in common, and I will concentrate on these rather than dwell on band saw versus circular saw.

To produce a 2 x 4 from my pine plantation, I need to have the following equipment:

- A chain saw to cut the timber.
- A truck to carry my equipment into the woods and the logs to the mill.
- A forwarder to move the logs out of the woods, load them onto the truck, take them to the mill, and load them onto the mill.
- The sawmill itself.
- A tractor with a loader to move sawdust and slabwood and plow snow.

I need about ten acres of flat, clear land for the sawmill, log deck, slab pile, sawdust pile, and lumber stacks. There also have to be large turnaround areas for big trucks and open areas for log sorting. This is all taxable as commercial property, a far cry from the 74 cents an acre we pay for forest land under Wisconsin's Forest Crop Law.

I give the sawdust away and, every winter, have to set fire to a huge slab pile nobody wants. Actually, nobody wants the free sawdust anymore, either. The people who picked it up before raised horses, which they raced at county fairs, etc. Now, with gambling legalized, people are too impatient to sit through horse races, preferring lotteries and slot machines, so the horse racers have gone out of business.

I have discovered my market niche now, and it's a nice one. I cut white pine boards. I buy all my logs, either cut or on the stump, which I then log myself. I hire out the hauling and skidding, and that requires a good knowledge of local contractors. With few loads a year, I have little clout with them, and they use my work as filler. This means I have to keep calling and pleading to get my logs delivered.

On the other end, the Amish man who kiln-dries and planes my lumber has constant problems with warping, moisture, and thickness (mainly because he won't use fans in his kiln and planes with a diesel-powered planer). My customer complains to me about these things and is threatening to cancel the whole business if the quality doesn't pick up, but there isn't much I can do short of investing in a commercial kiln and planer and doing it myself.

Another option for the sawmill is custom-sawing, either at your site or as a portable operation. If you set up permanently and have people bring their logs to you, your main problems have to do with the logs.

The typical sawmill customers are local farmers, not loggers or builders. Farmers don't own forwarders, so they drag logs out with their tractors, resulting in logs caked with dirt and with embedded stones and sand. This is especially bad if you have a band saw, but it isn't good with a circular saw either. Farmers don't have pulp piles, so the whole tree comes to your mill, as well as any other trees that they can find to make up a load. I've had farmers load 20- and 30-foot oak logs on hayracks with bumper jacks and then roll them off in my yard expecting me to—somehow—lift them onto my mill.

Thus, you may cut several nice butt logs, but for every one of those, you will cut five or six skinny, twisted sticks. Even though the logs may come from a blown-down tree in a backyard, the owner will swear that they contain no metal. They do, though, and so you risk serious damage to your mill on every pass. The worst case I ever heard of was a sawmiller who told me he had hit a metal maple sap "spile" in a red oak log!

There are further considerations regarding setting your mill up permanently. As long as the mill is "portable," it, and the land it sits on, are not taxed as industrial property, nor do you have to be zoned "commercial" to operate it. It might pay you to tow your mill off-site once in a while.

If you take your mill to the customer's site, you have the problems already mentioned and more. The farmer is responsible for loading my deck with logs and removing slabwood, sawdust, and cut lumber. It's not uncommon to find that, while he could drag big logs out of the woods, he can't pick them up and put them on the mill. It doesn't work to pick up one end at a time. The log has to go on straight or the mill may be damaged.

The customer is also supposed to furnish help, but do you really want his 12-year-old kid scrambling around your running sawmill? What does your liability insurance say about that?

Quite often, the farmer gets more lumber than he wants, or can pay for, and asks if you'll take part or all of your fee in lumber or logs. If that fails, he has you stop sawing, and you pull out having earned a lot less than you had been promised.

Finally, a word about production. Most ads for sawmills will say you can cut up to so many board feet per day. I don't know what my mill is rated at, but I would guess that it could produce up to 4,000 board feet a day. My goal is 1,200 board feet per day, and I can maintain that pretty consistently. This is one man sawing, loading logs, removing slab and sawdust, sticking and stacking the lumber, and maintaining the mill and equipment.

I saw one-inch boards out of eight-foot white pine logs. If, instead, I cut 2 x 12s out of large 16-foot logs, I could probably cut 4,000 feet in a day. Twelve hundred board feet of eight-foot boards is about two standard-sized pickup loads, and it requires slightly more than two cords of logs. The mill actually cuts about 250 board feet per hour with these sizes of logs and lumber. The rest of the time is spent on other tasks.

My customer prefers eight-foot lumber, and so that is what I cut. Eight-foot logs are easy to come by and handle. Even so, large mills prefer 16-foot logs. This obviously cuts the handling in half, but it also makes each log harder to handle. That's not a good tradeoff for me.

In addition, you get better lumber yield out of short logs. This is because the diameter of the small end of the log being sawed determines the width of boards you can saw off the entire log. If you have a 16-foot log, this diameter limits the width for the entire 16 feet. If, on the other hand, you saw this as two 8-foot logs, the limit on the width of the boards from the butt log is determined not from the top of the upper log, but from the point halfway, where you cut the 16-foot log in half. This can make quite a difference if your logs have a lot of taper to them.

Remember that the determining factor in deciding the lumber size you can cut out of a given log is not the width of the piece, but the diagonal between the furthest corners of the piece. (This is the hypoteneuse of the right triangle formed by the long and short sides.)

I also produce logs for log cabins. This is a good market. I produce mainly eight-foot logs because this is the length that loggers can supply in our area. I cut them flat on three sides and peel them. The big problems are the peeling and storing. Even though I only peel one side, it's still a lot of work. I use a peeler that consists of a drum with saw chain wrapped around it. It attaches to a chain saw and does a good job. After running the peeler over the log, I touch it up with a drawshave. This gives a smooth, hand-hewn look people like.

Builders generally prefer white pine logs. They say they twist less than red pine. There are problems with this, however, in that good white pine logs are hard to find. In addition, white pine stains worse than red pine and is subject to worm damage in the summer, so it's a chancy business.

I think the cabins made with my logs look great, and the people who live in them love them, but I have a lot of competition from log producers who have special equipment to produce logs with grooves milled in them and other exotic features. I supply the low end of the market, usually to guys who are moving up from mobile homes and building their houses themselves. That suits me fine. I like guys like that.

So there is no standard answer to the question, "Should you buy a small sawmill?" You have to decide that for yourself.

In recent years, most portable sawmills have been thin (1/8-inch) kerf band mills that usually cut horizontally, or circular saws with a 1/4-inch kerf that usually cut vertically. These mills all have various limitations. Most will not mill large logs, 6 or 8 feet, and sometimes not even 4 feet in diameter. The band mill blades dull quickly, and even when they're sharp, they tend to cut wavy lumber from very hard or knotty wood. The theory is that you can glean more lumber out of a log using a thin kerf because you lose less to sawdust, but if you need to run the rough boards through a planer several times to get rid of the "waves," you haven't gained anything.

Most circular portable sawmills cut straight, dimensional lumber, but

A Mighty-Mite portable band sawmill.

the kerf is 1/4 inch or wider. Like most band mills, they usually need to be set up permanently or on a trailer, which really limits their "portability." If you run a band or circular sawmill, you need equipment to transport the log to the sawmill, and some require a loader to put the log onto the mill.

Many of these mills employ hydraulic log arms (lifters) that put the logs up on the bunks of the sawmill and are also used to turn the logs as you cut. Many mills also use electronics to set the depth of cut on a log.

Unfortunately, when you involve complex hydraulics and electronics with milling out in the woods, there are plenty of things that can break down. Also, band mills require continuous log turning and resawing, so commonly the operator will just cut slabs and then cut boards from the slabs on a separate machine, an edger. Some popular portable circular sawmills have a pair of horizontal edger blades, known as a vertical edger, built into the headrig, to produce edged boards in one pass.

I recently learned about a fairly new, revolutionary "swing blade" portable sawmill concept invented in New Zealand by a man named Peterson, which has been refined in Australia by the Lucas family. The swing blade mill was created in that part of the world because the thin-blade mills could not efficiently mill the very hard, dense, heavy woods that are common in New Zealand, Australia, Africa, the South Pacific, and elsewhere. Some of these woods are so heavy that they won't float even when dry.

What they needed in these remote areas was a mill that was simple, economical, and productive; that would cut dimensional (not wavy) lumber from logs up to 8 feet in diameter; that was portable without a lot of extra equipment such as a trailer, skidder, or loader; and that would mill a log in place without continuous turning.

The Lucas Sawmill seems to fulfill these requirements. It does not require a trailer (you can just use your pickup with racks), and you take the mill to the log, so you don't need skidding equipment. The mill requires no log turning. The mill cuts with a five-bit-and-shank circular blade, using carbide bits, for longer life between sharpenings. Like some other portable circular mills, the Lucas Mill uses the five-bit blade arrangement, rather than the sixty or more cutters found on conventional circular sawmill blades. It's quicker to sharpen just five cutters, especially since sharpening is accomplished while the blade is still on the machine. The lumber produced contains no waves and is comparable to that milled on more conventional circular saws.

The Lucas Mill is sold in the United States by Bailey's Inc. of Laytonville, California. The company stocks several models and attachments for cutting slabs and bevel siding. The mill comes with three carbide blades and a 12-volt sharpener with a diamond wheel.

I haven't operated one of these Lucas Mills, but it would be worth your while to look into this relatively new mill before you invest in a portable sawmill.

I've been very satisfied with my own mill, a Mobil Dimension. It is a one-person operation, and I would recommend it highly to anyone considering buying a sawmill. It has more than paid for itself and continues to make money for me.

There's a saying: "If you are a hammer, the whole world looks like nails." Similarly, if you have a sawmill, the whole forest begins to look like 2 x 4s.

Running a sawmill is not a way of enjoying your woods. It is simply tending a machine, similar to running a machine in a factory—and a demanding machine at that. If you enjoy mechanical work, and I do, you'll probably enjoy a sawmill. If your goal is more forest- and nature-oriented, you may resent the time spent tied to a machine, and I do that, too. Good luck.

Solar-Drying Lumber

I once owned and operated a solar lumber kiln. I bought the plans and some of the hardware from a guy who later sold his design to the Wood-Mizer Corporation. The kiln is unique in that it utilizes two plastic sheets across the front rather than just one.

To dry lumber, you must heat it to drive the moisture out of the wood and into the atmosphere of the kiln. Then, you must remove the moisture you have driven out of the wood from the kiln.

Commercial kilns do this in various ways. All of them heat the lumber to drive out the moisture. Normally they do this with steam, heat-producing compressors, or electric heaters. To remove the moisture from the atmosphere, they either vent off the moist air, condense it with a refrigeration unit, or remove it with a vacuum process. Small, homemade kilns often just depend on uncontrolled air flow to continually (and inefficiently) remove the air.

The design I used formed an envelope between the two plastic sheets. A small fan constantly circulated air between these sheets. When the sun was shining, this air became heated as it passed between the sheets, and then exited to the main area where the lumber was stacked. I could sticker and stack about a thousand board feet of lumber in this area.

Another, large fan, which operated on a thermostat, started when the air was hot and circulated the heated air through the stack of lumber. At night, when the air cooled down, it shut off. On a sunny day, the air temperature would get up above 165 degrees F. This drove the moisture out of the wood into the kiln atmosphere.

At night, the large fan shut down, but the small fan continued to run, circulating the moisture-laden air from the day's heating between the plastic sheets. The cool night air cooled down the outer sheet to the point where the moisture passing behind it condensed and ran off. In this way, the atmosphere inside the kiln returned to normal humidity every night, ready to accept more moisture when the sun came up and again start driving moisture out of the wood.

A solar lumber kiln built into a house in Ohio.

All I ever dried in this fashion was one-inch white pine boards. It worked like a charm. I never had any problems with warping or staining. I always loaded it with air-dried boards, which would average about 20 to 25 percent moisture. They would come out of the kiln at from 6 to 8 percent. This was not "S Dry" or "Surface Dry" (also called "sorta dry"), which most lumber that you buy is. This would was dry clear through, ready to be used for cabinet work.

The kiln required no attention once you loaded it, and the power consumption was so low I never noticed it on my bill. When I went out in the morning, I would see moisture condensed on the inside of the outer sheet. This would lessen as time went on until, one day, I would see none. That indicated to me that the moisture level of the wood had reached 6 to 8 percent, and the drying was done.

The amount of time this kiln-drying took varied according to the number of sunny days and the outside air temperature. The lumber species, thickness of lumber, and initial moisture content also affected drying time, so I can't give you any hard numbers, but since it was essentially labor- and money-free, it really doesn't matter that much. Kilns like this are cheap to build, so if you need more capacity, just build another one. I tried to graph the amount of water removed every day, but my data were flawed by my dog drinking out of the collection bucket I was measuring. My results were puzzling until I caught him at it.

I built a wood-fired backup unit to supply the heat needed during the winter. It never operated very well. The plastic sheets were great conductors of heat, so most of the heat I generated was lost to the outside through them. I ended up mostly operating the kiln in the summer, although on sunny fall days, when the sun was low in the sky, it really worked well in spite of rather low outside temperatures.

I don't guess there is anywhere in North America where the problem would occur, but if it is too hot at night, the moisture will not condense and the kiln won't work. The simple test for this is dew formation. If dew forms at night in your area, it will work. If it doesn't, it won't.

I checked into this in Paraguay while serving there as a Peace Corps volunteer. I think that, even there, dew forms year-round, but I'm not sure. I never noticed whether it did in all seasons or not. Most people, apparently, don't pay much attention to dew. I asked dozens of people and the answers were about half and half. Half swore that dew formed, the other half swore that it didn't. The only way for me to know for sure was to check it out for myself for a year. I left before I could do that.

It doesn't make any sense to dry lumber down to 6 percent moisture and then let it sit around and reabsorb moisture from the atmosphere. Lumber, especially rough lumber, will do just that. Thus, you need some nice dry place to store the lumber you have dried. Normally, you don't have to sticker it, but you do have to stack it by width so that you can easily fill orders. All this has to be considered before you jump into kiln-drying.

Even if it all works out, though, there is a limited market for kiln-dried, rough lumber. To tap into the larger market, you need to plane the boards. I drew the line there. I'm not comfortable with the small tolerances planed-lumber customers require. Even though there may have been good money in it, it was a long way from the life I had intended to lead when I moved out into the country. We found other ways of making a living, ones which were closer to our original intentions.

Afterword

THERE'S A STORY ABOUT A POLITICIAN who was being heckled during a speech.

"Tell them all you know, it won't take long," shouted the heckler.

"I'll tell them all we both know; it won't take any longer," the politician shouted back.

Well, I've told you just about everything I know, and it didn't take long, but I'm not dumb enough to think that you couldn't add to my knowledge.

Most of what I have written here, I have learned from someone else. Some of it I just stumbled into on my own. The learning has never been easy. Woodcutters work in the woods, away from the public eye, so it's not easy to see what they do. For years it was thought that there really wasn't a whole lot to be learned. You just went out and did it. Woods workers in those days got no respect. It was considered to be just another form of manual labor. If you wanted a loan from the bank, it did you little good to list "pulp cutter" as your occupation.

Still, some of us persisted, and slowly built up a body of knowledge. Then, in the early 1980s, Søren Eriksson arrived and all the Swedish techniques became known. That was when I started to take a professional approach to my work. To this day, however, no books have been available to the general public that brought together the knowledge gained over these years. This book is intended to do that.

I hope you enjoyed reading it as much as I enjoyed writing it. Take what is in it seriously, but don't let it stop you from making your own discoveries and pushing the art forward. After all, nobody knows everything about woods work.

Index

adjusting screws
  carburetor, 30, 72–73
  chain tension, 76
  oil, 74
aerobic exercise, 16
age and fitness, 17
aiming line, 30, 91–92, 97–98
aiming with your ass, 92, 97
air-cleaning system, 31–32
air filter, 23, 31, 32, 73, 75, 76
air-fuel mixture, 71
American-made saws, 11, 29
American National Standards Institute (ANSI),
  27, 51
anaerobic exercise, 16
anti-vibration mounts, 21
automatic bar oiling, 23
automatic transmission, 181
axes, 64, 164

back
  correct use of, 60–61, 122
  problems with, 122–23
back braces, 122
Bailey's catalog, ii, 28, 33, 206, 216
ballistic nylon, 48, 49, 52
banders, 202
band mills, 205, 206
barber chair, 115
barking trees, 193
bar oil, 40–41, 73–74
bars
  banana-nose, 7, 107
  gauges of, 39, 40
  length of, 36–37, 38–39
  removing, 76
  repairing and replacing, 77, 78
  types of, 7, 37–38, 39
basal area, 145
bearings, 42, 77
bench chain grinder, 79, 80
benches, 119, 120
benching, 119–121 and bucking, 134
  and limbing, 125–26
bids, 142–44
Bilsom (company), 48
blocking, 155–58
blockwood, 155 rolling, 161–62
"blue label" chain, 27
body wood, 169

boiler, 166, 172, 174, 177
bones, 14
boots, 50–52
bore cutting, 106, 108, 111, 112
  modified, 110, 113–14
  standard, 109, 112
  uses for, 112
bow guide bar, 39
brakes. *See* chain brakes
British thermal units (Btus), 167, 168
bucking, 5, 66, 127, 130, 131
bunching, 17, 131, 134–35
bushings, 196
butt-log degrade, 116, 117, 121
butts, 63–64, 104–105
buying
  firewood, 169–70
  logs for milling, 200
buzz saws, 163–64

calorie, 157
calorie burning, 15
canola oil, 41
cant hook, 59, 61–62
cantilevering, 120–121
carbide-tipped chain, 25
carbohydrates, 18–19
carburetor
  adjusting screws, 30, 72–73
  all-position, 24
  damage to diaphragm, 40
carrying cases, 40
cart skidder, 186–87, 192
cellular phones, 184
centrifugal clutches, 23
chain brakes, 6–12, 70, 96
  inertial, 7–12
  standard, 8, 11
chains
  length of, 37
  replacing, 77, 78
  safety, 7, 27, 108
  sharpening, 28, 78–84
  tightening, 37, 76–77
  types of, 24–25, 27–28
chain-saw gloves, 52
chain saws
  carrying cases for, 40
  dealers of, 32–34
  maintenance of, 75–78

chain saws, *continued*
  parts of, 20–24
  starting, 69
  tools for adjusting, 42–43
  types of, 28–32
  See also bars; chains; sprockets
chain-saw safety boots, 50–52
chains, for truck, 181
chain tension adjusting screws, 76
chaps, 49, 50
chimney, 165, 173
Chinese loggers, 23
chipper chain, 25
chisel chain, 25, 27
choke, 70
circular portable sawmills, 205–206
circulorespiratory system, 15
cleaning routine, 75
clear-cutting, 98, 149, 150
clothing. *See* safety clothing
clutch drum, 24, 73
coast-down time, 3
color-visibility study, 156
combustion
  while exercising, 16
  in woodstoves, 165, 168
come-along, 103
compression bandage, 183
compression of wood, 132
compression releases, 31
conk, 93, 151
contractors, 141, 142, 143, 144, 145, 146,
  147, 169–70
conveyor, 153
cords, 154, 169
creosote buildup, 165–66, 173
crotches, 158
cubic inch displacement, 35
custom-sawing, 203
cutting firewood, 152
cutting the corners, 114
cutting with the top of the bar, 3–4
cutting with the tip of the bar. *See* bore cutting
cylinder, 73

dealers, 40, 42, 74, 79
  choosing, 32–34
dead trees, 169, 188
debarking, 17
delimbing. *See* limbing
diameter breast height (DBH), 140
diameter limit cut, 145
diameter of logs, 64, 67–68, 138–40
diet, 15, 18–19
discount houses, 32, 39, 201
displacement, 35–36
domino felling, 103–104
double-ended files, 43, 80
downed timber, 118
Doyle log scale, 143
drive links, 27
drop start, 70, 71
drying firewood, 169–70
drying lumber, 207–209
dump truck, 180, 194

earmuffs, 47
ear protection, 21, 47, 48
Echo (company), 10, 24, 28
economics
  buying firewood, 169–70
  sawmills, 199–202
  selling firewood, 153–55
  selling timber, 141–48
  value of wood, 136–38
  volume of wood, 138–40
electronic ignition, 23
engine displacement, 35–36
engine oil, 41
Eriksson, Søren, 64, 85, 86, 87, 88, 119, 120
escape path, 95
ethanol in gas, 40
European-made saws, 11, 29–32
exhaust, 21
exhaust ports, 36

face cords, 154, 155, 164, 170
facemask screen, 46, 47
falling object protection system (FOPS), 187
farmer, as sawmill customer, 201, 203–204
felling, 16, 17, 89–105
  accuracy, 91–92, 97–99, 100
  hung-up trees, 99, 101–105
  on hills, 117–118
  open-face method of, 90–95
  and retreating, 95–97, 100
  small-diameter trees, 99
  tools for, 60–62
  using bore cut for, 112
felling bar, 95
felling cut, 93, 94, 95
felling lever, 60–61, 62, 63, 93, 94, 95
felling pillow, 62
felling sequence, 101
fiberglass, 51
files, 25, 27, 42–43, 80, 81
filing, 81–83
filler cap, 23
filters, 23, 31, 32, 71
firewood, 149–164
  blocking, 155–59
  burning, 165–168
  buying, 169–70
  cutting, 152
  drying, 169–70
  loading, 153
  selling, 153–55
  scrub oak for, 104, 149–52
  splitting, 159–63
  stacking, 169, 170
flat-bed dump truck, 180, 194
flat file, 25
flat raker file, 81, 42, 43
flat tong, 59
flooding engine, 71, 72
Foley-Belsaw (company), 200
Forest Crop Law, 202
foresters, 145, 146, 147, 149, 152
forklift, 202
forwarders, 187–88, 192, 193, 194, 199
forwarding, 4, 131
4WD trucks, 179

front loader, 190
fuel, 40
fuel filter, 23, 71
fuel hole, 22
fuel pickup tube, 23, 71
fuel tank, 23
full cord, 169, 170

Game of Logging, 85, 86–87
gas for chain saw, 40
gauges
    of bars, 39, 40
    go/no-go, 5, 67, 131
    raker, 81
gloves, 49, 52
go/no-go gauge, 5, 67, 131
Goodwill, 54, 55, 56
grease, 41–42, 196–97
green firewood, 165, 166, 168
green lumber, 201
grinders, 43, 79, 80
groove in bar, 39, 76, 78
guard links, 108
guide links, 27
gunning the engine, 4, 70, 73, 125

handguard, 8, 21–22
hardhats, 45–48
hard-nose bars, 37
hard-toe boots, 50–51
hay-bale hook, 59
hay elevator, 153
heat, 166–67
heated handles, 53
heat lamp, 75
Heatmor (company), 177
Helly-Hansen logging top, 54
hinge, 92–93, 94, 95, 97, 98–99
hitching gear, 190
hitching points, 185–86
Homelite (company), 10, 11
hot water heating system, 166
hung-up trees, 6, 58, 61, 63–64, 94, 99,
    101–105
Husqvarna (company), 28, 30, 31, 32, 36
hydraulic log arms, 206
hydraulic systems, 190

ice tongs, 59
idle, setting, 72, 73
inertial chain brake, 7–12
International log scale, 143

jack, 62
Johnson, Marcia, 4, 5, 6
Jonsered (company), 28, 30, 31

kerf, 106, 132–33, 205
Kevlar, 48, 49, 50, 51
kickback, 106–108
    and bar length, 38
    and bucking, 133–34
    and prelimbing, 124–125
    protection from, 7–10
    and saftey tip versus inertial brake, 10–11
kickback zone, 3, 107
kiln-drying lumber, 207–209
knuckleboom loader, 137, 192

labels, on chain boxes, 27
laminated bars, 37–38
latent heat, 166, 167
leaning out, 71, 72
lie, 93
lifting techniques, 122
limbing, 16, 122, 124–29
    firewood, 157, 158
liners, 51–52
log-cabin logs, 130–31, 204–205
logger's stick, 5, 64, 65
logger's tape, 5, 64, 65, 66–67, 127
logging chain, 115–16
logging top, 54
logs
    moving, 58–60
    piling, 134–35
    sawing, 132–34
    sizing, 130–31
    sorting, 131–32
lopping the top, 133
Lucas sawmill, 206–207
lumber, 200, 201–203, 204, 205
lung capacity, 16, 17

McCulloch (company), 11
marking for bucking, 5, 65, 66, 127–28
marking trees for harvesting, 144, 146, 147
maul, 160, 161, 162, 163, 164
maximum bore cut, 111
measuring tape. *See* logger's tape
measuring wood, 64–68
mechanization of timber harvesting, 141
Mighty-Mite sawmill, 205
mill scale, 142, 143–44
MinMax sawmill, 200
mitts, 53
Mobile Dimension sawmill, 137, 200, 207
modified bore cut, 110
moisture content of wood, 168
mufflers, 21, 30
muscles, 13, 14, 15

National Institute of Occupational Safety and
    Health (NIOSH), 123
noses, 37, 38
    greasing of, 41–42
notching, 90–91, 92, 93, 97, 98–99

oak. *See* scrub oak
oak wilt, 151
Occupational Safety and Health
    Administration (OSHA), 10, 11, 29, 33,
    93, 102, 183
oil adjustment screw, 74
oil filter, 23, 41
oil-gas fuel mixture, 23, 24, 40
oil hole, 22
oil, natural alternatives, 41
Olympyk (company), 9, 28
one-piece mufflers, 30
"on-off" switches, 23
open-face notch, 90–91
oxygen requirement of body, 16–17

pads, 49–50
pants, 49–50
parlor stoves, 172, 173

peelers, 204–205
Peltor (company), 48
pickaroon, 59–60
pickup trucks, 179
piling, 131, 134–35
pine trees, 136, 138, 149
Pioneer (company), 28
pitch, 28
polyester, 55
polypropylene, 55
portable bench, 119
power grinders, 43
professional saws, 32
proposal for law mandating inertial
    chain brakes, 7–10
pole buildings, 201
portable sawmills, 203, 205–207
ports, 31, 36
Poulan (company), 11
power grinder, 43
power steering, 180–81
power takeoff shaft (PTO), 186, 192
prelimbing, 124–25
preventive maintenance of vehicles, 195–96
prying trees down, 60–61
pull cord, 23, 77, 170
pulp contractor, 169–70
pulphooks, 58–59, 60, 62, 63
pulpsticks, 5, 131, 139
pulpwood, 5, 131, 132, 142, 170
    handling, 58
    value of, 199
    volume of, 139–40
PVC pipe, as logger's stick, 5, 65

quality breaks, 5

raker, 25, 79, 81, 107
raker file. See flat raker file
raker gauge, 81
ratcheting suspension, 46
recoil mechanism, 23
replaceable-nose bars, 38
roads, 184–85
roller-nose bearings, 77
rollover protection systems (ROPS), 185, 187
roof boards, 201
rot, 93, 94
rotational kickback, 7, 11, 106, 107. See also
    kickback
round file, 25, 42, 43
round-ground chain, 25
rpm (revolutions per minute), 35, 72, 73
running the stick, 5, 127

Sachs-Dolmar, 9, 24, 28
safety
    awareness, 33–34
    "before-need planning" for, 182–83
    chain brakes, 6–12
    chains, 7, 27, 108
    and common errors, 2–4
    and dead trees, 188
    and fatigue, 89–90
    and hung-up trees, 101–102
    innovations for chain saws, 29
    and kickback, 7–10, 106, 107, 108

and operating vehicles, 185–89, 194–95
    rules for felling, 89–90
    and spring poles, 129, 188–89
    and working alone, 183–84
    See also safety clothing; safety glasses;
        safety manuals; safety tip guard
safety clothing, 48–52
    boots, 50–52
    gloves, 49, 52, 53
    pants, 49–50
    shirts, 50
safety glasses, 47
safety manuals, 101–102
safety tip guard, 10, 11, 106, 107, 108
sawdust, 202
sawlogs, 131
sawmills, 136, 137, 199–207
    economics of, 199–202
    portable, 203, 205–207
scaling logs, 142–44
scoop shovel, 63–64
screens
    air filter, 76
    hardhat, 46, 47
    muffler, 21
scrench, 42, 43
Scribner log scale, 143
scrub oaks, 149–52
secondary combustion, 175
selling
    firewood, 153–55
    timber, 141–48
semi-chisel chain, 25
sensible heat, 166, 167
shelf fungus, 93, 151
shirts, 50, 54–56
shovel, 63–64, 99, 100
side scarring, 114
sighting line, 91–92
Silvey (company), 62
single-cylinder, two-cycle engines, 23–24
skidders, 102, 192–93
skip link chain, 24
slab, 139
sloven, 99
snap-ring-removing tool, 43
snow blower, 187
snow mobiles, 184
snow tires, 181
solar lumber kiln, 207, 208–209
solid bars, 37–38
sorting, 131, 132
sound, engine, 197–98
spare parts, 43–44, 57
spark plugs, 43, 71
speed, 35
Spencer Manufacturing Company, 65
Spencer tapes, 65, 66
splitting, 159–63
spring poles, 128, 129, 188, 189
sprocket, 24, 28, 30, 77–78
sprocket-nose bars, 37, 38, 41–42
square-ground chisel, 25
stack damper, 173–74
stacking firewood, 169, 170. See also
    bunching; piling

stack temperature, 173, 175
stack thermometer, 173
standard bore cut, 109
standard cord, 164
starting chain saw, 69–74
    and adjusting speed, 72–73
    basic methods of, 69–70
    and flooding, 71
    and troubleshooting, 71–72
steel-toed boots, 50–51
Stellite-hardened noses, 37
stick. *See* logger's stick; running the stick
sticks (logs), value of, 136, 137. *See also* logs;
    pulpsticks; pulpwood
Stihl (company), 12, 22, 27, 28, 30, 31, 32
stretching exercises, 13–14
stumpage prices, 136, 141, 142
stump height, 101
stump pull, 116–17
stumps, 101
S (Surface) Dry, 208
suspension points, on hardhats, 45–46
Swedish Forest Operations Institute, 87
Swedish Forestry Institute Safety Manual, 122
Swedish logging tools
    double-ended file, 43, 80
    dragging tongs, 62, 152
    felling lever, 62
    portable bench, 119–20
    pulphook, 58–59, 62,
    toboggan, 63
    tree jack, 62
Swedish methods of logging, 36. *See also*
    Eriksson, Søren
Swedish studies
    calorie burning, 15
    color visibility, 156
    oxygen requirements, 16–17
    time-lapse photography of tree felling, 98
sweep, 130
swing blade portable sawmill, 206

teeth
    filing, 79, 80, 81–82, 83
    and kickback, 107–108
tension
    of chain, 37, 76–77
    and wood in, 132
Third World countries, 29
Thompson's Water Seal Preservative, 52
throttle interlocks, 12, 23
throwaway bars, 38, 78
Tilton, Dan, 87
timber on the stump, 141, 142
timber spikes, 39
Timber Stand Improvement (TSI), 150
tip guard, 10, 11
toboggan, 63
tongs, 59, 152
tool holder, 44
tools
    for adjusting chain saw, 42–43
    for handling wood, 58–64
    for measuring wood, 64–68
    See also Swedish logging tools
tooth profiles, 25, 26

tops, 54–56, 133, 138
traction, 181
tractors, 185–86, 188–90, 191
trailers, 137, 152, 153, 190–91, 192
training sessions, 1, 86–88
Tree Farm Family program, 145
tree jack, 62
troubleshooting
    chain-saw starting problems, 71–72
    vehicle problems, 196–98
trucks, 179–82
trunks
    splitting, 115–16
    twisting down, 61, 62, 99–100
turbo air-cleaning system, 31–32
twisting trees down, 61, 62, 99–100
two-cycle engines, 23–24
two-cycle oil, 40
T-wrench, 42, 43

ultraviolet rating, 46
utility poles, 131

value of wood, 136–37, 199
vehicles, 137
    forwarders, 187–88, 192, 193, 194
    preventive maintenance, 195–96
    skidders, 102, 192–93
    tractors, 185–86, 188–90, 191
    trailers, 152, 153, 190–91, 192
    troubleshooting, 196–98
    trucks, 179–82, 194
vertical edger, 206
vibration, 21
volume, of pulpsticks, 139–40

Wankel rotary engine, 24
water, 19
WD-40, 71, 196
wedges, driving, 61, 63, 93, 94, 98, 133
    making from brush, 64
wedge, from cutting, 90, 91, 92, 93
weight-to-power ratios, 35
wet wood, 165, 166, 168
white finger disease, 21
white oak, 151
white pine logs, 204, 205
white pine lumber, 203, 204
widow-makers, 97, 188
winches, 191
wind, 94
wind-thrown timber, 118
Wisconsin Department of Natural Resources,
    (DNR), 149
Wisconsin Woodland Owners Association
    (WWOA), 6, 7
wood burning, 165–68
woodfired boiler, 166, 172, 174, 177
woodlot, and contracting timber harvesting,
    142–48
Wood-Mizer (company), 200, 207
woodshed, 169
woodsplitting, 159–64
work habits, 17–18

"yellow label" chain, 27

CHELSEA GREEN

Sustainable living has many facets. Chelsea Green's celebration of the sustainable arts has led us to publish trend-setting books about organic gardening, solar electricity and renewable energy, innovative building techniques, regenerative forestry, local and bioregional democracy, and whole foods. The company's published works, while intensely practical, are also entertaining and inspirational, demonstrating that an ecological approach to life is consistent with producing beautiful, eloquent, and useful books, videos, and audio cassettes.

For more information about Chelsea Green, or to request a free catalog, call toll-free (800) 639–4099, or write to us at P.O. Box 428, White River Junction, Vermont 05001. Visit our website at www.chelseagreen.com.

Chelsea Green's titles include:

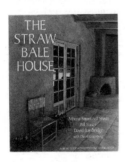

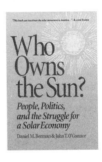

The Straw Bale House
The Independent Home:
  Living Well with Power
  from the Sun, Wind, and
  Water
Independent Builder:
  Designing & Building a
  House Your Own Way
The Rammed Earth House
The Passive Solar House
The Sauna
Wind Power for Home &
  Business
The Solar Living Sourcebook
A Shelter Sketchbook
Mortgage-Free!
Hammer. Nail. Wood.

The Flower Farmer
Passport to Gardening:
  A Sourcebook for the
  21st-Century Gardener
The New Organic Grower
Four-Season Harvest
Solar Gardening
The Contrary Farmer
The Contrary Farmer's
  Invitation to Gardening
Forest Gardening
Whole Foods Companion
The Apple Grower

Who Owns the Sun?
Gaviotas: A Village to
  Reinvent the World
Global Spin: The
  Corporate Assault on
  Environmentalism
Hemp Horizons
A Place in the Sun
Renewables are Ready
Beyond the Limits
Loving and Leaving the
  Good Life
The Man who Planted
  Trees
The Northern Forest
From the Redwood Forest:
  Ancient Trees and the
  Bottom Line